MW00785447

WHERE THE LAW IS:

AN INTRODUCTION TO ADVANCED LEGAL RESEARCH

Fifth Edition

■ ■ ■

J.D.S. Armstrong

Associate Director
Arthur W. Diamond Law Library
Columbia University School of Law

Christopher A. Knott

Professor of Law
Associate Dean for Information Services and Technology
Wake Forest University School of Law

R. Martin Witt

Head of Public Services
Arthur W. Diamond Law Library
Columbia University School of Law

AMERICAN CASEBOOK SERIES®

WEST
ACADEMIC
PUBLISHING

American Casebook Series is a trademark registered in the U.S. Patent and Trademark Office.

© West, a Thomson business, 2004, 2006
© 2009, 2013 Thomson/Reuters
© 2018 LEG, Inc. d/b/a West Academic
    444 Cedar Street, Suite 700
    St. Paul, MN 55101
    1-877-888-1330

West, West Academic Publishing, and West Academic are trademarks of West Publishing Corporation, used under license.

Printed in the United States of America

ISBN: 978-1-68328-525-0

To my family.

—JDSA

To Maggi, Acy, and Alexander.

—CAK

To all those who raised me.

—RMW

iii

ACKNOWLEDGMENTS FOR THE FIFTH EDITION

I would like to extend thanks to my co-authors Chris Knott and Marty Witt for the pleasure of working with them, and to Ian Armstrong for his updated graphical contribution.

—JDSA

Many thanks to my co-authors for making this process a real pleasure. I would also like to thank Dean Suzanne Reynolds and all of my colleagues at the Wake Forest University School of Law for their support and encouragement.

—CAK

Thank you to everyone associated with the Law Librarian Fellowship Program at the University of Denver, including the great librarians/instructors and my classmates-turned-colleagues. I knew it was a great opportunity at the time, but I've have come to appreciate it even more with years of perspective. Thanks too to Nickie Singleton, for being the best first director a new law librarian could hope for, and to the rest of the survivors for welcoming me into the profession. My colleagues at Columbia Law deserve recognition as well, for their support on this book and every other aspect of my day-to-day work. Finally, I am indebted to my co-authors for bringing me onto this ambitious project and for peppering the countless hours spent on this edition with good humor and insight.

—RMW

TABLE OF CONTENTS

LOCATION OF TABLES

WHERE THE LAW IS:

AN INTRODUCTION TO ADVANCED LEGAL RESEARCH

Fifth Edition

CHAPTER 1

ADVANCED LEGAL RESEARCH: GETTING STARTED

■ ■ ■

1.1   WHAT THIS BOOK IS ABOUT

As a lawyer, an important part of your job is to advise your client on the law and on its implications for your client's affairs, both prospectively and within the context of litigation. Your responsibility encompasses being as sure as possible about what the law is *not*, as well as what the law is, on any particular subject. Establishing a negative proposition through research, an exigency that arises constantly in legal practice, requires a very sure hand. In order to answer questions from your client or from the court about the law authoritatively and confidently, you must know that you have looked for the law in all the right places. Hence, the title of this book.

As a student of advanced legal research, you are already familiar with the nuts and bolts of legal information. Cases and statutes are no longer alien or frightening creatures to you, but rather the eagerly-sought tools that you know you need for your daily work. But as you shoulder more and greater research responsibilities, as you graduate from canned research exercises to the real world, you will want to ensure that you know where you have to look to do your job competently and reliably. This book, we hope, will help you learn to do just that.

In the old days, finding the law was a jumpy sort of process, involving the use of multiple sources, some of which were interconnected, that had grown up as historical fruits of the evolution of American legal publishing. Legal research instruction focused on how to use each of these legal publications, most of which were either unique or had rival publications that were essentially the same in structure. Many of the great research treatises of the past, such as Cohen, Berring, and Olson's *How to Find the Law* and Price, Bitner, and Bysiewicz's *Effective Legal Research*, concern themselves primarily with the description and illumination of these discrete publications.

Today, on the other hand, the information that emanates from the sources of legal authority is available from many suppliers, packaged in many different formats and combinations. Accordingly, today's legal researchers need to focus more on the information they are looking for, and less on any particular publication. In today's arena, you can no longer rely on any one publisher to have covered the field for you. The scope and coverage of works produced by a given publisher is influenced by competing licensing agreements, distribution networks, and both economic and political pressures that go beyond what the legal research market would seem logically to dictate. Researchers need to navigate through the shifting sands of the legal publishing world to locate all the information that they, as a matter of their own professional competency, deem necessary to the task at hand.

1.2   WHAT THIS BOOK IS NOT ABOUT

This book is about legal research, not about general research conducted by lawyers, which, of course, also happens all the time. Today's lawyer is called upon to argue from statistics, from marketing data out of the business world, from medical arcana, and from most other fields of human endeavor that furnish the background of discord. In order to construct their arguments and to master those anticipated from their opponents, lawyers may need to research facts or background in areas far afield from the law. Such research, since it is not specifically legal research, falls outside the scope of this book.

This book is also not about current awareness. All practicing lawyers have the responsibility of keeping up to date on legal developments in their areas of expertise, so as to be able to spot issues and recognize emerging problems or opportunities for their clients. Every area of practice has its own array of electronic news outlets and you will have the ability (and the obligation) to keep abreast of these. Moreover, many of the print sources discussed in this book arrive in the law practitioner's establishment fairly bristling with aids to maintaining such current awareness. Each volume of West's National Reporter System, for example, is chockablock with goodies intended for this purpose, e.g., tables of rules of procedure cited in that volume, words and phrases judicially construed in that volume, and so forth. These may, indeed, furnish the conscientious attorney with passingly interesting reading. However, they rarely figure in the process of active legal research, limited as they are to the tiny subset of materials (albeit recent materials) included in the selfsame volume. While we will occasionally mention some of these sources, we will focus instead on those elements that contribute usefully to research on a specific legal question rather than to speculative and abstract consideration of a legal authority's recent output.

1.3   WHY YOU MUST MAKE A RESEARCH PLAN

As advanced legal research students, it is you who are advanced. You are already somewhat versed in the law and know a bit about what you are looking for and about what problems you might encounter in finding it. Perhaps the most common problem expressed by students beginning a course in advanced legal research is the difficulty of knowing when to stop searching. We have already mentioned the frequent and demanding obligation to prove a negative through research. Yet the opposite, seemingly simpler and more inviting task of establishing a positive legal proposition is actually more fraught with peril because of this very problem of not knowing when to stop. When looking for legal authority for a proposition, the inexperienced legal researcher all too often falls prey to the *"EUREKA!"* syndrome, i.e., he finds something that supports his claim, and calls it quits right there. In trying to prove a negative, on the other hand, there is no treacherous *"EUREKA!* I have found it!" moment. There are only slowly mounting indications that you have, in fact, done enough: you start to see no new authorities cited, you have made a rational research plan, and you have carried it out.

The importance of making a rational and informed research plan cannot be overemphasized. By making such a plan (in writing, please, since this is tantamount to a contract with yourself!), you can avoid the pitfall of settling for the first (or fifth) plausible answer you encounter, when your conclusion is based on still incomplete research. This pitfall yawns all the larger in the electronic world. The speed and facility of flitting from one source to another in the multitasking environment makes it easy to fall into the trap of attempting basically random research stabs at each new source; this leads to sketchy results, inviting error and defeat.

The research plan can save you from this all-too-common fate. Basically, the purpose of the research plan is twofold. First, it ensures that you have built checks into your research that will keep you from reaching unwarranted conclusions. Second, once carried out, it provides the structure for logical and orderly documentation of what you have done. This documentation is particularly important when you do not find anything that satisfies the requested conditions, since the worth of your negative findings lies wholly in your testimony of where you looked. This also applies when you *did* find something, your document trail serving to validate its appropriateness and allowing others to build upon your work efficiently.

1.4 DOCUMENTING WHAT YOU FIND: CITATIONS

Documenting the fulfillment of your research plan should be done in such a way as to allow both today's and tomorrow's researchers to follow your trail easily. Such is the principle behind the sometimes irritating but nonetheless monumentally helpful rules of legal citation, such as (pre-eminently) those enshrined in *The Bluebook*. But in your own personal research writeups, you need not restrict yourself to leaving a trail universally legible to any and all researchers wherever they may be. You can and should feel free to enrich your paper trail with additional comments and details that pertain to your local environment. To be sure, you should always give full and correct citations to all references, so there is no possibility of error later. But you can also benefit by noting additional location information such as page numbers that are not part of the citation, hints on getting to a particular website, volume numbers, shelf locations, even color or other physical characteristics of volumes. The key here is to give such additional information in an easily strippable form, so that it can be removed at a stroke when adapting your research for a more generic reader.

At the other end of the spectrum from such private notes about exactly where the information you have found is enshrined, you need to be aware of the developing trend of universal citation systems. These systems derive from the star pagination schemes of yesteryear, which directed readers of a subsequent edition of a legal text, by means of graphical symbols interposed in that text, to the original location of the same text in an earlier edition. The "star pagination" concept was widely used during the last century to enable researchers to move back and forth between the West editions of published cases and their counterparts published by the government or by competing commercial publishers.

Today's universal citation systems, such as those adopted by the American Bar Association, the American Association of Law Libraries, and by some federal and many state courts since the early 1990s, seek to remove the "pagination" from the star pagination idea. Rather, the text itself gets divided up and labeled in manageable chunks (typically a paragraph), each of which is assigned an identifying number that is associated with the larger document and set of documents of which it is a part. One purpose of this graphically ungainly exercise is to remove the systemic preference that the traditional page-bound citation systems afforded to established print publishers of legal authorities. But by so doing, the new systems undercut one of the basic functions of citation: i.e., the referral of the researcher to an unchangeable physical reference standard, a tangible and yet distributed text of record. The world is grappling with this issue in a wide variety of contexts; suffice it for now to remember that, as of this writing, *The Bluebook* requires the legal writer to cite to physically printed texts when they exist.

1.5 DOCUMENTING WHAT YOU FIND: FORMATS

Such physically printed texts need not be consulted in paper format in order to furnish the desired unchangeable physical reference standard. The tangible reality of a book page is preserved for the researcher's purposes when it is reproduced in any analog-based format: thus, the longstanding acceptance of microformats (microfilm, microcard, microfiche) as reliably equivalent to the volumes they enshrined. To be sure, a manufacturing error can render an individual page illegible or misleading, and this has certainly created problems for individual researchers dependent on microformats for their information. But when it works, it works great. Even better for some purposes are electronically created image-based reproductions of print pages: digital graphic versions of the documents, such as Portable Document Format (.pdf) files, that capture the reality of the page content for digital reproduction and distribution. Since the publisher can see instantly that an error in image capture has occurred, the image can be redone on the spot, preserving the integrity of the document.

Increasingly, .pdf files of legal information are "born .pdf," i.e., they do not reproduce any pre-existing physically printed text but constitute the format of original distribution. Accordingly, establishing the authenticity of such materials is becoming more and more reliant on establishing the authoritativeness of the electronic issuer. The value of the .pdf files in these "born .pdf" instances, from the researcher's point of view, has to do with the ability of their issuer to provide credible evidence of such files' stability.

Thus, .pdf files and microfiche can be said to function as proxies and in many cases as full equivalents of their print originals for citation purposes. Yet no analog-based format can approach the flexibility, penetrability, and manipulability of text-based resources such as the full-text databases of Lexis Advance and Westlaw. These long-established online legal research vendors have been joined in recent years by other useful full-text providers such as Bloomberg Law, Casemaker Legal, and Fastcase. Bloomberg Law, especially, provides many documents in both text and as .pdf files. When a choice exists, the researcher needs to identify the best format for each stage of research. In many cases, the electronic text-based resources will be the sources of choice for location of information, while the print-origin sources (whether distributed in paper, fiche, or electronically) will still be relied upon for text verification and authentication.

1.6   WHAT SOURCE TO USE?

Although *The Bluebook* is now beating around the bush a bit on this matter of physical format, no such shyness is in evidence in preferring one source to another within format. The general principle in play is that the preferred citation is to the source authorized by the legal authority in question, even when that is not really the source that most researchers use in everyday life. Thus, when dealing with federal statutory law, *The Bluebook* commands the writer to "cite the *United States Code* (U.S.C.), the official federal code, whenever possible" (*The Bluebook* R. 12.3), compelling the researcher who has done all the legwork via, e.g., the United States Code Annotated (U.S.C.A.), to cross-check the text found there against the official text, the U.S. government-produced but comparatively unwieldy *United States Code*. All sources are clearly not created equal, and to avoid getting tripped up by a discrepancy, you need to keep strict track of which ones you actually perused with your own eyes. Looking at a reprint source may be the best you can do, or even the best thing that anyone could do, but you must acknowledge that you looked at that reprint source rather than at the original on which it was based. This comes up frequently in the case of the *United States Code Congressional and Administrative News*, the indispensable *U.S.C.C.A.N.*, frequently the first (and therefore for a while the only) widely distributed print source for United States federal statutes. You are specifically required to cite to *U.S.C.C.A.N.* if that is all that is available, rather than to use the Statutes at Large pagination indicated in U.S.C.C.A.N. to construct a hypothetical Stat. citation. To maximize usefulness to the subsequent researcher, you are to include the Stat. (i.e., Statutes at Large) pagination as a parenthetical part of your U.S.C.C.A.N. citation, but you must include your U.S.C.C.A.N. source (*The Bluebook* R. 12.6).

This principle is generalized in *The Bluebook* Rule 1.6 (a)(ii), governing the use of material conveniently reprinted in a non-official source. The third example given, citation of a U.S.C.C.A.N. reprint of a Congressional Committee Report, comes up frequently. Moreover, the notion of using a U.S.C.C.A.N. reprint of a Committee Report without indicating U.S.C.C.A.N. as its source vividly demonstrates the dangers of not acknowledging your actual source. The U.S.C.C.A.N. versions of the reports are generally excerpts, and even though the precise text quoted may have survived the transplant intact, the context in which it appears may be different enough to affect how it is read and understood. The same dangers are posed by using materials culled from casebooks, treatises, or looseleaf services. You should always either go the extra mile of referring back to the original source for the reprinted material, or acknowledge what you have done and either take the rap or accept the praise for having engaged in such a shortcut.

1.7 FOLLOWING TANGENTS:
HOW MUCH IS TOO MUCH?

Don't let your research plan keep you from doing *more*. You must be prepared to recognize new opportunities for investigation as they present themselves in the course of your research. You cannot allow the plan (your own or any canned instructions or checklists for legal research) to turn you into an automaton. Grappling with the implications of the legal authorities you uncover is the heart of your professional function, and you cannot abdicate this responsibility. That said, you need to be able to decide when to stop.

You can and should stop a line of research when you get to a point where the facts you are encountering, the law you are finding, or both, are no longer relevant to your research question. This is a judgment call that will become easier to make as you become more familiar with the subject at hand. More straightforwardly, you should stop when you come full circle and are back at your familiar core of material again. Once you are in a closed system of this type, you need to step back and consider whether it would be prudent to take a fresh approach.

On the other hand, you should not stop when you get to a point where you continue to find new cases but they are all similar. The temptation here is to get overwhelmed by the multiplicity of similar cases, and to stop reading. Instead, you can spot-check them for relevant variables such as similar facts or analogous law, and then narrow them down by applying combinations of criteria that make them ever closer to your situation. Another way to narrow down a potentially overwhelming array of seemingly similar cases is to run them through a citator to see which ones are of lasting importance. Which ones have been recently cited? Which ones have been voluminously cited, cited in law review articles, cited by higher courts, or in other jurisdictions? These are the cases that are likely to be the bases for the next stage of your research.

Another factor to consider in deciding when your research is finished is what kind of assignment you received. Different types of research are called for at different times. "Get me a case" means something very different from "what is the law on x." The former is clearly calling for a more abbreviated research foray than the latter. But beware! "A case" doesn't mean any old case relevant to the matter, but one *good* case. A "good case" ideally means one with a desirable interpretation of the law from the client's point of view, especially when it explicitly criticizes undesirable interpretations. As compared with the client's situation, the ideal "good case" will involve similar facts, a relevant jurisdiction (maybe even the same judge!), and still be valid, i.e., still "good law." Obviously this latter point, if explored in detail, takes you over into the other sort of research, the more exhaustive "find me the law on x." It is all a matter of degree.

1.8   HOW TO MAKE A RESEARCH PLAN

As you start to make a research plan you will need to determine first who it is that has authority to speak on your issue. Often more than one legal authority has a legitimate claim to speak to an issue, so you should plan to address them in descending order of authority. As a simple example, if one legislative body, e.g., the United States Congress, has preemptive authority over a particular subject matter, you should research its output before considering the output of other lesser, probably more local, authorities. As a less-simple example, if there is reason to anticipate that a normally higher authority would afford deference to the opinion of a nominally subordinate one, you should start with the output of the latter. Thus, for matters of local court rule interpretation, you would start with the opinions of the local court involved, rather than go straight to the United States Supreme Court to see what it has to say. Similarly for substantive issues of state law.

Once you have decided upon the authority in which you are interested, you next need to consider what are the different places where you could look for its output. As you will see in the following chapters, the output of most legal authorities is now available in many different places and formats. You will need to consider the differences between the options and whether there is anything to be gained by looking in multiple places.

Finally, you should consider whether somebody has done this work before. Other attorneys in your workplace may have considered this same issue last week, and you will want to find out how that work may be accessible to you. The armies of law students, law professors, and practitioners toiling away to produce law journals may have done a lot of the legwork on your subject already. And of course, librarians and other legal writers sustain a whole industry of publications aimed at distilling and distributing legal research to the profession. Make sure you are not reinventing the wheel, at least where an appropriate wheel already exists!

When you have considered all the factors above, you are ready to set down a logically ordered and thorough plan. Your plan should account for all the elements in our diagram in **Table 1.A**. It should specify where and how you are going to look for each of the following: the primary source that determines the legal issue, its history, its commentary, and its progeny or applications. Although each of these should be accounted for, elements that may not be necessary should not be sketched out in detail unless they prove to be so, e.g., mention "legislative history to be investigated if necessary," but only plan legislative history out if you, the courts, or commentators find some ambiguity, error, or omission in the governing statute.

Writing out a research plan will probably prove discomfiting to many at first, since it calls for a possibly unfamiliar assertion of researcher control over the process. The untutored legal researcher of today first dives instinctively into exploratory full-text searching of legal databases. This may or may not be a good idea, depending on the problem at hand. Whether it is a good idea or not can become apparent to the researcher in the course of writing out the research plan. You will need to consider the best uses of full-text searching, and what is its optimal place or places in your plan. You do not usually want to be in the situation of having full-text searching as the only arrow in your quiver.

1.9   BEST USES OF FULL-TEXT SEARCHING

That said, the full-text searching of large legal databases is understandably a mainstay of legal researchers today, and the unique functionalities that such searching provides should be exploited in almost every research plan. When doing case law research, full-text searches can be used by the clueless to mount fishing expeditions to figure out what the blazes is going on, albeit often at a financial cost. Plugging terms from your situation's fact pattern into a query put to a large case law database without any constraining knowledge of the law will usually retrieve other cases from similar situations; these can illuminate for you broadly what the legal issue in the case might actually be. The simplest form of this kind of search would include distinctive keywords from the facts, especially in combination with each other. Terms of art, either factual or legal, are particularly powerful when used in this way.

At the other end of the process, full-text searching should always be employed as a check on the completeness and validity of subject index-based research. Once you are approaching the end of research through other means, you should do a full-text search to see whether completely different subject indexing terms come up in cases retrieved via the full-text search, and, if so, figure out why. This use of full-text searching allows you to reap the benefits of subject indexing without suffering its limitations.

Beyond fishing expeditions, and beyond checking up on your other research, full-text searching can be especially effective in areas with which you are already quite familiar. In such cases you are really using it as an updating and current awareness tool to supplement your own knowledge of the area, and it is a powerful tool indeed. However, as a beginning lawyer, such areas will take a while to accumulate.

Finally, full-text searching can be the best way to go in areas of the law that are poorly or unsuitably subject indexed. This is an example of how the elimination of the middleman (the subject indexer) can pay off in certain circumstances. Subject indexing has necessarily focused on areas of greater industry demand, usually as a result of the economic or political environment. But cases of all types come to trial and get published, even some that do not have a powerful economic or political constituency behind them. For finding these kinds of cases, the full-text database search can be the best way to go.

1.10   BEST USES OF FIELDED SEARCHING

While full-text searching offers some indispensable capabilities, the more focused results offered by fielded searching are usually what the researcher wants and needs. While many fields offered in the large legal databases are specific to certain types of documents and will be handled in the appropriate later chapters, some general observations are in order at the outset. The concept of fields, that is, particular categories of information about or from documents that can be searched in isolation from other categories, is not limited to the electronic environment. Highly developed print indexes of fielded information have long been available in American law. Some of the most important fielded searching in law is done in indexing documents which are also available in print in West's American Digest System. The electronic environment, however, offers both newly-created fields and the ability to combine fielded searching with full-text searching.

Newly created fields, i.e., fields that are only accessible in the electronic databases, allow searching by judge's name, by date of decision, and by submerged party names (i.e., parties not included in the short title of the case). The essence of focused and effective searching consists of combining fields effectively in a number of ways. One field-combining technique that speeds case location is to combine a distinctive word in the title field with a range of dates in the date field. Full-text searching and fielded searching can also be combined to help research efficiently—a full-text search of keywords or terms of art paired with a fielded search for the names of attorneys involved in the current matter can be useful, since those attorneys may have been called in to deal with familiar, i.e., similar, legal issues. Other complex exploratory full-text searches could include terms associated with particular procedural postures in combination with a fielded search for a judge's name, to see how a judge has ruled on similar issues in the past.

Many field-combining techniques boost the effectiveness of subject-oriented research. One such technique is to require multiple subject headings that must all be present. Another is to focus the search by limiting it to the headnote/summary field. The language in the headnotes is extracted for the most part directly from the language in the case; since the headnotes refer only to the significant legal points made by the court in the opinion, a search limited to the headnotes field will only pick up cases where the search terms relate to the main thrust of the case, not to passing asides.

1.11 BEST USES OF SEARCHING SUBJECT INDEXED/EDITED DATA

American common law is a huge edifice and its key is the indexing that has developed over the last 150 years. A principal branch of that indexing, the West Key Number System, dates back to 1907, and continues to evolve (conservatively) to this day. The enormous utility of the West Key Number indexing has prompted competing publishers to develop analogous indexing systems, such as the "Topic" terms added to documents in the Lexis Advance database. Whichever indexing scheme is used, there are several common circumstances in which resort to searching the subject indexing fields is strongly indicated.

First, the use of subject indexes is invaluable to the researcher who is learning about the structure and development of the law in a particular area. Even if the area may have been preliminarily identified via a full-text fishing expedition, mapping it out in a coherent fashion will be expedited by the use of subject-indexed information. The indexing schemes are built on hierarchical subject arrangements, so incorporation of that structure into your search will present you with the case law arranged in a meaningful order.

This meaningful order means that you don't need to hit the bullseye every time. Because of the structure of the index, if you don't come up with just the right legal authority on your first try, the material preceding or following your targeted material might well be better for you than what you came looking for. This serendipity factor, made possible by the ability to rummage around in the subject structure of the indexed resource, can help you get your bearings in a new subject.

Subject indexing can also enable the researcher to narrow down a large body of case law to a specific point, especially when few or no distinctive keywords are anticipated in the judicial language. Again, the hierarchical structure of the indexing system enables you to progress from general areas of law to highly specialized points of legal doctrine, based on the refinements of the subject headings assigned to each case by specialized indexers. The difficulty of doing similarly refined searching in just the full texts in a database is compounded when the researcher is not sufficiently familiar with the language used in a particular area to distinguish between apparently minute or inconsistent variations in terminology.

When, on the other hand, the range of vocabulary that can be used in a given legal situation is unusually varied, indexing again comes to the rescue. Even though the judge in one case wrote "lawyer" and "dereliction" and the judge in another similar case wrote "counselor" and "malfeasance," both cases can be found through the good offices of the indexer who put them both (as well as many others) under the rubric of "attorney" and "misconduct." This collocation function of subject indexing is particularly important in our country, with its 51 principal jurisdictions, each of which can develop its own strain of terminology for the same legal reality.

Finally, subject indexing collocates cases not only across jurisdictions, but also over time. The language of indexers needs to be responsive to new developments in the law, but it also needs to enable us to reach across the generations to understand the foundations of today's law in the cases of yesterday. Indexes change slowly, in order to facilitate the comparison of cases from different stages of the law's development. While context and, especially, language change in response to the life of the world outside the courtroom, the indexing terms provide enough continuity to enable the researcher to recognize the legal identity of issues considered.

1.12   WHAT YOU ARE GOING TO LOOK FOR

Please be forewarned that this book is not about checklists or flow charts. Such cookbook instructions may have their place, but they will not teach you how to think about doing legal research. You must yourself be able to generate the checklist, the flow chart, and the research plan, since this process contributes to your professional work product.

That said, even the simplest, most bare-bones research plan will likely involve at least these three elements—1) jurisdiction; 2) subject or topic; 3) keywords or terms of art.

Before diving into research, in either full-text databases or subject-organized resources, you should have a good idea of which jurisdiction's law is likely to apply. Though this always includes some geographic aspect (e.g., New York vs. Texas vs. North Dakota), it should also be considered in the context of federal vs. state vs. municipal or local. At the outset, particularly when conducting research into an area with which you are unfamiliar, you may only be able to identify "Iowa" as a jurisdiction, without any idea whether state or federal law is likely to control. As you become a more experienced researcher, you will likely be able to identify certain areas of law that fall under federal jurisdiction (e.g., copyrights), others that fall under state jurisdiction (e.g., torts), and others that fall under municipal/local jurisdiction (e.g., zoning). Even at the outset, however, identifying as narrow a jurisdiction as possible will be helpful, and you should do your best to be able to answer that question before you ever run a search or look at a subject index. You will, after all, use different authorities to support a point of law in Texas than you would in New York.

Subject or topic is, naturally, very important when you are using indexes based on subjects, but even full-text searching will be improved by an understanding of what general legal subject encompasses the issues you are researching. This can often be best understood by thinking about law school classes—if you were reading about a case involving the same issues as described in your case file or research assignment, what class would you likely be reading for? Contracts? Intellectual Property? Criminal Procedure?

Finally, keywords, or terms of art, are the specific terms or legal concepts that you generally think of when contemplating a full-text search.

The unique opportunities in case law research provided by full-text database searching have led us to address case law in many of these opening observations. However, the point about being able to understand the law's development across a span of time can usefully be extended to all sources of legal authority. You will always want to be armed with an understanding not only of the applicable legal authorities, but of the antecedents, the commentary on, and the applications of those authorities. In order to emphasize this injunction, we are willing, despite our aforementioned aversion to formulae for the researcher, to present one simple diagram (see **Table 1.A**).

This diagram, which represents graphically the sources you need to account for in your research plan, can be adapted to the different types of legal authority that you will be using. The sources represented in it are conceptual and general enough that they will not relieve any researcher from the burden of thought about what they are doing. Rather, it is hoped that the diagram will stimulate thought about how the law you are researching has developed over time, and how it is likely to develop in the future.

1.13   TABLE

TABLE 1.A

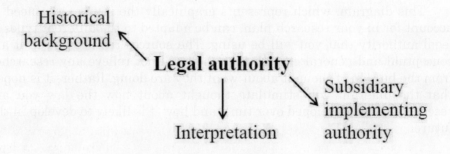

Legal authority
- Historical background
- Interpretation
- Subsidiary implementing authority

CHAPTER 2

STATUTES

■ ■ ■

2.1 STATUTES FIRST

American legal research today starts with statutes. The first step in deciding legal obligations and rights is to determine whether there is a statute that governs the situation. A statute is a decree by the sovereign establishing a legal requirement of those subject to its authority. In the United States we have many kinds of statutes, and many sorts of legal requirements, but ultimately their authority can all be traced to the granting of legislative powers by "[w]e the People of the United States," in our Constitution. The humblest parking ordinance passed by a one-stoplight hamlet gets its teeth from the nation's consent to be so governed.

How that consent gets translated into the myriad levels of legislating and regulating is treated later in the chapters on Legislative History and Administrative Law Research. But its most direct and unalloyed product is the legislation that emanates from our sovereign political body, the United States Congress. In the following discussion of statutory law, we will focus primarily on the statutory output of the federal legislature, as exemplar of the legislative function in this country, and comment only secondarily on state statutory research as differences require. Be aware, however, that the code/session law structure is typical of state law as well as federal. Be aware also that it is frequently better to get your hooks into statutory law via the use of secondary sources. Nonetheless, you will always need to know how to work with the primary sources so you can absolutely scour them for every relevant provision, once you have found a way in to the statute via your chosen starting point.

2.2 CODES

As legal researchers, our work with statutes usually begins (and often ends) with a by-product of legislation: the statutory code. The United States Code ("the Code") is a confection based on the legislative output of Congress, but infinitely easier to digest. Since the Code takes the raw federal statutes and incorporates them into a subject arrangement of the law, it is the usual starting point for federal legal research. The researcher needs, of course, to concern herself as well with the statutory sources of the code, and with statutes that are not incorporated into the code, but those concerns should usually be addressed after thorough exploration of what the Code itself has to offer.

Three different publishers produce versions of the United States Code (all of which also include the U.S. Constitution), and each of them offers it both in print and electronically. Additionally, archival editions of each version are available on microfiche. The most useful and most frequently consulted versions of the Code are the annotated versions, which are commercially published and continually updated. The *United States Code Annotated (U.S.C.A.),* published by West since 1927, was for many years the most widely used tool in American legal research. It now appears on the Westlaw platform as well. The United States Code Service (U.S.C.S.), currently published by LexisNexis and available in paper and via the Lexis Advance platform, offers a variety of different features. Finally, the United States Code itself (U.S.C.), as published by the U.S. Government, is produced in print and also distributed electronically by a number of different entities (see **Table 2.A**). It appears in a new edition every six years, and is supplemented annually between editions.

2.3   WORKING WITH A STATUTORY CODE INDEX

The researcher seeking to identify a statute that will control the legal situation she confronts must choose whether to start looking from the bottom up—i.e., from the details of the situation—or from the top down—i.e., working through the logic of the hierarchical structure of the code. In most instances, researchers new to a subject will start from the bottom up, working from the salient details of the situation at hand. The most efficient way to locate statutes pertaining to a particular set of circumstances is through a code index. Thus, the very first step in most legal research using primary materials is to consult the index of the appropriate statutory code.

What does the index do for you? It pulls together all the code sections on a given topic from wherever they may appear in the code. Since a code is a subject arrangement, this may seem redundant. However, a quick examination of the U.S. Code's structure will reveal the reason for the considerable utility of its index. The Code is built on the basis of 53 "Titles," or broad subjects. These 53 Titles are ordered mostly alphabetically and each is assigned a number. Within each Title, the Code sections are to some extent arranged hierarchically and thematically. General provisions on a given subject come before more specific ones, and new sections are jammed in between existing ones where necessary to preserve thematic continuity. Thus, browsing the Code will play an important part in statutory research, as sections proximate to a retrieved section will quite probably also be relevant to a researcher's concerns.

However, not all Code sections with bearing on a particular topic will necessarily be found proximate to each other, nor even within the same title. The process by which new statutes are incorporated into the Code requires each statute to be worked into the Code sections and areas it most clearly affects. A statute can be chopped up and incorporated into a number of different titles if necessary. But if the subject of interest to the researcher is one that does not fit wholly within the boundaries of a given title, a tool is required to launch the researcher into all the different titles that have incorporated statutes on said subject. That tool is the index.

Typically, statutory codes like the United States Code will have a General Index that covers the whole edifice. Thus, the *U.S.C.A.*, the *U.S.C.S.*, and the *U.S.C.* all have multiple volume General Indexes that direct the researcher to particular Titles and sections. The commercial versions (the *U.S.C.A.* and *U.S.C.S.* indexes) are republished annually; the *U.S.C.*'s periodic updating supplements get their own indexes. In addition to the General Indexes, the *U.S.C.A.* and *U.S.C.S.* have indexes at the end of each Title in the main volumes. Since each of these individual title indexes is only updated when the main volume containing it is updated, the General Index is usually more up to date. Changes to the Code that appear in a pocket part are therefore usually indexed only in the General Index, with limited exceptions, e.g., Titles 26 and 42, whose length and complexity have led the *U.S.C.A.* to issue revisions to those Titles' indexes in their annual pocket parts.

Code indexes cannot be mere concordances: they need to do more than just register and sort the actual language of the statute. They need to include or omit a section in which a particular term is used from an index heading depending on whether the section is really *about* that subject or, on the contrary, just mentions the term. The best indexes also use alternate language so that a researcher without prior knowledge of the statutory terminology can find some way in to the code's content.

2.4   TERMS TO LOOK UP IN CODE INDEXES

First and foremost, you should be looking for terms that you anticipate finding in the code language itself. Distinctive terms from the code language are almost always picked up in the code indexes. Abstract legal concepts are sometimes picked up, but by no means always. Moreover, the language you seek may only be represented in the index by a subheading, without an alphabetical main entry of its own. If you can't find the term you seek, think more generally about what larger subject headings should contain your term as a subheading. If the language that you expect to find in the code is not turning up in the index at all, try looking for synonymous terms.

Occasionally interpretive, analytic, or synthesizing terms are used to draw terms together. For example, in the *U.S.C.S.* General Index the entry for the insanity defense is a subhead under the MENTAL HEALTH heading, with a reference leading there from the heading INSANITY DEFENSE REFORM ACT OF 1984. Unfortunately, this helpful drawing together of code sections pertaining to all manner of mental health-related topics points up a big drawback with indexed materials: the potential for editorial error. The researcher who duly proceeds to "MENTAL HEALTH— Defense of insanity, 18 § 20" is left dangling: 18 § 20 proves to be titled "Financial institution defined," and contains nary a mention of the insanity defense. Depending on your opinion of the institutions of capitalism, this index heading may or may not have a certain poetic resonance, but it probably does not accomplish the task you had in mind. Somehow, the current number of the section of the Code, 18 § 17 (changed to this from § 20 in 1986 by an act of Congress) was not updated by the index compilers. Happily, we have the opportunity to do an end run around the sloppy indexer by searching in the full text of the code database when the index lets us down (if not before).

2.5   DISTINCTIONS BETWEEN CODE INDEXES

As mentioned above, in the commercial codes the most important distinction between the General Indexes and the title indexes is the potential difference in currency. The General Index is updated annually, and therefore will cover additions and revisions to the Code that appear in the pocket parts to the main volumes. The title indexes, however, are only as recent as the main volume that they appear in, and the pocket parts do not generally contain their own indexing. The title indexes also contain listings only for code sections within the confines of that one Title. For example, the General Index to the *U.S.C.A.* lists Copyrights—Civil Air Patrol, 36 § 40306. There is no cross reference to this section within the title index to Title 17, Copyrights, because it falls outside of Title 17.

The title indexes do offer some entry points that are absent from the General Index. Despite the claim in the *U.S.C.A.* General Index's prefatory matter that "it incorporates index references for ... selected Code of Federal Regulations' promulgations and other materials set out in the Code," the title indexes contain many more references to CFR sections reprinted in the Code volumes than does the General Index. For example, the title index to Title 17, Copyright, contains numerous subject subheadings that lead to CFR sections; these entries do not appear in the General Index. And, of course, the title index offers easy portability! Despite these title index features, however, the more up-to-date coverage of the General Index makes use of the latter indispensable.

It is important to note that the index is not itself a legal document, but a separate and independent work of authorship. Different indexes can use different terms to point researchers to the same code sections. For example, compare these entries from the indexes of the different publications of the Code:

> *U.S.C.A.:* WEAPONS—Look-alike firearms, definitions, 15 § 5001;

> *U.S.C.S.:* WEAPONS AND FIREARMS—Replicas or imitations, 15 § 5001, 18 § 921;

> *U.S.C.:* WEAPONS—Look-alike firearms, definitions. 15 § 5001 & WEAPONS—Replicas, antique firearms, 18 § 921.

On the other hand, the same (or equivalent) terms can point to different sections according to different indexes. Compare, for example, *U.S.C.A.:* WEAPONS—Records and recordation, 18 § 925 and *U.S.C.S.:* WEAPONS AND FIREARMS—Records, 18 § 923.

The indexes also differ in the granularity with which different subjects are handled, although not consistently: each of the three indexes contains a different combination of headings. For example, the *U.S.C.A.* and *U.S.C.* both contain entries for "WAX," but the *U.S.C.S.* contains no equivalent entry. The point to remember here is that while, as you would expect, the index language does closely track the statutory language to which it refers, the indexes of different code versions still differ. If you are not finding what you need in one version, it may prove fruitful to try another. Do note that the indexes to the *U.S.C.A.* and the *U.S.C.* are far more similar than are any other pair of indexes; there is an overlap, as will be seen, between the production process of the two publications. Since the *U.S.C.S.* index is more different from the other two than they are from each other, combining a *U.S.C.S.* index search with one of the other two is more likely to add something to your search than would searching the other two alone.

2.6   USING A CODE INDEX ONLINE

Both the Lexis Advance and the Westlaw versions of the Code offer two distinct ways of accessing subject indexing material online. When using the United States Code Annotated Index on Westlaw, you first see only main subject headings from the print General Index with one letter per page. You cannot see the subheadings that break down the subjects into detail and actually lead you to Code sections. The browsing feature of this index view only allows you to scan the already visible alphabetical list of main subject headings, not the underlying subheadings. In order to get to the subheadings and Code references, you have to choose a main heading and click on it. If it doesn't turn out to have anything of use to you, you have to go back to the main subject heading screen and look again. This inability to scan subheadings from the start makes use of the online index clunkier and more time-consuming than it would be to sweep your eye over the equivalent amount of material in the print indexes.

Your second option is to conduct a search of this index using the main search box toward the top of the page, but only after first navigating to a page that allows you to browse the index headings. Importantly, however, this search is limited to those same main subject headings. Take, for example, a search for the term "Transfers." That search in the United States Code Annotated Index yields four results: 1) Generation-Skipping Transfers; 2) National Commission on Electronic Fund Transfers; 3) Voluntary Transfers of Leave; 4) Wire Transfers. Second-level results, such as the index entry for COPYRIGHTS > Transfers cannot be located via a search for "Transfers."

The electronic version of the U.S.C.S. Index on Lexis Advance displays differently than does Westlaw's U.S.C.A. Index in that you can use the arrow to the left of an entry to expand particular entries, allowing you to browse within them instead of clicking a link and being taken to a new page. You can repeat this step with the initial letters, main subject headings, and all subheadings, drilling down as many levels as exist for the narrowest relevant term, without ever losing the trail. You can also click the hyperlinked main subject heading or any subheading to be taken to that specific entry listing, which includes every available subdivision. Don't be thrown off by the Lexis Advance search/browse page's referring to this material as "TOC" (Table of Contents): it consists, as does the "index" view in Westlaw's U.S.C.A., of the alphabetically arranged principal headings from the print index, individually linked to pages showing each term's alphabetically arranged subheadings from that same index. None of this content relates to the Tables of Contents in the print codes, which are structurally based (and little-used) signposts to the page number location of material in each individual print volume.

Most importantly, with both the U.S.C.S. and U.S.C.A. online versions, the number of index headings and subheadings viewable at a glance is significantly smaller than with the print index. The print index offers the ability to sweep over large portions of subject matter, capsulized in the form of index subject headings and subheadings, and thus to see your sought-after topic in context. Here, in our very first research tool encountered, we meet up with the issue of serendipity versus targeted searching discussed in the first chapter, and see the different problems and opportunities offered by each. In this case, the balance is unusually skewed in favor of serendipity, since in statutory searching, the language being searched is typically so taut and precise that the structure of the index adds more value than does the ability to zero in on particular language used in the statute but not in the index.

2.7   FINDING THE STATUTE BY FINDING A CASE

The other principal way to figure out what statute may be applicable to the facts of your particular situation is to find cases in which the facts are close to yours, and then ascertain what statute or statutes were found applicable or at least discussed in those cases. Finding a case with good fact pattern resemblance is discussed in **Chapter 5** below. Once you find such a case, on Westlaw, Lexis Advance, and Bloomberg Law you will be able to click through to the statutes cited, but remember that you should not restrict yourself to those precise sections alone. As ever with code-based research, you should take advantage of the subject arrangement and peruse both all the proximate sections and the larger structure of the code to make sure you are finding every relevant portion.

2.8   WORKING WITH THE STRUCTURE OF THE CODE

You can think of both the similar case method and the code index method as being "from the bottom up" techniques for finding relevant statutory law. These methods are definitely the way to go when you are unfamiliar with the law in a given area. But once you are reasonably well-versed in some area of the law, you will probably feel the urge to use a more "top down" method when working with statutory codes. This would mean working from the structure within the code itself to arrive at the sections you need.

As mentioned above, the U.S. Code is arranged in 53 named Titles, which are mostly alphabetically arranged and then numbered. For the most part, the numbers and the names of Titles have remained fixed since the Code was created in 1926, at which time it fit into one physical volume! Some of the Titles have become enormous and complex since that time, necessitating elaborate elongated section numbering schemes to accommodate burgeoning legislative developments within particular portions of the Code.

Title 42, Public Health and Welfare, for example, has seen lots of growth and has a correspondingly complex structure: 42 U.S.C. § 1395i–2a has a subsection 1395i–2a (d)(1)(B)(i), and 42 U.S.C. § 1320a–7a has a subsection 1320a–7a(i)(6)(A)(iii)(I). Title 15, Commerce and Trade (which covers securities) also fairly bristles with letters and numbers, as in 15 U.S.C. § 77bbbb, which is preceded by § 77aaaa, which is in turn preceded by sections 77aaa through 77zzz, sections 77aa through 77mm, sections 77a through 77z–3, and plain old section 77. Some of these fancier section numbers pose more of a problem than others: considerable care is needed to make sure, e.g., that section 77lll is not misrendered somewhere along the line of transmission as simply a five digit number or that reference to

Title 15, section 77d(d) undergoes a slight change to morph into the completely different section of 77dd!

Some Titles of the Code make up in variety of subject matter (each covered in a separate section) what they lack in organizational complexity: Title 36, Patriotic and National Observances, Ceremonies, and Organizations marches straight up to § 300,113, though it skips many numbers along the way. On the other hand, some Titles, rooted in a different historical world, are almost moribund. Title 27, Intoxicating Liquors, has seen few changes since its inception, as can be seen by its current iteration in one slim volume of the *U.S.C.A.*, with a copyright date of 1927, accompanied by a slim current pocket part.

This particular unassuming volume of the *U.S.C.A.* illustrates the difficulties of pinning down authority in an immutable form. Although the latest printing of this volume consulted during the preparation of this book, the 1927 edition in its 1987 (25th) reprint, retains the original copyright date and, therefore, one would assume, the original content, it has a reset title page and has dropped one of the publishers both from the title page and from the copyright page. Nowhere in the formal citation to this source would the distinction between this printing and the earlier printings be evident. This brings up a very practical reason the official *U.S.C.* is preferred for authentication purposes: no reprinting is involved, since each edition is published separately.

Title 34, which became Crime Control and Law Enforcement in 2017, used to be Navy, until Congress eliminated that Title in 1956 and distributed its provisions within Title 10, Armed Forces (formerly Army). A similar fate befell Title 6, Surety Bonds, in 1947. After many years, that title number has now been reassigned to Domestic Security. Beginning with the 2014 Supplement to the U.S.C., two new Titles appear as part of the Code. Provisions relating to voting and elections were taken from Titles 2 and 42 and combined in a new Title 52, Voting and Elections. Title 54— National Park Service and Related Programs—was also created in 2014. Further additions are in the works as well, including Title 53—Small Business and Title 56—Wildlife. For more details on these projects, visit http://uscode.house.gov/ and select "Positive Law Codification" from the menu on the left. Despite this recent flurry of activity, changes to the Title arrangement have historically been infrequent; when they occur, tables are published showing the distribution of the code material to new sections, or its other disposition (see **Section 2.13**).

When working from the top down, the first step is to pick which Title to examine. Electronically, this is just a matter of consulting a menu in whichever U.S. Code database you have selected to use. In print, the commercial publishers make Title location easier by putting the names of the Titles on the spine. *U.S.C.A.* generally puts no more than one Title in a volume, except for the foundational Titles 1–4; both *U.S.C.S.* and *U.S.C.* include some mixed-Title volumes throughout the Code.

If you are really at a loss for which Title to examine, you can do a full-text search of the Code database as a fishing expedition for suggested Titles. But searching the entire Code for most terms is an awkward, confusing, and frustrating enterprise which—except for this limited preliminary step—we counsel against.

Having determined a Title of the Code in which to begin, the structurally-oriented researcher turns next to that Title's table of contents. In print, the table of contents appears at the beginning of the Title, and (in the commercially published versions) any changes to the table of contents appear in an updated version at the beginning of the pocket part for the Title's first volume. In the electronic versions, the entries are likewise descriptively-named groupings of sections. You can drill down from these groupings to an array of individual sections and thence to the text of those sections.

The groupings listed in the first level of the table of contents are most often called "Chapters," with a capital "C." They appear in the official Code and are uniform throughout the different publications. The original Chapters were devised by the codifiers. Sometimes changes and additions are devised by the Code editors, but more often they are included in the legislation that is changing or adding to the text of the Title. The Chapters tend to be very broad in scope. Sometimes, as in the new Title 6, Domestic Security, they are further divided into subchapters. The numbering of some Chapters occasionally furnishes the beginning of the section numbers that fall within them, but more usually they are unrelated. In some Titles, Chapters do not make up the first level of the table of contents, but are located further down. For example, in Title 10, Armed Forces, there are Subtitles and Parts before you get down to the Chapter level; in Title 26, the Internal Revenue Code, there are only Subtitles between Titles and Chapters. Though the precise terminology may vary, the important underlying principle of Code organization remains constant: group like with like, related materials close to one another, to allow the researcher to conduct efficient statutory research.

But while the Chapter or Subtitle structure is crucial for "top-down" research, it does not comprise part of the citation scheme for any section. Nor are Chapters themselves usually cited formally as a unit, although they can be used as informal shorthand: think of "Chapter 11 reorganization" as a term in bankruptcy discourse. Instead, if you want to discuss the group of Code sections that make up Chapter 4 of Title 17, Copyright, you would cite to Title 17 U.S.C. §§ 401–412. This is in order to provide maximum precision in what you are telling the reader. The Chapter 4 of today is not necessarily the Chapter 4 that existed last week, and by specifying the sections under discussion you eliminate the need for the reader laboriously to reconstruct what Chapter 4 looked like at the moment you were writing. Note also that the General Index, discussed in **Section 2.3**, provides references to a specific section or a range of sections, rather than to Chapters or Subtitles. Similarly, the table of contents of the print code does not send you from a Chapter number and name to a page number, but rather to a starting section number for that Chapter. The fluid and dynamic nature of the Code, subject to constant revision, addition, amendment, and deletion, means that page numbers would be more confusing than helpful. Instead, the section numbers themselves form the basis for locating text within the volume or the database, and thus constitute necessary elements for citation to the text.

Having found the right Chapter or Chapters, the structurally-oriented researcher skims the individual section names for likely-looking ones, reads those, and then reads outward from them in an expanding circle. The subject-hierarchical structure of a statutory code means that linear proximity is usually a good indicator of relevance. This is one reason why working with statutory codes is easier in print than electronically. Taking advantage of these features in print is intuitive, but it requires an extra step in electronic format. Navigation buttons exist in both Lexis Advance and Westlaw, but as a user you must seek them out to benefit from them. Having the whole Chapter physically before you as you work through it in print gives you a tangible sense of where you are in relation to the section you started from, and thus how all the bits that you are finding fit together. By contrast, the item-by-item reading style necessitated by screen formats can make it hard to keep each section you read squarely in its appropriate context. Moreover, the order in which things are stated in a code can be significant when construing the statute, and that sense of order is harder to perceive and keep track of in the electronic text, especially when you've reached a section of the Code via a search rather than by drilling down to the relevant section.

2.9   CODE CURRENCY

Both "top-down" and "from-the-bottom-up" researchers will eventually arrive at the sections they want to use. The text of those sections, however, may vary depending on which version of the Code you have chosen to look at. Electronic versions may already have incorporated changes to the Code text effected by statutes that were enacted after the most recent print versions went to press. Thus, the electronic version of the U.S. Code incorporates changes made by Supplements to the current edition before those supplements have been distributed in print. The as-yet electronic-only content added to the U.S.C. database at the website of its creator, the Office of the Law Revision Counsel (see **Table 2.A**), gets incorporated into the structure of the code. Electronic versions of the commercially published codes include updating statutory material that varies in its currency.

The code-updating structure online can be less streamlined in the state law context. For example, while Lexis Advance and Westlaw offer New York statutory databases that integrate the code with recent statutes up through a date that can be considerably later than the date of the last printed pocket part to the code, both services put even newer statutory enactments, unedited, into databases separate from the code. You are then alerted via graphical symbols or an instruction to update when that separate database contains material that affects the code section you have retrieved. We shall return to this point in the section on how to find session laws.

Although updating code text online is obviously an easier process, some researchers prefer to go as far as possible with the paper sources before resorting to electronic databases for final updating. When you have a series of paper sources in front of you, each containing an updating change to a code section, it makes the timing and interrelationship of the changes graphically clear, and facilitates comparison of the different evolving versions of the text. How, then, to go about updating the Code using paper sources? We will assume, for this purpose, that you will use a commercially produced version of the Code, since the official U.S. Code has such a significant publication lag.

Before you begin, make sure that the version of the Code that you are using is the most recent one. This can be ascertained by referring to the website of the publisher. As soon as you think you have found a relevant section or sections, you should check for updates. Do not get caught up in spending too much time parsing a section that has perhaps already been superseded. The first step in updating is to consult the pocket part, the unbound supplement tucked into the slot at the back of the book. Every volume of the commercially published codes has such a slot to accommodate pocket parts. Every such slot must either (a) be filled with a current pocket part, (b) be filled with a cardboard tag alerting you to the existence of a freestanding paperback supplement for the volume, a "proxy pocket part," if you will, or (c) be in a main volume that was published within the current year. You must ascertain which of these alternatives is in play and consult the appropriate material because the next step, supplementation *beyond* the pocket part (or its proxy, the freestanding paperback supplement to the volume), does not include the contents thereof.

The process of going "beyond the pocket part" in print varies slightly in the two different commercial Code publishers, but only after the point when the code component of the statutory law is exhausted (which will be covered in **Section 2.15**). The search for updated Code sections is the same in both versions: after the pocket part you turn to a separate set of paperback updates, periodically issued and typically shelved at the end of the set. The *U.S.C.S.* updating volumes, entitled "Cumulative Later Case and Statutory Service," include the "latest statutory additions, amendments, and repeals classified to Code titles and sections. . ." As with the pocket part, all you need to do here is to look up the Code section of interest, and any changes or additions will be laid out in code format. The *U.S.C.A.* updating supplements, called "Pamphlets" although they can be hefty paperback volumes of well over a thousand pages, are similar, although non-cumulating as between themselves.

You can also consult these paperback updates for changes to the Code by looking in their subject indexes: unlike the pocket part supplements, these volumes do have their own indexing, which is more up-to-date than the annual General Indexes. Do not restrict the language you use to that which proved successful in searching the General Index, since new developments since then may have suggested new indexing terms. Since these Code updates are already laid out in Code format and have been subject indexed, i.e., since substantial (and therefore time-consuming) editorial work has been done, they cannot get you all that up-to-date. To improve your currency further, you need to go beyond the Code into the as-yet uncodified Public Laws, which will be discussed in **Section 2.15**.

2.10 CHOOSING A FORMAT IN WHICH TO DO YOUR CODE RESEARCH

When deciding how to do your code research, check a variety of sources to make sure that the code you are using is as up-to-date as possible. If you are researching in print codes you should definitely plan to check your work for currency by comparing it to what is available in the online code databases (and beyond). The other advantages of online code searching include easier accessibility (always available on your desktop or laptop, no problem with missing volumes, no multiple volumes to haul around), and the perennial electronic advantage when you are trying to locate specific language within a haystack of verbiage. Searching for a term in a full-text code database can, under some circumstances, speed the finding of a code section, and can also help with pinpointing a particular portion of a lengthy code section. The latter task is usually not onerous enough to constitute a serious advantage for the electronic code searcher, but that situation changes radically when the context changes to session laws, typically much longer and more convoluted than code sections.

In the code context, however, you should give serious consideration to the advantages of paper research for at least the initial stages of your research. We already saw the greater functionality of the print code indexes, the most direct way into the code when you seek statutory law on a given subject. But the print code publications offer other advantages as well. Seeing the code in paper makes it much easier to understand the context of any given section. Instead of seeing only the section retrieved by your query, you are made unavoidably aware of the sections surrounding your own. The electronic versions do offer various means to get to those surrounding sections, but, since it takes an active choice to do so, many researchers will be tempted to skip that added step, or to give it short shrift.

The print researcher is automatically exposed not only to surrounding sections, but also, within longer stretches of statutory language, to the context of the language within the section itself, without the need to scroll through multiple sections to see the whole thing. On a larger scale, clearly and graphically seeing the end of one section or subsection and the beginning of another as one does in the print volumes makes it easier to grasp the organizational logic and structure of the code. Finally, having different subjects and different chronological iterations of the code available in different physical volumes makes comparison of the same handy and efficient—once, that is, you have assembled all the relevant volumes and cleared off enough desk space to arrange them all usefully!

2.11 CHOOSING A CODE SOURCE

In addition to choosing between print and electronic versions of the statutory code, you may need to choose a publisher. As mentioned at the outset of this discussion of codes, the text of the United States Code is available in print and electronically from three different publishers. Each of the three versions has different things to offer, speaking strictly from the perspective of the code text itself. Clearly, the *U.S.C.* offers authoritativeness, as the very output of the U.S. Government. In print, both the *U.S.C.A.* and the *U.S.C.S.* offer greater currency within a single iteration of the code. The *U.S.C.A.* and *U.S.C.S.* have historically varied in terms of the source of their code text, and this may actually lead to differences in the language they publish. The *U.S.C.A.*, published by West, uses as its source the text of the *U.S.C.*, which from the beginning has been produced for the government largely by employees of West. This close connection between West and the official Code may also explain why the indexes of the *U.S.C.* and the *U.S.C.A.* are much more similar to each other than either is to the index of the *U.S.C.S.* The source of the code language in *U.S.C.S.*, by comparison, is drawn from the language of the Statutes at Large, in case of conflict between those Statutes and the *U.S.C.* language. Typically this comes up where the codifiers have altered subdivision labels or devised them from scratch in non-statutory language to make them more "code-like." For one example, see 2 U.S.C. § 30a versus 2 U.S.C.A. § 30a versus 2 U.S.C.S. § 30a versus P.L. 101–520, Title III, section 310, 104 Stat. 2278, where only the U.S.C.S. section heading is based on the language used in the underlying statute.

Usually, legal researchers will start off their print-based code research with a commercial version of the code (more current, more convenient), switching over to the official version only to verify that the text found in the commercial publication is accurate. Recent informal surveys have suggested that while large law libraries will have all three print versions of the Code, smaller ones will most often have only the *U.S.C.* and the *U.S.C.A.*, or even just the *U.S.C.A.* The annotation material in the commercially published codes is much more likely to vary than is the code text, and this will be discussed in the chapter on case law.

So why would you use the official *United States Code* itself? The quick answer would be "because *The Bluebook* requires it," Rule 12.3 instructing the writer to cite the official code whenever possible. In any serious legal research, you will eventually need to obtain access to a print copy of the *United States Code*. No matter what combination of other Code versions you consult (the online U.S.C.A. or U.S.C.S. for currency, the print *U.S.C.A.* or *U.S.C.S.* for clarity of organization, or the online U.S.C. for a combination of authoritativeness and moderate currency) you will always need to check the print *U.S.C.* as a final check of accuracy and authenticity. In the language of the Office of the Law Revision Counsel's own website: "While every effort has been made to ensure that the Code database on the web site is accurate, those using it for legal research should verify their results against the printed version of the United States Code available through the Government Printing [sic] Office." Note that Rule 12.2.1(a) specifies *The Bluebook*'s order of preference for statutory sources where the official version is not yet available: commercially published print codes are preferred over other quickly-updated sources.

In the state law context, researchers may also have the choice of more than one version of the state's statutory code. Sometimes the state publishes an official code, or designates one of the commercially published versions as "official." In some states there is no official code at all, but only commercially published ones. Typically, Westlaw and Lexis Advance each include the version of the code published by their affiliated print publishers. In print, the different publishers are associated with different updating methods, with some specializing in pocket part or looseleaf updating and others reprinting the code in full each year. The availability and official or unofficial status of these different code versions can be reviewed in the annually updated book by Kendall F. Svengalis, *Legal Information Buyer's Guide and Reference Manual*.

2.12　CODES OF THE PAST

When you need to figure out what the statutory law was at some specific earlier time, previous editions of the relevant code can often provide the easiest way to pin down the statutory environment as of the time in question. While the *United States Code* itself is only available online from GPO from the 1994 (plus Supplement II) edition on, all editions from 1925 through 2016 are included as .pdf files in the U.S. Code collection of HeinOnline. Each print edition of the *United States Code* is designed for permanent retention, along with all supplementary volumes. All editions are also available in microfiche. Lexis Advance and Westlaw both provide "archived" versions of their previous editions of the United States Code, no longer being updated with new developments, but closed as of a certain date. These files are only available for the years since 1992 for the U.S.C.S. (Lexis Advance) and 1990 for the U.S.C.A. (Westlaw) (and for similarly limited ranges of dates for states). Different steps are taken to access these archived versions in each database. On Lexis Advance, you can first identify the code section in the current U.S.C.S. From there, you will be provided with a link to "Archived code versions" that can be sorted by year. Alternatively, you can run an Archived Code Search using the link on the main Statutes and Legislation page. On Westlaw, you first select a year within the "United States Code Annotated—Historical." An advanced field search here allows you to enter a citation and arrive at a particular Code section as it existed in that year. Westlaw also offers, for an even more limited range of years and jurisdictions, a beautifully designed search option that retrieves code material that was in effect on a specific date in the past. This "Effective Date" option is available for the U.S.C.A. starting with 1996 (and for 34 states and the District of Columbia, beginning with 2007 for all, and earlier for many). In the state law context (outside the limited date ranges of the Westlaw "Effective Date" option described above), consult a bibliography of the state's statutory law to see which code edition or which collection of revised statutes would most likely contain the law that was applicable during the period in which you are interested (see **Appendix**). Both Westlaw and Lexis offer online archives of some prior state codes, starting with the late 1980s and the early 1990s respectively.

For years earlier than those covered by the effective date functionality just mentioned, the commercial federal Code publications, designed for completely dynamic and ongoing revision, are trickier to capture in amber. When individual volumes are replaced and retired from the *U.S.C.A.*, they are preserved in a microfiche set by W. S. Hein. Those pocket parts that were in the main volumes at the time of their replacement are included in the set, and Hein also produces a separate set that includes as many of the intervening pocket parts as can be located. By far the trickiest maneuver in this area of research is to locate code text that came into and went out of existence between publications of revised main volumes. Such fugitive text can most easily be tracked down in the *U.S.C.A.* by consulting superseded volumes of its General Index, which comprises part of the Hein microfiche set. Some law libraries also retain superseded print volumes of the *U.S.C.S.*, as it is not republished in microfiche. In the state law context, note that Hein also publishes a microfiche set of superseded state codes.

2.13 RENUMBERED CODES

Researchers into the law as of a particular date in the past may encounter old citations to code sections that have since been re-numbered. Re-numbering is not done often, but when it does occur, it usually affects a whole Title (or large subdivisions thereof) at once. The subject arrangement of the code may require shifting of some code sections to open up space for newly developing areas of law. Renumbering sometimes accompanies a Title's revision and re-enactment as positive law (see **Section 2.23**).

All the print versions of the Code contain a table at the head of each renumbered Title, showing the disposition of all the previous sections of the old Title. In the electronic versions of the Code, these disposition tables also appear at the head of the relevant Title. Additionally, in print the *U.S.C.* and *U.S.C.S.* also have consolidated lists of all renumbered code sections in the Tables volumes. This kind of shifting of the numbered ground under the researcher's feet doesn't happen often, but it does happen often enough that if the reference you are pursuing seems weirdly inappropriate, one of the first things you should do is to poke around in the prefatory material to that Title to see if a renumbering has occurred.

2.14 SESSION LAWS

Most legislatures publish their output in two ways: originally as session laws, then reworked as a code. While a code is arranged by subject, involving complex and time-consuming editorial work to fit it all together and make it work, the session laws are simply the raw output of the legislature's session, published in chronological order with only minimal editorial work. There is no subject arrangement or any other arrangement imposed on them. As they fall off the government's assembly line, they go into the session laws. The convenient subject arrangement of the U.S. Code, the increasing percentage of it that has been enacted as positive law, and the electronically enhanced speed of access to updated code sections are forcing the session laws of the United States—the Statutes at Large—ever further into the background. Many a third-year law student has never cracked open a volume of same. Yet, knowledge of how to work with session laws (see **Table 2.B**) is indispensable.

One of the most common ways that researchers encounter the session laws is when they seek to update known code sections beyond the most recent version of the code: you will need to use the session laws for statutes that have not yet made it into the code. But you will also need to use the session laws for statutes that will never go into the code, and for statutes that are unwieldy and dispersed in the code. Finally, you will need to use the session laws to verify the accuracy of statutory language from any Title not enacted into positive law (see **Section 2.23**).

2.15 USING SESSION LAWS TO UPDATE THE CODE

Because of the minimal editorial work required to publish session laws, they can sometimes be ready for consultation much faster than the code sections to which they will contribute, especially during times of heavy activity, such as at the end of a legislative session. Since as a collection they may, therefore, be more current than the code, the legal researcher must supplement any code work with a search of the relevant session laws. The simplest part of the task is that of seeing whether any session law has been enacted that explicitly alters the text of the code section on which you are relying. We saw in **Section 2.9** how in the electronic databases the code sections are flagged in various ways when a subsequent session law not yet incorporated into the code has altered it. The process is a bit more laborious using print, and this is one reason why the finishing touches to your statutory research are probably best done online, when that is feasible. If you do have to use print for this, you must use a commercial product that specializes in rapid publication of current session laws, since you need to obtain specifically those session laws that postdate the most updated version available of the code. In most jurisdictions this print product is a separate publication from the code, frequently a freestanding supplement to the session law set that it updates.

In the states, these publications are frequently titled "Session Law News" or "Advance Legislative Service," and the latter is the generic term for them. Newly-minted state session laws are sometimes presented in these publications as "redlined" versions of the pre-existing code. The new session law specifies how an existing section of the state's statutory code is to be changed, typically by underlining the new additions to the text (or, online, by highlighting them in a different color or rendering them all caps) and by crossing out the parts of the previous statutory language that it repeals or changes (or sometimes, online, by putting the excised language in parentheses, not a happy graphic device). When viewing session law material on the open web, be especially careful about using a reputable source. Availability of current, reliable, and authentic state session law material varies tremendously from one jurisdiction to another.

In the federal jurisdiction, changes to the existing Code are described in the words of the amending session law, rather than graphically shown by redlining. There are several federal advance legislative services available (see **Table 2.C**). One is provided by the softcover supplements published to accompany the *U.S.C.S.*, entitled *U.S.C.S. Advance.* This publication, which comes out monthly, includes a feature entitled "Table of Code Sections Added, Amended, Repealed, or Otherwise Affected," the "TCSA." The TCSA shows, for each affected section of the U.S. Code, which Public Law is responsible. The analogous tool in the West system is the table within the monthly advance sheets to *U.S.C.C.A.N.* entitled "U.S. Code and U.S. Code Annotated Sections Amended, Repealed, New, Etc." The *U.S.C.C.A.N.* table is a bit faster to appear than is *U.S.C.S.'s* TCSA, and includes page references to the Statutes at Large pages where these Public Laws will eventually appear. Another print tool that can be used to ascertain whether a given code section has been changed by subsequent session laws is the Shepard's citator for the code. *Shepard's Federal Statute Citations*, for instance, notes for each section of the U.S. Code when it has been amended by a session law that will appear in the *Statutes at Large*. KeyCite and Shepard's serve the same purpose on Westlaw and Lexis Advance respectively.

2.16 USING SESSION LAWS TO FIND NEW LAWS WITHOUT REFERENCE TO EARLIER CODE SECTIONS

Useful though these finding tools may be, you cannot rely upon them entirely to find all new statutes that affect your situation. Remember, you originally found your code section either by consulting a subject index, by reference from a secondary source or other citing source, or by full-text searching. There is nothing to say that some new statute, which on its terms does not affect the code section you identified by any of these means, could not be equally germane to your research. You will need to delve more deeply into the session laws than merely looking for statutes that specifically and explicitly affect your code section.

As in your code research, consultation of the subject index to the session laws can be an efficient way in. The critical difference is that there is no overarching subject index to the session law set, no "General Index" that covers all the volumes. Rather, each publication unit comes with its own index. Thus, each volume of the *United States Statutes at Large* (which in reality means the physical book containing the last "Part" of each volume) contains a Subject Index. That index covers only the statutes published in that volume. The same is true for *U.S.C.C.A.N.*, the commercial publication that issues the Statutes at Large in permanent form. How, then, can we say that the subject index to session laws can be efficient, if each volume has a separate index that must be searched separately?

The non-cumulative nature of the session law indexes is not a problem for most legal researchers because usually they will only need the indexes to the most very recent publication units of the session laws, namely the indexes in the paperback issues of the commercial services that undertake to provide print coverage of current statutes. In the West system, that would be the "advance" paperback volumes of *U.S.C.C.A.N.* These are published monthly, and the indexes in the back cumulate until the publication of the final, hardback, edition. Pagination of the statutes published currently in *U.S.C.C.A.N.* is the same as the pagination that will be used in the *Statutes at Large* when they are eventually published. *U.S.C.S.* also offers publication of new Public Laws, and indicates their ultimate Stat. paging as well, in their *U.S.C.S. Advance* pamphlets, mentioned above. The indexing in the *U.S.C.S. Advance* issues, as in the *U.S.C.C.A.N.* advance issues, cumulates from issue to issue.

We did not refer to any subject indexing of session laws in the electronic databases of the same, because it does not exist. On Westlaw, neither the U.S. Public Laws database (for the current session of Congress) nor the "U.S. Public Laws—Historical" have indexes available; the current session's public laws can be selected by number from a list or searched, and the historical public laws can only be accessed via search. On Lexis Advance, the Public Laws from the U.S.C.S. Advance can be searched directly (see **Table 2.C**) but do not include an index. Nor does the federal government's electronic database of public and private laws (accessible via the Federal Digital System (FDsys) and numerous other online venues) include a separate index. So again, as with the codes, if you want to use a subject index, rather than to search the full text of the session laws directly, you will do it in print.

One of the main reasons one would wish to use a subject index rather than simply to search the full text of the session laws, would be if one wanted to have access to alternative search terms. If one has not correctly anticipated the actual language that was used by the legislators, one may miss the statute by putting in the wrong search terms. One looks to the indexer for assistance in suggesting other search terms. The indexers of session laws do not disappoint. The indexing in the advance sheet pamphlets does not necessarily use the same terms as does the indexing in the statutory code (which is not terribly surprising), nor even as does the indexing in the permanent edition of the session laws (a bit more surprising). This is especially true in the advance sheet pamphlets of state session laws, commonly referred to as "Advance Legislative Services" (ALS). Sometimes an ALS indexer will even add outrageously lay language to the index, to try to ease the use of the index for the uninitiated. Thus, in one extreme example, where the code indexer had demurely put licensing laws under "taverns," the ALS indexer had added an additional heading for a brand new licensing provision, filing it under the considerably more informal "booze shops."

2.17   CITATIONS TO SESSION LAWS

The index, a full-text search, or a secondary source citation can each eventually lead you to a page number or to a law number within the session laws. The numbering systems used with respect to session laws tend to be bipartite, with the first element referring to the date or to the numbered session of the legislature and the second element being the number assigned in sequential order to this particular statute. Thus, since 1957 the Public Laws of the United States have been numbered in the form

[number of Congress]—[order of this public law in the numerical list of public laws from this Congress]

The laws are "through-numbered" within a two year Congress: if the first session of the 149th Congress ends with P.L. 149–312, the first law passed by the second session of the 149th Congress will be P.L. 149–313. The Office of the Federal Register, which is part of the National Archives and Records Administration, assigns law numbers to the bills once the latter have received Presidential approval (or have been passed over a Presidential veto), and posts the newly-assigned law numbers on their website.

Citations to session laws, though, don't stop with just the law number. *The Bluebook* requires all session law citations to include identification of the volume in which the law appears, as well as the law's name and number. You can think of this as being like the name and address of the session law. For example, in citing the Museum and Library Services Act of 2003, Pub. L. No. 108–81, 117 Stat. 991, all three elements of the citation are mandatory. The "108" is like the family name, in that it indicates the law's provenance is the 108th Congress. The "81" serves as the law's first name, particular to that law within the "108" family. "117 Stat. 991" is like the law's home address, with the volume number, "117 Stat." serving as the street name, and the page number serving as the law's particular address on that street. Note that the home address alone cannot adequately identify the session law because more than one law may commence on that same page, so it is not a unique identifier.

Session laws differ from codes in this respect, since codes are identified only by code titles and section numbers, and their tangible enshrinement on a physical page is indicated only by a mention of the publication year of a code version, if that. Code sections need to remain untethered to page numbers so that as their surroundings swell, shrink, and shift they can still be found in their right place in relationship to those surroundings. Session laws, by contrast, are immutable. They may lose all or part of their clout, thanks to subsequent actions by the legislature or courts, but their passage is what the session laws memorialize, and that cannot be affected by anyone after it has occurred. A page number in a physical volume, widely distributed among the population through the Government Publishing Office's Federal Depository Library Program, ensures that this historical fact of the session law's passage remains verifiable by all.

2.18 CHOOSING A SOURCE FOR SESSION LAWS

As ever, the problem with the GPO's official version is the slowness of its publication. Prior to the appearance in print of the *United States*

Statutes at Large, the researching public has already long had access to what it will contain, both on government and commercial databases, and in the print *U.S.C.C.A.N.* and the *U.S.C.S. Advance.* Since 1975, *U.S.C.C.A.N.* has provided a mockup of the actual page setups of the eventual Statutes at Large, and therefore of the expected pagination of the official source. Prior to 1975, the page numbers of session laws published in *U.S.C.C.A.N.* were completely independent of Statutes at Large pagination. Even with the current close physical resemblance between the *U.S.C.C.A.N.* pages and the eventual official publication, the rule of *The Bluebook* we mentioned in our first chapter remains: you cannot read the statute in *U.S.C.C.A.N.* and cite as though you had read it in the *Statutes at Large.*

Although many print and online sources offer faster access to the Public Laws than does the *Statutes at Large*, these other sources also vary greatly between themselves in the speed of access they provide. You always need to check the data source that you are using to see how up-to-date it is that very day. In the legal databases, there is generally an "information" link for each file that tells either specifically or as a matter of policy how up-to-date the information in that file is. You are always more interested in specific information about currency than in an updating policy that might be merely aspirational! Sometimes individual documents within the files have a note at the top about the specific currency of the database from which the document is drawn. However, even specific information about currency may be inaccurate: sometimes adding new laws to the database appears to be a higher priority than does adding the notice to a coverage information page that this has been done.

As of this writing, there is no more up-to-date database for newly enacted public laws than those on Lexis Advance and Westlaw. They incorporate language from enrolled bills passed by Congress and signed by the President before even the government's fastest public law website does, although the government does offer the same text still in its bill format. The language for these versions is taken from the Congress.gov database of the Library of Congress, and so despite its labeling in both Lexis Advance and Westlaw as Public Law (and indeed its rapid incorporation into especially the U.S.C.S. database) it is actually, at least at first, only the final language of the bill as signed. The Westlaw session law database of U.S. Public Laws is generally just as up-to-date as that of Lexis Advance, but the corresponding U.S.C.A. database lags a bit behind the U.S.C.S. database in incorporating these new laws, perhaps waiting for them at least to be released officially as Public Laws before incorporating them into the code. In all the databases, in order to be sure of having the very latest material, you must continue your research into the realm of pending legislation. This is discussed in **Section 2.29** on researching bills.

For updating statutory law beyond the code, therefore, you will almost always be using unofficial sources like electronic databases, *U.S.C.C.A.N.*, or *U.S.C.S. Advance*. Where do the official volumes of the *Statutes at Large* come into play? We mentioned at the end of **Section 2.14** that there were four principal reasons why you need to use session law sets. The first, to find laws that have not yet made it into the code, will never involve use of the actual *Statutes at Large*, simply because of the time lag in publication of the latter. But, as discussed in **Sections 2.19–2.23**, the other three uses of the session laws can all obligate the researcher to refer to the official set.

In the state law context, note that some states offer only an official set of session laws, published by the state. Others offer competing versions produced by different publishers (New York, for example, offers an official publication and two competing commercial publications!). As usual, Westlaw and Lexis Advance offer the versions published by their affiliated print publishers; Bloomberg Law and the states' own websites offer the official texts. The Svengalis *Legal Information Buyer's Guide* offers a frequently updated overview of state session law publication.

2.19 FINDING LAWS THAT WILL NEVER MAKE IT INTO THE CODE

Codes aim to include statutes of a general and permanent nature. "General" means applicable to everyone that comes under a statute's substantive terms: this is what is meant by the "Public" law nomenclature in the *Statutes at Large*. The alternative is a Private Law, and while these are not as common as they once were, they are still enacted and still published in the *Statutes at Large*. These Private Laws provide for the specific relief of named parties in their dealings with the government. Historically, many of them provided pension coverage to widows of Civil War veterans; today the typical Private Law involves immigration relief for an individual.

Private Laws are published in slip (uncollected) form and in the official *Statutes at Large*, which contains the only index to them. This single point of entry to the printed record illustrates the precariousness of access to non-commercially significant information. In the First Session of the 107th Congress, one Private Law was passed, Act for the Relief of Rita Mirembe Revell, Private Law 107–1, 115 Stat. 2471. In theory the best way to find your way to this law in the *Statutes at Large* would be to look in the index for each year. In the subject index to vol. 115, there is an index entry under "Revell, Rita Mirembe" . . . the only problem is that the page number to which it refers is 200 pages off (2671). Nor can you find the correct page number by searching for and finding this Private Law in the database of government publications provided via FDsys, since the .pdf files of the Private Laws do not provide page references to the *Statutes at Large*. On

FDsys though, you can search .pdf files directly, including those of the Statutes at Large. Another option would be to search for words in the statute's title in the Statutes at Large Library on HeinOnline (see **Table 2.B**), and click on "View Matching Text Pages." And, finally, one counter-intuitively efficient way to find this Private Law would be to look through the Private Laws section in each date-appropriate volume of the *Statutes at Large*. Private Laws being as few and far between as they are these days, that practice is actually even quicker than looking at an accurate index would be.

While few will ever be concerned with finding Private Laws, the non-"general" statutes that don't go into the Code, many may at some point wish to find one of the non-"permanent" laws that also are not Code candidates. Prominent among laws that are not destined for the Code are such one-off statutes as appropriations acts, appointments, and laws that by their terms apply only for a very short time. For seeking out the likes of these, the researcher may need access to the whole chronological stretch of uncodified statutes. The problem that could basically be laughed off in the context of pre-codified session laws looms a bit larger in the world of never-codified statutes. How does one search for them in the absence of a unified index? Clearly one would want to search the full text across a database comprising all the session laws.

The only way to do such a search is via HeinOnline's U.S. Statutes at Large collection, which offers the whole set as .pdf files. The entire collection can be searched for files in which the search term is present. Since the files can be very lengthy and sometimes contain more than one law, you should use the "View Matching Text Page" feature to locate your search term within an individual result file.

Other searchable text of the Statutes at Large is only shallowly available online. The uncodified Public Laws are available in searchable text on Westlaw only back to 1973, on Lexis Advance only back to 1988, and on FDsys back to 1951. The Library of Congress's American Memory website offers access to image files of the first eighteen volumes of the Statutes at Large (covering the first forty-three Congresses, 1789–1875), along with searchable indexing of each. The first eight volumes included in the American Memory project share an online index. With that one small exception, however, for statutes prior to 1951 one would have to use HeinOnline, search the separate subject indexes for each Congress, or obtain citations through research in secondary sources.

2.20 UPDATING UNCODIFIED SESSION LAWS

Whereas amendments to, or repealing of, codified laws are indicated in the ever-changing code itself, amendments to or repealing of never-codified session laws must be researched differently. Notice that even though an uncodified session law may be reproduced in a "note" to the Code, it is still updatable only via the Public Law number. For this task there is only one tool specifically made for the job: *Shepard's Federal Statute Citations* in print. Neither Shepard's on Lexis Advance nor KeyCite on Westlaw offer updating of the uncodified sections of the *Statutes at Large*, even for those portions that are represented in the statutory databases of the respective services. By using this Shepard's print product you can check to see if an uncodified Public Law has been amended or repealed, in whole or in part. Since Shepard's publication involves editorial work that requires time, you should also do a keyword search in the full-text session law databases to verify that nothing new has come up that could affect your statute since Shepard's did their work.

In the state law environment, as you would expect, the technique for updating non-codified statutes will be different in each jurisdiction, and can get quite complicated. In New York, for example, session laws not part of the Compiled Laws of New York (the New York equivalent of the United States Code) are updated via *Shepard's New York Statute Citations* in print, but cannot be updated on Shepard's on Lexis Advance nor (except for a limited subset described in the next paragraph) on Westlaw.

The commercial publishers who produce the collected Compiled Laws of New York have each cobbled together a set of Unconsolidated Laws that they have selected from those session laws that are not assigned by the Legislature to an existing part of the Compiled Laws. The complication is that the two publishers have selected different laws to treat in this way, so their numbering systems are completely different from each other. In *McKinney's Consolidated Laws of New York*, a session law selected for this treatment will be assigned a McKinney's Unconsolidated Laws number that will then function within McKinney's as a code section number, i.e., subsequent session laws that amend the original session law will be used to refashion the existing McKinney's Unconsolidated Laws section, and will be added to the list of underlying statutory authorities for that section in the parenthetical information following the text of the refashioned section. Subsequent citation to this subset of the session laws outside the Compiled Laws can be researched via KeyCite, but no others can.

A similar approach is used in the *New York Consolidated Laws Service* (CLS) volume of Unconsolidated Laws, each of which gets its own CLS Unconsol. Law number and gets similarly updated. The *CLS* print set provides a helpful table correlating its own Unconsolidated Laws with those of McKinney's (no equivalent table exists in McKinney's), and with the underlying session laws. For details on this process in each of the several states, consult a research guide for the particular state (see **Appendix**).

2.21 STATUTES MORE CONVENIENTLY DISCUSSED IN THEIR ORIGINAL SESSION LAW FORM

The third use of the session laws is for those laws that are more usefully cited to the session law than to the code. A session law citation would usually be more useful than a code citation when the original statute was broken up and the pieces scattered into far-flung corners of the code, such that lining them up to talk about them collectively would be awkward. *The Bluebook* discusses this in Rule 12.2.2(a), giving in its examples some idea of how scattered the sections have to be in order to be considered unwieldy. The other chief circumstance in which a session law citation would be more useful than code citation would be when you wish to discuss the history of the actual passage of the statute. The session law citation, tied as it is to a particular date, gives a historical precision that is indispensable in the historical context.

2.22 SESSION LAW NOMENCLATURE VS. CODE NOMENCLATURE

Once one is cognizant of both the session law version and the codified version of the same law, one is struck by the very different numerical labels that get affixed to the same language in its different contexts. It is crucial that the researcher keep these different labels straight and distinct; confusion between a session law and a code section is one of the easiest and most common mistakes made by beginning legal researchers. We have already seen that a code section is labeled by the title of the code in which it appears, the name of the code, and finally its own section number. We saw, too, that the code sections can be grouped together in subgroupings called subtitles, chapters, or subchapters, but that these subject groupings do not function as part of the citation to any section. By contrast, a session law is labeled by its own name and law number, and then with a citation to where it is physically printed, i.e., a volume and page number of a particular statutory set.

The complications arise when we look within the individual statutes: session laws can be very long indeed, and require multiple subdivisions. And here's the rub: the principal subdivisions within individual Public Laws are (like the subdivisions of the entire U.S. Code) known as Titles. This kind of Title can indeed be properly incorporated into a citation of that particular portion of a session law. Sometimes these subdivisions are the most useful way to refer to a particular set of provisions, and so they enter the common legal parlance. For example, consider Title VII civil rights actions. To be precise you would need to say Title VII of what specific statute you were talking about, but within the civil rights area, say Title VII and everybody knows what you mean: Title VII of the Civil Rights Act of 1964. In order to avoid confusion in any particular instance about whether you are looking at something that pertains to a big portion of the U.S. Code or, rather, to a subdivision of an individual session law, note that the former always involves a regular number (e.g., Title 17) and the latter a capital Roman numeral.

The other form of confusion that arises from statutory labels is caused by chapters. The kind of chapter that denotes a grouping together for arrangement purposes in a statutory code gets a capital "C," as though you were talking about a chapter in a book. However, some session law series use a numbering scheme where each statute is assigned a chapter number as its individual identification number. The *Statutes at Large* used this system until 1957. Many state legislatures still assign chapter numbers to each enacted law. What you need to remember here is that the sort of chapter number that refers only to an individual statute gets a lower-case "c," and is frequently abbreviated "ch.," or even "c." Since your research may well need to go back and forth between the session laws and the code, you will need to keep all these labels straight so that it remains clear to you and to your readers which you are talking about at any particular time.

2.23 SESSION LAWS AS AUTHENTICATION OF CODE LANGUAGE

The fourth reason you will need to use the session laws is to verify the accuracy of language in the code. As of this writing, 27 of the 53 Titles of the U.S. Code have been enacted by Congress as positive law, meaning that the language in these Titles is the official text of the law. Thus, the researcher must rely on that language, without reference back to the *Statutes at Large*. Titles that have been enacted as positive law are identified by asterisks on the Title list maintained by the Office of the Law Revision Counsel at http://uscode.house.gov/browse.xhtml. Subsequent enactments on subjects pertaining to the enacted Titles must be framed by Congress as amendments to the appropriate enacted Code Title, rather than leaving this task to the Office of the Law Revision Counsel to do *ex post facto*. All other Code Titles are only *prima facie* evidence of the law they contain. This means that Code sections from Titles that have not been enacted as positive law can be rebutted as evidence of the law if their language conflicts with that of the *Statutes at Large*. This, in turn, means that if you are relying on language from such a code section, you are supposed to verify its language against that of the *Statutes at Large*. If the language of the two is conflicting, the language of the *Statutes at Large* governs (*The Bluebook* R. 12.2.2(c)).

Once a statute is passed by Congress, its text receives first official publication as a freestanding "slip law," identified by its law number. That text is then sent both to the National Archives and Records Administration for incorporation in session law format into the *Statutes at Large*, and to the Office of the Law Revision Counsel of the House of Representatives for codification, i.e., to be added, as the Counsel sees fit, to the edifice of current general and permanent federal statutory law, the United States Code. Sometimes the new law needs to have a little something added, or subtracted, or changed in order to make it fit coherently into the existing body of the Code. Sometimes (or always, with respect to those Titles of the Code that have already been enacted as positive law by Congress) all the codifiers have to do is to give effect to language specifically stating how a particular portion of the code is to be amended by the session law in question. Other times the codifiers have to choose, based on the subject matter of earlier code sections, where to put the new content and what might need to be excised from the existing code. Making these changes frequently obliges the codifiers to alter the language of the code to accommodate the additions, changes, and deletions while maintaining a logical and readable whole. It is the job of the Office of the Law Revision Counsel to make all these changes as unsubstantive as possible. Nonetheless, it is here that the possibility of error arises.

As Charles J. Zinn, long the Law Revision Counsel, wrote in his Law Library Journal article titled *Codification of the Laws*, 45 Law Libr. J. 2 (1952), "[c]lassification is a matter of opinion and judgment." Occasionally (only very occasionally, in light of the amount of codification that has to be done), the Counsel goes astray, and makes what turns out to be a substantive change to the statute in the course of revising it for the code.

This is why the statutes in their original formats are the governing authority. The original legislation is the expression of both houses of Congress, but the Titles of the Code not enacted as positive law are in part merely a creation of the codification scribes. The statutes in their original format (*Statutes at Large*) are "positive law." The Code, as it emerges from the hands of the codification body, is just a useful system of evidence as to what the positive law is, which must be verified in the last analysis, against the positive law of the *Statutes at Large*.

2.24 GETTING FROM A CODE SECTION TO ITS SOURCE IN THE SESSION LAWS

In case you do need to verify the accuracy of a code section, you will have to find out where exactly in the Statutes at Large your code language came from. At the end of each code section, in all versions, there is parenthetical information that can vary slightly between the services, and that is sometimes all you need to get to the original language of the session law. This information contains one or a series of citations to Public Laws: these are the session laws that furnish the basis for the code section in question. The first citation given was the original source for the code section; any subsequent session laws cited furnished the basis for amendment of or addition to the original language of the section. In the U.S.C.S. on Lexis Advance and the U.S.C. on Bloomberg Law you can click through from the parenthetical information following each code section to .pdf files of the source public laws in the Statutes at Large. In the U.S.C.A. on Westlaw you can only click through to the text versions of the source laws in Westlaw's session law database. The U.S.C. online at FDsys gives the parenthetical source information, but without offering any click-through functionality. Cornell's Legal Information Institute project version of the Code, at https://www.law.cornell.edu/uscode, also includes links to .pdf files of the Statutes at Large, as made available by the Office of the Law Revision Counsel.

In all but the simplest cases, however, you may need to go further to identify what was added when. After the parenthetical information comes a section (which in the print editions, helpfully, is in a different font to differentiate it from the code itself) called "Historical and Statutory Notes" (*U.S.C.A.*), "History; Ancillary Laws and Directives" (*U.S.C.S.*), or "Historical and Statutory Notes" and "Amendments" (*U.S.C.*): these sections give brief indications of which statutes did what to the code section in question. This section of the annotations is also where a lot of statutory material not incorporated into the code is presented, in the form of a "note" to the code. These notes (references to which frequently refer to "nts") often include language of purpose from the statute. They are cited by courts, but are not covered by any citators, so tracing the judicial impact of a "note" requires either working with its source in the Statutes at Large or, when it is not taken from there, by a full-text search of the appropriate case law database.

On Bloomberg Law and on Lexis Advance, you can click through from these notes to .pdf files of the source public laws. Neither Westlaw nor the Office of the Law Revision Counsel nor FDsys offer links to the Statutes at Large, but they do provide citations. If you are using a source that does not link directly to the Statutes at Large, HeinOnline is your best bet. It is home to searchable .pdf files of the Statutes at Large, from inception through the most recent volume. It also links out to FDsys for those laws that are more recent and so not yet published in the Statutes at Large. Searching by term or keyword can still be onerous, given the commonality of language among disparate legislation. Happily, there is a separate tool that will enable you to find the appropriate language relatively easily: the Tables volume of the Code.

Each of the three publications of the Code has a volume or volumes entitled "Tables." The Tables lay out where everything in the Statutes at Large has been placed in the U.S. Code, including in the notes to the U.S. Code. The breakdown of the Public Laws for this purpose is down to the individual section number, which is given with the actual page of the

Statutes at Large on which it appears. Since the principal purpose of the Tables is to show the disposition of the Statutes at Large in the Code, the Tables are arranged in Public Law number order. But the savvy researcher will also resort to the Tables when trying to pin down a particular location within the Statutes at Large for a known code section. In the print Tables, once you know which Public Law is involved, you can then sweep your eyes over the Code sections listed for that Public Law in the right hand column. When your eye alights upon the desired code section number, you can look back to the left to see which exact page in the Statutes at Large was the source for your code section. Though this method be slightly unsystematic, it still beats skimming through the statute itself! This technique works both in print and online, and covers the full range of dates of the Statutes at Large in both. For long and very long statutes, this locating function is extremely helpful.

Not only is the arrangement of the information different in the U.S.C.S., U.S.C.A., and U.S.C. Tables, but their content varies slightly as well. This means that if there is an error in one, it can be worthwhile to try one of the others. As ever, the U.S.C.S. Tables vary more in content from the other two than the other two do from each other. The U.S.C.S. Tables on Lexis Advance (called U.S.C.S. Statutes at Large Table and findable by typing USSALT into the first search box) include an additional column that usefully characterizes what the given Public Law did to each code section indicated, not just those that are repealed or unclassified. The U.S.C.S. Tables also go into much more granular detail than the others, both as to which subsection of the Code was the destination of a given section of the session law, and indicating such subdivisions as Titles on the session law side of the Table. On the other hand, the *U.S.C.A.* Tables in print are conveniently reprinted *in toto* frequently. The online Tables produced by the Office of the Law Revision Counsel (appearing as "Other Tables and Tools > Table III—Statutes at Large") go back to 1789, but, uniquely, under "Classification Tables" you can also view yearly tables beginning from 1995 that offer a choice between arrangement in Public Law order or in U.S. Code order.

2.25 MONSTER SESSION LAWS: OMNIBUS STATUTES

Our concern over the difficulty of locating statutory language precisely within a long law may seem overwrought, but only until your first encounter with an omnibus statute. *Black's Law Dictionary* defines omnibus as "[o]f, relating to, or involving numerous objects or items at once; including many things or having various purposes," and an omnibus bill as either "1. A single bill containing various distinct matters, usu. drafted in this way to force the executive either to accept all the unrelated minor provisions or to veto the major provision," or "2. A bill that deals with all proposals relating to a particular subject, such as an 'omnibus judgeship bill' covering all proposals for new judgeships or an 'omnibus crime bill' dealing with different subjects such as new crimes and grants to states for crime control." Some states have long had constitutional "single subject" provisions prohibiting such legislation, precisely to counter their obfuscatory and logrolling potential.

The most difficult problems when working with omnibus statutes involve legislative history, but looking for uncodified topics or even looking for codified language within them to check the accuracy of code sections can be brutal. Whether by design or by necessity (of cramming things in before the end of the legislative session so all that work need not have been in vain), these omnibus statutes can be incredibly long. **Section 2.17** notes that the law number is a necessary part of the session law citation so that you can know which law is meant when more than one law starts on the same page. No such problem arises with these omnibus monstrosities: some of them (e.g., the Omnibus Consolidated Appropriations Act of 1997) tip the scales at over 700 pages of pure law, couched in unremitting statutory English.

The titles of the omnibus acts can seem bizarre when one peruses the components that get shoehorned into them. The outlines or tables of contents included at the beginning of such statutes are usually skeletal and not much help. Also, there is no provision of running heads of the subdivisions throughout the text, and there are so many different levels of subdivisions (including the subdivisions of the Code or of earlier session laws that are being designated for amendment) that flipping through the pages of these statutes looking for the subdivision indicated in the table of contents is confusing and frustrating. Finally, the typefaces used to differentiate subdivisions are inconsistent, which further complicates finding them. This is a situation where full-text searching is truly indispensable.

2.26 READING THE SESSION LAW AS AN AID TO UNDERSTANDING THE CODE

Another kind of verification of accuracy involves reviewing the whole original session law for its internal cross-references. For situations where you want to read an original statute as a unit, the best solution is to use the Popular Name Table in any of the versions of the Code. This gem of a publication (discussed further in **Section 2.27**) includes citations for named "acts" subsumed into larger Public Laws, showing not only their dispersal into the Code, but also both which subdivision of which Public Law contains it and what its initial page is (i.e., within that public law) in the *Statutes at Large*. The desire to read the whole statute together as originally passed probably most often arises when the codification process has created some ambiguity about the coverage or applicability of a particular provision. References to "herein" or "hereinafter," for instance, may be clearer or indeed different in the session law than in the Code.

2.27 FINDING STATUTES BY "NAME"

The Popular Name Table, a feature in all editions of the Code (each offering a slightly different array of names), introduces us to the last major access point in indexes generally: name of item. We have seen in **Section 2.3** through **Section 2.8** how to find statutes by subject either through use of a subject index or through a subject hierarchy structure. We saw in **Section 2.14** that the chronological arrangement of the *Statutes at Large* enables you to find statutes by date or by law number. Finally, we come to a resource that permits us to look for a statute whose name we know, through an alphabetical index of statute names. The Popular Name Tables in the commercially published print codes take you from the statute name to session law and code citations for the original act and all subsequent amendments; the one in the official U.S. Code takes you to the original session law citation only.

What are these "popular names" that are indexed in the Popular Name Table? Often they are names given by Congress to statutes in the language of their own opening section: "This Act may be cited as the 'Consolidated Omnibus Budget Reconciliation Act of 1985'" (Pub. L. No. 99–272, § 1, 100 Stat. 82 (1986)). Within the statute, such statements usually bear the caption "Short Title." But on the street the statute is called "COBRA," and this even more "popular" name is also indexed, referring the reader to the entry under the official short title. Occasionally the Office of the Federal Register of the National Archives and Records Administration, which edits the *Statutes at Large*, creates a title for a statute where the legislature was silent on the matter, and puts that title into the margin of the session law. This goes into the Popular Name Table as well.

The commercially published Popular Name Tables often include variants that are not found in the U.S.C. Popular Name Table, for one reason or another. A prime example of this is "Obamacare." The federal government under former President Obama made great efforts to refer to this act by its formal name of Patient Protection and Affordable Care Act, or the shortened Affordable Care Act, rather than Obamacare. As such, the U.S.C. Popular Name Table includes no entry or reference to "Obamacare." The U.S.C.S. and U.S.C.A. Popular Name Tables on the other hand, include references for all three popular names—Obamacare, Patient Protection and Affordable Care Act, and Affordable Care Act in an effort to get researchers to the appropriate section no matter where they begin. But the commercially published Popular Name Tables are not always identical when it comes to these unofficial names. For instance, the U.S.C.A. Popular Name Table includes an entry for the Switchblade Knife Act (actually the

Ballistic Knife Prohibition Act of 1986), which is not found in the U.S.C.S. Popular Name Table, while the U.S.C.S. Popular Name Table includes an entry for the Swine Flu Act (actually the National Swine Flu Immunization Program of 1976), which is not found in the U.S.C.A. version. Notably, neither of those unofficial names appears in the U.S.C. Popular Name Table. Contemplation of the Popular Name Table gives rise to an appreciation of the wide ranging activities of Congress: consider the Popcorn Promotion, Research, and Consumer Information Act (Pub. L. 104–127, Title V, Subtitle E, Apr. 4, 1996, 110 Stat. 1074.) It also cuts through all the byzantine layers of legislative action, so that you can easily find the "Use of Assisted Housing by Aliens Act of 1996" nested within the "Illegal Immigration Reform and Immigrant Responsibility Act of 1996," which in turn resides within the mammoth "Omnibus Consolidated Appropriations Act, 1997" (Sept. 30, 1996). But do not mistake the Popular Name Table for a title index to all of the *Statutes at Large*: many Acts within the latter are denominated simply "Act of [date]," and consequently make no appearance in the Popular Name Table.

2.28 GETTING FROM A SESSION LAW TO THE CORRESPONDING CODE SECTIONS

We have seen that the arrangement of the Tables to the Codes is in Public Law number order; now we will get to the uses for which that order is actually designed. We started out with the Code for reasons of efficiency, and then needed to get from the Code to the session law for a variety of reasons. What about when you are starting off with a session law?

There are three main reasons why you would be interested in proceeding from the session law to working with the Code, and they comprise the reasons why a code system was devised in the first place. The first reason would be to see the current state of the law on the subject matter that was covered by your session law: since a code collates the various general and permanent laws on the same subject, it should fill you in on later enactments that have affected your original statute. Secondly, locating your statute within a code enables you to see it within its larger subject context, i.e., in the context of other laws on related matters. Finally, because of the subject collocation provided by a code, it enables you to go on to find other related legal authorities and annotating materials.

How, then, do you go about finding where your session law was put into the U.S. Code? The easiest case is when the Code destination is indicated within the language of the session law itself, sometimes even in its title, as in Public Law 108–92, titled "An Act To amend chapter 84 of title 5, United States Code. . . ." We saw above how the language of the session law is frequently framed in terms of how a particular section or subsection of the Code is to be amended thereby. However, where the destination in the Code is a section that has not been enacted as positive law, the Code section (or sections) where the new statute will reside is not necessarily spelled out in its own language. In some versions of the session laws, marginal notes created by the codifiers and indicating code destination may be included alongside the text. But the most thorough and comprehensive source of code destinations is the aforementioned (in **Section 2.24**) Tables component of every version of the Code. They offer a high level of precision of location, and since they are updated periodically, they are kept up-to-date with changes to the Code. Superseded paper editions, moreover, can provide navigational aid to those working with archival back editions of the Code.

2.29   FINDING BILLS

Sometimes your situation dictates that you must be concerned with laws that are on the horizon as well as with laws that are already in effect. In such circumstances, the final step in researching statutory authority on a subject is finding any germinating statutes, i.e., current bills, that deal with your subject. Moreover, the search for bills can also reap a bonus: you may come up with an actual law that has only just been enacted, and has not yet been incorporated into either the latest session laws or—*a fortiori*— the Code.

When looking for possible imminent changes to the legislative landscape, you are concerned only with those bills pending in the current legislative session, and will want to look for them by subject. You will of course want to look for bills that on their terms propose to affect an already existing statute. But if you only look for bills that on their terms would affect a particular section of the Code or an existing Public Law, you might miss something relevant to your subject. **Section 2.18** above on choosing a source for session laws notes that in the U.S.C.A. database you would be obliged to look into the Public Laws database to get the latest statutes, since there is a lag between their appearance there and in the U.S.C.A. on Westlaw. In fact, you would be just as well or better served to do your updating search in the bills database, since then you would find in one search everything too recent to go into the Code: bills, very newly enacted Public Laws, everything. To narrow your results down to just those bills that have already become law, you can filter the results list by limiting to "Enacted Legislation" on Westlaw or "Enrolled" on Lexis Advance. Note that "Enrolled" captures all bills that passed Congress, even if subsequently vetoed by the President.

2.30   FINDING A BILL BY SUBJECT

The electronic legal databases offer a variety of ways to look for bills on a subject. The text for all of these services originates in the U.S.

Government Publishing Office (GPO). The GPO's FDsys website offers full-text searching of the text of bills going back to the 103rd Congress. The documents accessed via FDsys also include a digital signature designed to "assure users that publications available from GPO websites are as official and authentic as publications that have been printed and disseminated by GPO for 150 years. . ." The Library of Congress's Congress.gov website also offers full-text searching of bills from 1973 to the present. Lexis Advance and Westlaw also offer full-text searching of bills, and the bill texts get picked up by a variety of other sites (see **Table 2.D**).

Of course full-text searches make you completely dependent on the actual language employed by the bills. In order to search bills by subject headings that may not track the bill language exactly, you need to consult a subject index to bills. Congress.gov allows for browsing legislation by subject terms, geographic entities, and organization names going back to the 111th Congress (2009–2010), as well as by more general policy area going back to the 93rd Congress (1973–1974). These terms are assigned to each bill and resolution by legislative analysts from the Congressional Research Service, and are added to the legislation cumulatively as it wends its way through the legislative process. Similarly, ProQuest Congressional adds subject terms from the 7,500 word CIS Index Controlled Vocabulary to the bills in its database.

Subject indexing has also been offered since 1937 by the *Congressional Index*, a CCH looseleaf publication available in print only, updated weekly with a wide variety of information about current legislation in the U.S. Congress. Each volume contains, among other things, a subject index to bills introduced in one of the houses of the current Congress. The subject headings used in the index include broad terms that group bills under general topics, such as agriculture or education, with subheadings for more specific topics within them.

One peculiarity of this index is its division into a number of layers of currency (a typical CCH technique, used to avoid excessive weekly republication of the same material): you will need to look through as many as three layers of alphabetical subject indexing in each chamber of Congress to do a thorough subject search. As with the electronic sources, note the date of currency of these indexes. You will want to do a full-text search in the online bill databases for material that was too late to be caught in the most recent issue of the *Congressional Index*. Also, since the *Congressional Index* contains only summaries describing the content of each bill very briefly, you will need to retrieve the full text of the bill from one of the sources listed in **Table 2.D**.

2.31 FINDING A BILL BY BILL NUMBER, BY DATE, OR BY SPONSOR

You may already have information about a bill that would make it more efficient to locate the bill text or other information by bill number, by date, or by sponsor. You can use any of these access points in the electronic bills databases and in the *Congressional Index*. Bill numbers are typically composed of, first, an abbreviation denoting the legislative chamber into which the bill was originally introduced and, second, a sequential number in order of the bill's introduction into that chamber. To make the citation complete, you need to add information specifying the legislature during which the bill was introduced, and the year of publication. Since the bill numbers are assigned in chronological sequence, a numerical list of bills will also enable you to pick out a bill by its date, if that is all you have to go on (frequently the case if you are working from, e.g., a newspaper story). If you want to find a bill by a known sponsor, you can consult the "Author Index" in the Senate volume of the *Congressional Index* (this covers House authors as well), or browse the By Sponsor lists on Congress.gov.

In the state law context, the states vary in how they make public the text of proposed legislation, but in no state is the documentation as highly developed as it is in the federal jurisdiction. For information about the different ways that you can access pending state bills, consult a bibliography like William H. Manz's *Guide to State Legislation, Legislative History, and Administrative Materials* (7th ed., AALL Publications Series No. 61. Buffalo, N.Y.: W. S. Hein, 2008) or a state legal research guide (see **Appendix**). Common bill retrieval methods in the state context include use of the state legislature's website, employment of a specialized document delivery service, or telephone contact with the state legislature.

For possible future statutes that are even farther out toward the horizon, perhaps just a glimmer (but a persistent glimmer) in a legislator's eye, you would need to look further than the bill resources. Don't overlook the value of full-text searching in newspapers of record, principally (for this purpose) the *New York Times* and the *Washington Post*. In the state law context, check out the websites of interest groups focused on your subject of concern, and the website of the National Conference of State Legislatures, which frequently comments on matters that are expected to be the subject of upcoming legislation in more than one state.

2.32 CASES INTERPRETING STATUTES

As advanced students of legal research, you know that mere awareness of the current statute relevant to your situation is not enough. In our common law system, you need to know what precedents, if any, exist in the application of that statute by the courts. So important a role does this court interpretation play in determining the significance of your statute, that finding all relevant cases construing it is as indispensable to legal research as is finding an absolutely current statutory text. While there are many different ways to find case law (see **Chapter 5**), there are a number of specialized ways to sift the case law for those cases that apply (or construe, perhaps declining to apply) your statute.

When all you want is the famous, leading cases interpreting an important statute, you should think in terms of looking in law review articles for exactly those cases, the cream of the crop, that can furnish the basis for much of your further research. Another important type of secondary resource for such research consists of the many treatises on statute-based subjects that are arranged by code section, and which offer selective annotations either in a separate section or in footnotes (e.g., works on federal or state practice, evidence, copyright, the U.C.C., etc.). See **Chapter 4** on law reviews and **Chapter 6** on treatises for more on this type of research.

2.33 FINDING CASES IN AN ANNOTATED CODE

Let us assume, however, that you are looking for more and that you are ready to do some detailed research. The *sine qua non* of this type of research is the annotated code, already encountered in the form of the U.S.C.A. and the U.S.C.S. Annotated codes follow each section of code text with references to sources that will aid in the interpretation of that section. Chief among these interpretive sources are citations to relevant cases with brief summaries of how the statute was applied in each. Typically, these case descriptions come after all the information about the code section itself (the text, the derivation information, the legislative history information, and the references to commentary on the statute).

In the *U.S.C.A.*, the case descriptions are called Notes of Decisions, and are preceded by an alphabetical table of contents that groups the decisions under hierarchically numbered subject headings called "catchlines." In the *U.S.C.S.* they are called Interpretive Notes and Decisions, and the table of contents is just numbered hierarchically, with no alphabetical arrangement. The significance of this distinction is usually *de minimis*, but when you come to a section with hundreds and hundreds of case descriptions, and a correspondingly high number of subject headings classifying them, the difference may loom a bit larger (e.g., 42 U.S.C.A. § 1983, with an alphabetical table of contents that covers nearly 120 pages in the *U.S.C.A.*).

Note that these numbered subject headings are used only in this one context, and have no connection to any other numbered subject heading scheme (like West's Key Number System, or the subject headings in other publishers' annotated codes). The subject headings used (as well as the actual cases identified in the annotations) are different, for instance, in the two electronic annotated codes, so you may want to check both in case the concept or point you are interested in is not addressed in the one you try first. In the Westlaw default hierarchical view, you can easily click the specific subject heading to retrieve only annotations related to that one subject. If you prefer a closer counterpart to print, you can switch to a list view that includes the numbers from the print *U.S.C.A.* list of subject headings. There, clicking the number will have you jump down the page to the part of the annotations that falls under that subject heading, but the alphabetical organization of the print list is not available. A similar method, using icons rather than numbers, is used on Lexis Advance. Since the Lexis catchlines are in a hierarchical arrangement, reviewing the annotations in their assigned order is a bit more like the scanning experience in the print process, which is easiest of all. Where both online sources shine, of course, is in the ability to click through from the case descriptions to the cases themselves. Hard to argue with the convenience of that!

Each case description in the U.S.C.A. (and in other West annotated codes) is identical to a headnote in the cited case, and thus to a digest entry for that case, with only one significant difference. The headnote in the case reporter and the entry in the digest both list all the statutory sections cited by the court for the point of law discussed therein. The case description in the code annotation, on the other hand, omits this list. Consequently, you may wish to click through to see the original headnote (or pull the case, if working with print sources) so that you get the full list of statute sections and don't focus your attention prematurely on only the section under which you found the case.

Whenever (as here) you have a lot of cases to look up from a source that is on Lexis Advance or Westlaw, you should consider working at the computer with the analogous print source in your hand. That way you can, for instance, scan the Notes of Decision in print (often faster than scrolling and reading online), and when you identify a case you want to look at in full text, enter the case citation, e.g., 5 U.S. 137 or 248 N.Y. 339, into the main search box of your preferred database to go directly to that case. If it still looks relevant, you can save it for future reference by using the database's organizational tool (called folders) or print it, in whole or in part (the latter if you prefer to read from the print volumes). This technique, marrying the most convenient parts of print and online formats, minimizes the chance that you will allow gaps in your research either through error or frustration.

Where a case cites to a whole act (whether the choice to do so is technically correct or incorrect), and the act has been codified into numerous sections, the case will usually be noted under the first of the code sections, frequently the introductory one. Therefore, you should make a practice of looking not only at the notes of decision listed for your particular code section, but also under those listed for the adjacent sections and for the introductory sections to the Chapter (finally a use for those chapter subdivisions!). If you don't have a code section but only a Public Law number to work with, first determine the relevant code section (see **Section 2.28** for instructions on how to do this), and then look up case annotations in the annotated code. Remember also that citation rules dictate using the code citation, except in limited exceptional circumstances. If you confirm that there actually is no code citation for your statute, then you will need to resort to other techniques to find cases tied to it (see **Section 2.38** and **Section 2.39**).

2.34   CURRENCY OF THE CASE ANNOTATIONS

Searching the U.S.C.A. or U.S.C.S. online for case annotations, you will need to be concerned (as you were when looking for the current statute) with the currency of the database. Online, in both the U.S.C.A. and U.S.C.S., the information provided does not give a "current through" date. Once you get to an individual code section, the heading at the top of the document tells you up through which public law number this section has been updated. However, neither database offers information about the currency of the case annotations. By contrast, in both the print *U.S.C.A.* and *U.S.C.S.*, each volume or issue contains not only information about the currency of the statutory text, but also information about the cutoff point for case annotation, given in terms of the last page of each case reporter reviewed for relevant cases for the U.S.C.S. and in terms of last publication date included for the U.S.C.A. While the database is as current in its case annotations as the latest print supplement to the *U.S.C.A.* or *U.S.C.S.*, without access to the print books you would have no way of knowing how current that actually was. This is another instance where you can usefully supplement the convenience of the online format with the fuller documentation associated with the print format.

Of course, no matter how up to date the annotations are, you can get cases that are more recent by mining the most recent cases in the case law databases via a full-text search for references to your statute. This is analogous to searching the most recent public laws for subject terms, in order to get more current than the most updated version of the code. You are essentially eliminating the editorial middleman, and going straight to the data as yet unsifted by that middleman. While you do sacrifice the orderliness of the subject arrangement of the catchlines, you gain not only in currency but in the ability to customize your search by the inclusion of particular terms.

2.35 REVISION OF THE ANNOTATIONS

The annotated codes, as we saw above in the section on using codes, are not republished on a fixed schedule as the official code is. Rather, each volume is republished as the need arises, usually when the annual pocket part that is cumulating all changes to that volume since its last republication gets too fat for the book's spine, or when a wholesale revision of a title makes it indispensable to republish right away (as with Title 17, Copyright, following enactment of the Copyright Act of 1976). When the pocket part gets too fat, the first step is often to publish a softcover supplement that takes the place of the pocket part; this gets shelved adjacent to the supplemented volume. Usually the existence of such a supplement indicates that republication of the main volume in question is on the way.

When republication of an annotated code volume occurs, what changes does it include? Obviously all the material that is still valid from the most recent pocket part is incorporated into the appropriate section of the new main volume. But other changes can occur at this point as well. Errors that crept into the original volume can now be corrected, significant subsequent history of annotating cases can be appended to their case descriptions, and, curiously, the catchlines for annotations within the sections can be renamed, reorganized, and reassigned. This latter revision occurs with surprising frequency, and the text of the annotations themselves have sometimes been rewritten, but the actual selection of cases from earlier editions is usually carried forward into all successive editions. Occasionally there is an exception, so if you want to find absolutely all cases that have ever been selected to annotate a given code section, you can consult superseded volumes of the *U.S.C.A.*, available in the Hein microfiche set. As we saw above, the *U.S.C.S.* is not preserved in microfiche, so you would need to seek out a library that has retained archival copies of superseded *U.S.C.S.* volumes in order to do an exhaustive historical search.

2.36 CASES INCLUDED IN THE ANNOTATIONS

The selection of cases for annotations varies from publisher to publisher. The two annotated versions of the U.S. Code have historically differed in their approach to case annotations. Of old, the *U.S.C.A.* aspired to "completeness," while the *U.S.C.S.* aimed to be more selective. Currently, the *U.S.C.S.* is also being marketed as having "comprehensive" annotations. In fact, however, neither set is comprehensive, whether through active editorial discretion or just the exigencies of dealing with the tidal wave of decisions that must be sorted through: while the *U.S.C.A.* will frequently have more annotations after a given code section, the *U.S.C.S.* often has cases that the *U.S.C.A.* does not. The obvious moral: check both codes for the most complete picture possible, and don't assume that even the combination of the two is comprehensive. You will always want to make use of the full range of case-finding tools at your disposal.

2.37   CASE ANNOTATIONS IN SPECIALIZED SOURCES

You may also wish to look for case annotations in more specialized sources, many of which offer such annotations in code section order. For example, the *CCH Standard Federal Tax Reporter* offers case annotations arranged under thematic catchlines after each section of the Internal Revenue Code (Title 26 of the United States Code). The catchlines are devised from a more specialized viewpoint and, since it does not limit itself to officially published cases, the coverage of the annotations is broader. Similar services exist for annotations to such statute-like authorities as rules of procedure and evidence. For more information on this kind of research, see **Chapter 9** on looseleafs.

In the state law context, the annotated code (and some states, as with the federal code, have codes published by more than one publisher) is again your primary tool for finding judicial interpretations of statutes. However, there are also some additional resources for the state law researcher. If your statute was based on a uniform law (see **Chapter 11** for more on this concept), the *Uniform Laws Annotated* set will provide annotations to cases from a range of jurisdictions that have statutes based on the uniform source. Similarly, the various U.C.C. services such as West's *Uniform Commercial Code Reporting Service* and LexisNexis's *UCC Reporter-Digest* provide citations in code section order to cases from a variety of jurisdictions. But even using specialized annotation services (see **Table 2.E**) cannot assure you of complete coverage because of the editorial time required to put the annotations together, if for no other reason. To be sure that you have found absolutely every relevant decision, you will need to supplement your annotation search with either or both of the other two principal methods of finding cases pertaining to your statute.

2.38   USING A CITATOR TO FIND CASES INTERPRETING A STATUTE

The first of these alternative methods should be the use of a citator. The citator process will catch the newer judicial applications of your statute faster than the code annotators will, so you can gain valuable currency of coverage without sacrificing the organizational efficacy of an edited resource. Shepard's and KeyCite will both provide you with citations to cases (including cases not yet published) that construe your statute. The reason they should be regarded as secondary to use of the annotations is that unlike the annotations they provide only finding information, no description of content. Even when working electronically with a citator, where you can simply click through from each citation to the underlying case, you would waste a lot of time compared with the quick sweep you can make of an annotation to determine whether it is possibly relevant.

When working with a citator, make sure to check under all the possible ways that your statute could have been cited, i.e., as the section as a whole, as the specific subsection invoked in the case, or as the section in context of a sequence of sections identified by a section number followed by "*et seq.*" Again, it is definitely worthwhile to check more than one online citator, since they do not necessarily pick up the same cases, and they certainly do not necessarily pick them up at the same time. The online citators have overwhelming advantages over the print alternative: they furnish you with the case name of the citing reference and with its initial page as well as the page on which your statute was cited, and they allow you to see all the citing references in one pass, instead of obligating you to look through multiple volumes and supplements (any of which could be off the shelf just at the moment you need it!). They also come with powerful filtering tools that allow you to limit unwieldy result lists by, e.g., jurisdiction down to specific courts or by date down to specific time frames and allow searching of the full text of just those decisions that have been identified as citing to your statute. Despite the clear superiority of online citations, however, Shepard's in print (in the federal context, *Shepard's Federal Statute Citations*) remains the only resource available for the researcher needing to find cases construing an uncodified session law. Also, for those who like to get a sense of what sort of context you are dealing with, it can be easier to pick up on the magnitude of judicial commentary on a particular statute by taking note of how many pages of citations there are to it as opposed to scrolling through a long, long list of them. After a certain amount of scrolling, all such lists tend to seem equally endless!

2.39 USING FULL-TEXT SEARCHING TO FIND CASES INTERPRETING A STATUTE

The final way to find cases applying a given statute, and by far the most problematic, is to do a full-text search in a case law database. This is something you will definitely need to do at some point, so it is important to consider the challenges it poses. Fully aware of the potential difficulties, you will be better prepared to avoid the pitfalls that lie in wait. The twofold lure of the full-text search consists of the more current database you will be using, and the opportunity to bypass the possible errors of the editor (or the algorithm) that prepared the annotations or the citator. On the first count, the case law databases of Westlaw and Lexis Advance are updated in something much closer to real time than are their code databases, so you have additional, fresh material to look at. On the second count, since you get to choose how to look for the statutory references in the cases, you may think of some way to do so that catches something that others missed.

But herein lies the problem: the authors of decisions, *The Bluebook* notwithstanding, refer to statutes in many, many different ways, and you must cover them all to be successful in a full-text search. You can, of course, reasonably expect that every case dealing with your statute will cite to it in some manner. If you search for the code section number in some reasonably close proximity to the title number, you should get most of the relevant cases. But be warned that you will probably not get all of them, since you will miss the ones where for some reason only the underlying session law was cited, or where some fanciful version of the citing information is used, or where the statutory authority cited was a much broader grouping of code sections than you anticipated. Moreover, you may also retrieve many false drops, documents that also include those two numbers in the requested degree of proximity to each other but that do not concern your statute. You need to acknowledge to yourself that whenever you get a lot of false drops, your potential disposition to err shoots up, since the parade of irrelevant material up your screen can make your head swim just long enough to miss the one relevant item that is caught up in that crowd.

One way to try to achieve greater precision in a full-text search for cases construing a statute is to base the search on the precise statutory language that is of interest, rather than on the statute's citation, or to combine both these elements into a single search or series of searches. The downside of this is that here, too, you will probably miss some relevant cases, since the court cannot be assumed in every case to have actually quoted the statute. You have to be creative in doing this kind of full-text searching, and you also have to reconcile yourself to the idea that you cannot rely on this kind of searching alone. Once you have run whatever course of research you have set for yourself along these lines (e.g., annotations plus citator plus full-text search), one final step remains to check that your work is complete: you can do case law research on the subject matter of the statute, without mentioning the particular statute. Full advice on this kind of case law research is included in **Chapter 5**.

2.40 SPECIAL ISSUES IN STATE STATUTORY RESEARCH

Throughout this chapter on statutes we have raised points pertaining to state statutory research when they have varied from the federal model, or to confirm their similarity. Now we will address the single biggest issue in working with state statutes: the difficulty of comparative research. The legal researcher has many different reasons to want to do comparative state statutory research. She may wish to locate the ideal jurisdiction for a certain kind of activity, or a certain kind of lawsuit. She may wish to draw upon the statutes of different states as part of the work of drafting a new statute. She may wish to explain why the statutes of some states result in the different case law jurisprudence of those jurisdictions.

Doing this kind of research—locating the statutes from different jurisdictions that address the same legal issue though possibly couched in different terms (e.g., "criminal" rather than "penal")—is more difficult than case law comparative research for a number of reasons. First, there is no national index to statutes that assigns subjects to them as do the case indexing systems. Second, language is used differently in statutes than it is in cases: the statutory language of a jurisdiction is liable to be more standardized than the judicial language within that jurisdiction; as a result, the full-text researcher is less likely to get a hit based on the smaller universe of possible terms that will be used with respect to a given topic. The reasons we gravitate away from full-text searching in the Code databases as a whole are still in play here, but the need to cover a lot of ground pretty much compels you to do full-text searches in statutory databases that cover all states at once. Third, the variations of language between jurisdictions are more likely to remain hermetically sealed off from each other. Whereas judges in one jurisdiction may cite (and quote from) cases from elsewhere as persuasive authority, it is far rarer for a judge to even mention a statute from another jurisdiction.

How, then, to accomplish this difficult legal research task? The first step, as ever, is to ascertain whether someone else has already done it for you. Comparative state statutes on a particular topic are a relatively common subject of law review articles (see **Chapter 4**). Many of these comparative analyses of state statutes are indexed in a series of bibliographies entitled *Subject Compilations of State Laws* (see **Table 2.F**). These bibliographies also index other sources of comparisons of state laws on particular topics, including charts and tables in subject treatises. Another good source is the websites of interest groups with a brief on that particular topic. Groups of legislators, such as the National Conference of State Legislatures, are another source of information on comparative state statutes. Finally, both Lexis Advance and Westlaw offer 50-state surveys of different areas of law, designed to provide quick access to relevant statutes from each state (see **Table 2.F**).

2.41 TABLES

TABLE 2.A: SELECTED SOURCES FOR
THE UNITED STATES CODE

1. United States Government Publishing Office

   http://www.gpo.gov/fdsys

   [Select "United States Code" under "Browse"]. The site includes .pdf files beginning with 1994 and authenticated .pdf files beginning with the 2006 main edition.

2. Office of the Law Revision Counsel of the United States House of Representatives

   http://uscode.house.gov/

3. Cornell Legal Information Institute

   http://www.law.cornell.edu/uscode/

4. *United States Code: Containing the General and Permanent Laws of the United States Enacted Through the 112th Congress (ending January 2, 2013 [. . .]).* Prepared and published under authority of Title 2, U.S. Code, Section 285b, by the Office of the Law Revision Counsel of the House of Representatives. Washington, D.C.: Government Publishing Office, 2013–. (This is the "2012 Edition." New main editions are published every six years. Supplements appear yearly, also with a significant delay between enactment and official publication.)

5. *United States Code Annotated.* St. Paul, Minn.: West Publishing, 1927– (This set is currently published by Thomson West).

6. Westlaw:

   United States Code Annotated: Statutes & Court Rules > United States Code Annotated (USCA) United States Code—Unannotated: Statutes & Court Rules > United States Code Annotated (USCA) > United States Code—Unannotated (under "Tools & Resources" on the right)

   United States Code Annotated Index: Statutes & Court Rules > United States Code Annotated (USCA) > United States Code Annotated Index (under "Tools & Resources" on the right)

   United States Code Annotated Popular Name Table: Statutes & Court Rules > United States Code Annotated (USCA) > United States Code Annotated Popular Name Table (under "Tools & Resources" on the right).

United States Code Annotated Tables: Statutes & Court Rules > United States Code Annotated (USCA) > United States Code Annotated Tables (under "Tools & Resources" on the right)

United States Code Annotated—Historical: Statutes & Court Rules > United States Code Annotated (USCA) > United States Code Annotated—Historical (under "Tools & Resources" on the right). Historical versions of the USCA from 1990 to 2016 are only accessible by searching, not browsing. The most useful options are full-text, Citation, e.g., 18 USCA 101, and Credit, which allows you to pull code sections using the citations for the Public Laws on which they were based, e.g., 94–553.

7. *United States Code Service.* Charlottesville, Va., 1998– (This set is currently published by LexisNexis).

8. Lexis Advance:

   United States Code Service: Statutes and Legislation > Codes > USCS—United States Code Service—Titles 1 through 54

   United States Code Service Index: On the home screen main search box, type "USCIDX" then select "United States Code Service—Titles 1 through 54—Index" from the drop-down menu. If you click the name, you will add that source to your search; if you wish to browse the index to look up a term, click the Table of Contents icon to the right of the Title. United States Code Service Popular Names Table: Statutes and Legislation > Codes > USCS Popular Names Table

   Shortcut: type "USNAME" in the home page main search box.

   United States Code Service—Statutes at Large Table: Statutes and Legislation > Codes > USCS Statutes at Large Table Shortcut: Shortcut: type "USSALT" in the home page main search box. United States Archived Code Search: Statutes and Legislation > Archived Code Search (under Related Resources on the right) > limit to U.S. Federal and the year you want (back to 1992)

9. Bloomberg Law: Federal Law > Federal Legislative > United States Code (USC)

10. HeinOnline: U.S. Code > United States Code (image files of all main editions and supplements, beginning with 1926 to the most current print edition).

TABLE 2.B: SOURCES FOR UNITED STATES SESSION LAWS

1.   United States, *United States Statutes at Large*. Washington, D. C.: United States Government Publishing Office.

     Coverage begins in 1789 (1st Congress)

2.   United States Government Publishing Office, FDsys

     http://www.gpo.gov/fdsys/browse/collectiontab.action

     Select "United States Statutes at Large" for .pdf coverage beginning with 1951 / volume 65 / 82nd Congress, 1st Session. You can also retrieve a session law from the Statutes at Large using the RETRIEVE BY CITATION function available at https://www.gpo.gov/fdsys/search/showcitation.action.

     Note also that while many of the FDsys Statutes at Large materials are digitally signed as an indicator of authenticity, the website itself calls attention to 1 U.S.C. 112 and alleges that it makes "the printed edition" of the Statutes at Large legal evidence of the laws and other materials therein.

3.   Library of Congress, Congress.gov

     https://www.congress.gov/

     [Select "Public Laws" under "Bill Searches and Lists."] Coverage includes all public laws since 1973.

4.   HeinOnline, U.S. Statutes at Large Collection. This subscription database offers .pdf files of the Statutes at Large beginning with volume 1 and is currently up-to-date with the GPO series.

5.   Westlaw:

     United States Statutes at Large (1789–1972): Statutes & Court Rules > United States Code Annotated (SCA) > United States Statutes at Large (under "Tools & Resources" on the right). The full text is available only in non-searchable .pdf files. Even when downloaded, the optical character recognition on the .pdf is generally of exceptionally poor quality, making locating a phrase within an Act difficult indeed. Note that the Public Law Number field can only be used to locate acts from between 1957 and 1972. Earlier session laws can be retrieved using Congressional chapter citation. For Statutes at Large citations, you must include the quotation marks around the citation to avoid unwanted results.

     United States Public Laws—Historical (1973 to the most recently concluded Congress): Proposed & Enacted Legislation

> Federal > U.S. Public Laws > U.S. Public Laws—Historical (under Tools & Resources on the right). Only the 10 most recent documents are displayed, but you can click on "Advanced" towards the top to allow for search by citation or for terms in the text. You can use the *P.L.* or *Stat.* citation, but there are no .pdf files available.

United States Public Laws—Current Congress: Proposed & Enacted Legislation > Federal > U.S. Public Laws. You can browse by year or click on "Advanced" towards the top to allow for search by citation and you can conduct full-text searches. There are no .pdf files available.

United States Code Congressional & Administrative News: Legislative History > U.S. Code Congressional & Administrative News > Public Laws. Coverage begins in 1973. There are no .pdf files available. You can conduct full-text searches. You can also search by Public Law Number or Statutes at Large citation (curiously named "Stat Page Number" though obviously requiring a volume as well for best results, e.g., 90 Stat. 2541).

6. Library of Congress, American Memory: Statutes at Large

    http://memory.loc.gov/ammem/amlaw/lwsl.html

    Coverage is from 1789–1875, 1st–43rd Congress, image files only.

7. *United States Code Congressional and Administrative News*. St. Paul, Minn.: Thomson West

    Coverage begins in 1952 (82d Congress, Second Session). Its predecessor publications were the *United States Code Congressional and Administrative Service* (1951) and the *United States Code Congressional Service*, beginning in 1941 (77th Congress).

8. Lexis Advance:

    USCS—Public Laws: Statutes and Legislation > Public Laws/ALS > USCS—Public Laws.

    Shortcut: type "PUBLAW" in the home page main search box. Coverage is from September 9, 1988 through "current." Full-text searchable, but no .pdf files.

    United States Statutes at Large: Statutes and Legislation > Public Laws/ALS > United States Statutes at Large. Coverage begin from 1776 and new updates come after the printed version is released by the GPO. This database is only searchable by Title, popular name, or brief synopsis, not full text. Once a particular document is identified and selected, a .pdf file is available. The U.S.C.S. History notes for each code section will also include hyperlinks into this Statutes at Large database, where .pdf files can be downloaded.

9. Bloomberg Law: Federal Law > Federal Legislative > U.S. Public Laws & Statutes at Large. This database supports full-text searching from 1788 to present. Though files are available for the full range, the source and quality of the files varies. Very old laws have simple image files; some recent laws lead to authenticated .pdf files from the GPO, though others do not.

10. LLMC Digital: subscription database. Includes scanned .pdf files of the U.S. Statutes at Large, volumes 1 through 125, although volumes are often broken up into multiple parts (e.g., Volume 124, Part 1; Volume 124, Part 2, etc.). The full text of a particular "part" can be searched only after you click into that part.

11. *United States Code Service: Advance*. Charlottesville, Va.: LexisNexis

TABLE 2.C: SOURCES FOR NEW FEDERAL SESSION LAWS

1. United States Government Publishing Office, FDsys

    http://www.gpo.gov/fdsys

    Called "Public and Private Laws" under "Browse."

2. Library of Congress, Congress.gov

    https://www.congress.gov/

    [Select "Public Laws" under "Bill Searches and Lists."]

3. *United States Code Congressional and Administrative News.* St. Paul, Minn.: Thomson West. Newest session laws are published in the softbound supplementary volumes.

4. Westlaw:

    Proposed & Enacted Legislation > Federal > U.S. Public Laws

    Includes Public Laws from the current legislative session only.

5. *United States Code Service: Advance.* Charlottesville, Va.: LexisNexis

6. Lexis Advance

    USCS—Public Laws: Statutes and Legislation > Public Laws/ALS > USCS—Public Laws.

    Shortcut: type "PUBLAW" in the home page main search box. Coverage is from September 9, 1988 through "current." Full-text searchable, but no .pdf files.

7. Bloomberg Law: Federal Law > Federal Legislative > U.S. Public Laws & Statutes at Large

TABLE 2.D: ONLINE SOURCES OF CONGRESSIONAL BILLS

1. Library of Congress, Congress.gov

    https://www.congress.gov/

    Includes bill information starting with the 93rd Congress (1973), and bill texts starting with the 101st Congress (1989) with .pdf files starting with the 103rd (1993).

2. United States Government Publishing Office, FDsys

    http://www.gpo.gov/fdsys

    [Choose collection "Congressional Bills."] Coverage begins with the 103rd Congress (1993–94). Offers both text and .pdf files.

3. Westlaw:

    Congressional Bills: Proposed & Enacted Legislation > Federal > Congressional Bills. Coverage is for the current session only, with text but not .pdf files. Links through to bill tracking information.

    Bill Tracking: Statutes & Court Rules > Bill Tracking (Under "Tools & Resources" on the right) > U.S. Congress. Coverage is for the current session only, with text but not .pdf files.

    Bill Tracking: Historical: Statutes & Court Rules > Bill Tracking (Under "Tools & Resources" on the right) > Bill Tracking: Historical (Under "Tools & Resources" on the right) > U.S. Congress. Summary coverage begins in 2005, but full text is only sometimes available (not in .pdf)

4. Lexis:

    Bill Text: Statutes & Legislation > Bill Text. Arranged by Congress number, Bill Text archives go back to the 101st Congress.

    Bill Tracking: Statutes & Legislation > Bill Tracking

    Arranged by Congress number, Bill Tracking Reports go back to the 101st Congress. Does not include full text.

5. Bloomberg Law: Federal Law > Federal Legislative > U.S. Congress > U.S. House & Senate Bills

    Text and .pdf files, coverage starts with 1993. New bill summaries are sometimes available before the full text is.

TABLE 2.E: EXAMPLES OF SPECIALIZED SOURCES OF STATUTE ANNOTATIONS AND HOW THEY WORK

Case annotations of statutes can be found in many treatises, as well as in looseleaf services, specialized reporters, and specialized statutory compilations like those listed here.

1. *Copyright Law Reporter*. Chicago, Ill.: CCH

   This looseleaf service is a good example of the multi-step process used to get from statutory section to interpreting case in such publications. The copyright statutes appear in one volume, and each section of the statute is assigned a paragraph number. Cases are found by consulting a list of cases organized by the paragraph number(s) (and therefore the statutory sections) to which they are relevant. The payoff for going through this comparatively cumbersome process is subject access to many cases not published in print elsewhere and thus not picked up by the general indexing systems.

2. *Federal Rules Service*. St. Paul, Minn.: Thomson West

   Here, too, a multi-step finding process leads to "unpublished" cases. In this set, the text of each Federal Rule is followed by a detailed breakdown of subject headings pertaining to that section (analogous to the catchnotes following the statutory sections in the annotated codes), and then cases are listed in a "Findex" under those numbered subject headings.

3. *Uniform Laws Annotated*. St. Paul, Minn.: Thomson West

   This set covers only those laws that have been adopted by states on the basis, to at least some extent, of a Uniform Law (these are discussed at some length in **Chapter 11**), but in the familiar format of a West annotated code. The text of each section is followed by official commentary and then by notes of decisions.

TABLE 2.F: SOME SOURCES OF COMPARATIVE STATE STATUTES

1. Cheryl Rae Nyberg, *Subject Compilations of State Laws, 2014–2015*. Getzville, N. Y.: W. S. Hein, 2016.

   This is the latest in a series of annotated bibliographies of different sorts of subject compilations of statutes that cover multiple states. Compilations indexed include law review articles, appendices to treatises, and websites. There is some cross-referencing and some cumulation of the indexing within the set. Also available on HeinOnline.

2. *National Survey of State Laws*. 7th ed. Richard A. Leiter, editor. Getzville, N. Y.: W. S. Hein, 2015. Available in the National Survey of State Laws collection on HeinOnline.

   Citations and summaries of state laws arranged in tables for 54 topics.

3. Inter-state political, advocacy, and governmental organizations are often useful sources of information on recent and proposed legislation on a particular subject. One particularly useful site is that of the National Conference of State Legislatures:

   http://www.ncsl.org/

4. Westlaw:

   50 State Statutory Surveys: Statutes & Court Rules > 50 State Statutory Surveys (under "Tools & Resources" on the right). Includes lists of statute sections from the state level arranged within 20 broad topics, with hyperlinks to the statutes themselves within Westlaw. Also includes State-by-State Analysis tables that includes some explanation with the references. Also reachable via Citing References > Secondary Sources from the statutes included in a survey.

5. Lexis Advance:

   50 State Surveys: Statutes & Legislation > 50 State Surveys (under "Related Resources" on the right) > LexisNexis 50 State Surveys: Statutes and Regs

   Lexis 50 state surveys include a brief introduction and background and then have tables with state-by-state explanations and hyperlinks to the relevant state statutes on Lexis Advance.

CHAPTER 3

LEGISLATIVE HISTORY

■ ■ ■

3.1 LEGISLATIVE HISTORY: WHEN AND WHY?

Legislative history takes a back seat to case law as an interpretive tool for statutes. Unless there is arguably an ambiguity on the face of the statute, the first place to look beyond the statute's own text for legal authority is to judicial interpretation, not legislative history. That said, in the proper circumstances an argument from legislative history can be decisive. The idea behind it is that the judiciary must give effect to the will of the sovereign legislature and so must ascertain that will correctly, even if it involves looking beyond the language of the statute for the legislature's intent.

This idea has had far longer play in the United States than in closely related jurisprudential systems such as the United Kingdom. Up until the 1993 turning point of the English House of Lords case *Pepper v. Hart* [1993] 1 All E.R. 42 (H.L.), the use of legislative history as an aid to statutory interpretation was traditionally viewed as barred from English courts. See, e.g., Michael P. Healy, *Legislative Intent and Statutory Interpretation in England and the United States: An Assessment of the Impact of* Pepper v. Hart, 35 Stan. J. Int'l L. 231 (1999).

Even here in the United States, there has long been lively debate about the proper role of legislative history in statutory interpretation. But the demand by researchers, both legal and historical, for the stuff of legislative history has been strong enough over a long period of time to support the creation of a robust and thorough publication system for this type of material, at least in the context of the U.S. government. The situation in the states, we shall see, is rather different.

3.2 TYPES OF LEGISLATIVE HISTORY DOCUMENTS

The underlying quest of the legal researcher is for material that indicates what the legislature had in its collective mind when it voted to enact a certain statute. Of course, the cold hard truth is that different legislators may well have had different things in mind. The exploration of that reality, however, is really more the province of the political historian, who will concern herself more with the machinations of individual legislators and of the large supporting cast of figures peripheral to the legislative process.

In the strictly legal researcher's pursuit of the theoretical contents of the fictitious collective legislative mind, the evidence that legislative history musters comprises the material that was available to the legislators generally when they were casting their votes. The U.S. Congress can generate a lot of documentation in the course of its work. The legal researcher must be able to identify which kinds of documentation may arguably be probative of legislative intent, and it is under this lens that evaluation of the relative value of the different kinds of documentation can be made.

The principal kinds of legislative history documents for the U.S. Congress are (in rough chronological order by their sequence of production):

— Bills

— Committee hearings

— Committee prints

— House or Senate Documents

— Committee Reports

— Floor debate

In this chapter, we will address these types of documents in order of their relative importance, which varies considerably from their chronological order.

3.3   THE IMPACT OF TECHNOLOGY ON LEGISLATIVE HISTORY RESEARCH

Perhaps more than any other aspect of legal research, the process by which one identifies and locates the full text of legislative history documents has been made immeasurably easier by technology. In years past, researchers had two primary options: 1) hope someone had done the hard work of collecting the relevant legislative documents for a particular statute and published it in print (a compiled legislative history); or 2) making extensive use of multiple print sets (some of which had lists of documents, others of which had excerpts of Committee Reports) and compiling a legislative history from scratch. Unless you happened to be looking for a particularly significant act, there was no such thing as "one-stop research."

Today, a commercial product called ProQuest Legislative Insight (PQLI) has made many of those earlier resources superfluous. . . if you are fortunate enough to have access to it. Alas, such a collection costs a pretty penny and so many institutions may find themselves without access to this

Cadillac of legislative history databases. Even so, the Yugos of the world have made tremendous strides as well, and will perform satisfactorily for many less elaborate needs. This chapter will discuss the various electronic resources, but will not delve into the convoluted world of print except where necessary.

3.4 PROQUEST LEGISLATIVE INSIGHT

For the researcher identifying legislative intent, PQLI is worth its weight in gold. As of this writing, it is home to legislative histories for over 27,000 federal laws. For those laws, the key to accessing all the relevant material you need, in searchable .pdf files, is the Public Law Number. Remember, if you are starting with a section of the Code, the parenthetical information that follows the Code text will include the desired Public Law Number(s) (see **Section 2.24** for additional detail). Using just the Public Law Number, you are able to browse for your act by clicking on the appropriate congress and then scrolling through the numeric listing (with titles, to make sure you have the number right). Alternatively, you can run a Search by Number if you have a Public Law Number, Bill Number, Public Resolution Number, Statutes at Large Citation, Publication Number, or a few other numeric identifiers. In either event, in PQLI you'll be looking for a Publication Type called Legislative History, because it is this document that includes a summary and links to all relevant legislative history documents described in this chapter.

3.5 COMPILED LEGISLATIVE HISTORIES

If you are without access to PQLI, all is not lost. In that circumstance, you should still ascertain whether someone has already compiled a legislative history that you can use. Many important federal statutes have been subjected to this kind of research, and the results have often been published. Compiled legislative histories may consist of reprints of full documents, a selection of particularly important excerpts, or simply of a list of citations to the documents identified. Absent access to PQLI, you can check other specialized resources to see whether they include the work you've set out to do.

Compiled legislative histories are indexed in specialized subject bibliographies and in general bibliographies of federal legislative histories (see **Table 3.A**). In the latter category, the standard sources are Nancy P. Johnson's *Sources of Compiled Legislative Histories* (2014) and Bernard D. Reams Jr.'s *Federal Legislative Histories* (1994). In electronic format, HeinOnline includes the U.S. Federal Legislative History Library. Within that library you can find a unique adaptation of Nancy Johnson's Sources of Compiled Legislative Histories to the electronic format. Arranged by Congress or in an alphabetical list by act title, the Sources of Compiled

Legislative Histories Database is a finding aid that leads directly to .pdf files on HeinOnline of the compiled legislative histories and related journal articles. If the act you're interested in isn't listed, be sure to check the U.S. Federal Legislative History Title Collection, as it does (rarely) house compiled legislatives histories not included in Nancy Johnson's work or its electronic counterpart. Legislative history compilations can also often find their way into journals, so you can check law review indexes for appropriate pieces not yet listed in the legislative history indexes (see **Chapter 4** on law reviews); book-length compilations that have not yet been included in indexes can be sought in library catalogs and on publisher websites.

3.6   COMPILING YOUR OWN LEGISLATIVE HISTORY

If you don't have a compiled legislative history available for your act, then it falls on you to identify what legislative history documents were produced in connection with it, to determine what your access options are, and to weigh properly the relative value of types of documents in determining legislative intent. If you do not have access to electronic resources like those developed by ProQuest, this can be a daunting task. There are, however, tools out there that can help you perform it efficiently. For more detail on those tools and all the nitty gritty information you need to identify documents and compile a legislative history from scratch (i.e., "the old-fashioned way") please see Chapter 3 from the 4th edition of *Where the Law Is*. Let us turn now to a brief discussion of the types of legislative history documents, presented in roughly declining order of importance.

3.7   COMMITTEE REPORTS

Of all the legislative history documents potentially created, the Committee Reports are universally regarded as by far the most important: this is what the legislators were made aware of as they decided how to vote on a bill, and it therefore furnishes evidence of their intent. So significant are the Committee Reports that the text of the reports, or of excerpts from them, are made widely available in conjunction with the statutes in whose construction they aid. For recent Committee Reports, FDsys has many freely available, and, for laws starting with those in 1948, U.S.C.C.A.N. remains a valued source for Committee Reports (selected, and often edited), that help ascertain legislative intent. In many instances, these Committee Reports, or even just U.S.C.C.A.N.'s selected excerpts of them, may be enough to compile a basic legislative history yourself (see **Table 3.B** for other sources of Committee Reports).

Note that, although Committee Reports are widely cited in court decisions, these Reports cannot be systematically traced through to the body of case law to see how the courts have made use of them. No citator, in other words, undertakes to provide citing references for Committee Reports. Finding court citations to these Reports will require full-text searching. There are myriad ways you could approach such a full-text search. You could run the statute through the citator of your choice, and then limit the results to those cases that include the word "Report" (or its variants, such as Rep't, Rept., or Rep.) and other important words (or numbers) from the Report citation. You could also do a full-text search in the appropriate case law database looking for cases that use the word Report (or its variants) in proximity to the Report number.

Doing the searches described above can be done without reference to a Report number, because the citing court will of necessity also cite the underlying statute. But a Report number will make the search easier by enabling you to use the close proximity between the word "Report" and the Report number to minimize false drops. And of course you will need the Report number to find the text of the Report first yourself, if, for example, it transpires that no court has ever cited any Committee Report on your statute.

3.8   COMMITTEE HEARINGS

After Committee Reports, the type of legislative history material that is logically the next most likely to furnish evidence of legislative intent is the committee hearing. Some sorts of hearings are more likely to be important than others. Congress holds periodic supervisory hearings that are mandated by law, and it holds hearings in contemplation of confirming executive appointments of officials. Neither of these would be useful for establishing legislative intent. The kind of hearings you are looking for are the hearings on proposed bills and investigative hearings held in contemplation of the drafting of bills, whether those bills become law or not. While open committee hearings are more widely available, the committees of Congress also often conduct closed hearings, usually involving material sensitive because of concerns over national security or personal privacy, or during the working markup sessions in the final stages of legislative drafting. The records of this kind of hearing, captured and maintained with varying degrees of attention over the years, were historically treated by the committee involved as internal documents for the committee's use only, and retained only as archival records of the committee's operations. Nevertheless, these unpublished hearings are also sometimes included in PQLI or in compiled legislative histories, which raises an important question: how useful are these unpublished hearings?

Well, we can logically compare them to other sorts of legal research materials. While the publication of statutes is not specifically mandated by our Constitution, a statute intended to be unpublished is completely antithetical to our system of government. Statutes are the state speaking in a normative vein to those subject to its authority, and publication of those statutes is the broadcast that allows the distant public to hear the promulgating speech. While the statute may exist, in some sense, even without publication, its effect would be curtailed by (among other things) the Due Process Clause of the Fifth Amendment. For a historical overview of the needfulness of publication of statutes, see *U.S. v. Burgess*, 1987 WL 39092, 1987 U.S. Dist. LEXIS 11227, No. 133066 (N.D. Ill., Dec. 1, 1987). For a case to be unpublished, by contrast, is extremely common. Only the tip of the iceberg of judicial opinions gets published as case reports. An unpublished case may or may not be citeable, depending on the jurisdiction. To be sure, even if you are not permitted to cite a case, it still retains some importance to the researcher as an indicator of how that judge (or others of similar inclination) is likely to lean in particular circumstances. An unpublished hearing, however, loses almost nothing of its probative value by virtue of being unpublished. Whatever effect the closed hearing had on legislators when they were forming legislative intent is at least as likely to be significant as with open hearings (see **Table 3.C** for sources of committee hearings).

3.9   COMMITTEE PRINTS AND HOUSE AND SENATE DOCUMENTS

Next most significant, logically, are other materials relied upon by the committee during its deliberations and in preparing its reports. These run the gamut from investigative reports to statistical tables, from draft bills to annual reports of executive agencies submitted to Congress as mandated by law. These sorts of materials may be selected for publication either as committee prints, only some of which are numbered (Senate only), or as House or Senate Documents (especially the communications from the executive branch to Congress), which are deemed to contain information that will be in wider demand. Note that "Documents" here is a specific class of publications, and not a reference to legislative history documents generally.

3.10   BILLS AS LEGISLATIVE HISTORY

All of the legislative history sources explored above contain commentary or background of one sort or another relevant to Congressional thinking concerning proposed legislation. Another sort of source to consider is the actual texts of the proposed legislation as it developed into the form that was eventually enacted into law. Many of the techniques used when searching recent bills for relevant pending legislation (see **Sections 2.29–2.31**) can be projected back into the past to find variant bills on a subject, the differences between which can shed light on Congress's intent in making the changes that were eventually made. You may find useful information by comparing different states of the same bill at different stages in its evolution, or by comparing related but unsuccessful bills in earlier Congresses. Particularly useful, of course, would be finding that Congress had specifically rejected a text that supports an interpretation proposed by your opponent.

3.11 FLOOR DEBATE, AS CAPTURED IN THE CONGRESSIONAL RECORD

Finally, we consider the chronicle of Congressional activity presented in the Congressional Record. When the *Congressional Record* commenced in March of 1873, it was the first publication to contain the full text of Congressional floor debate and comment. It was preceded by four earlier publications, the *Annals of Congress* (1789–1824), the *Abridgement of the Debates of Congress* (1789–1850), the *Register of the Debates in Congress* (1824–1837), and the *Congressional Globe* (1833–1873) which were primarily paraphrased reporting of what had transpired on the floor, and are available in .pdf files at the American Memory website of the Library of Congress.

Novice legal researchers frequently make the mistake of thinking that what they are going to do when looking for legislative intent is to look in the Congressional Record. They expect to find clarification through floor debate of what was in the legislative mind at the time of passage. But we have saved floor debate and the Congressional Record for last in this consideration of legislative history sources precisely because it offers a lot of very questionable evidence of legislative intent. The bill texts reproduced therein, to be sure, offer both high evidentiary value and convenience. Occasionally some last minute colloquy between members of Congress about the intended meaning of some wording in the legislation about to be voted on can indeed provide a solid gold nugget of evidence as to intent. Even so, courts are often reluctant to accept the statement of one legislator as evidence of the entire body's collective intent.

Further, the bulk of material contained in the Congressional Record can be completely discounted as a source of such evidence, for the simple reason that it only occurred *ex post facto*. Much of the content of the Congressional Record consists of the "extensions of remarks" that Members of Congress are entitled to insert into the Record even though they never delivered the same on the floor of Congress nor, therefore, into the ears of their colleagues in preparation for a vote. Even material not designated as an extension of remarks may not actually have been uttered on the floor, thanks to the extremely liberal editorial license granted the Members of Congress. While their subsequent remarks may be rich fodder indeed for the political historian, their timing makes them pretty slim pickings for the legal researcher. This is not to say that nothing of any value can be gleaned from the extensions of remarks. Since they frequently deal with politically significant aspects of the topic under discussion, even *ex post facto* remarks can act as signposts to important issues that should be researched carefully in the more probative documents such as Committee Reports (see **Table 3.D** for sources of the Congressional Record and floor debates).

3.12 CONGRESSIONAL RECORD PAGINATION

In the course of your research, you will probably notice that most sources pointing you to the Congressional Record references for a particular bill or law do so by date only, not by page. This is because the Record goes through two different iterations, and each is paginated differently. The Congressional Record appears first in a Daily Edition, which is paginated in separate sections for the House and Senate. Once material is carried over to the Bound Edition (the compilation volumes that have been amended and added to by members of Congress and are repaginated in one continuous sequence), *The Bluebook* requires citation to the Bound Edition (called there the permanent edition), rather than to the Daily Edition (Rule 13.5). This has posed a problem from the mid-eighties on, when production and distribution of the Bound Edition became intermittent and spotty. Currently, the best way to get access to the Bound Edition is via the U.S. Congressional Documents library on HeinOnline (covers 1873–2011). HeinOnline also offers a very helpful "Congressional Record Daily to Bound Locator," which can pinpoint the location of specific language in the desired edition. If you don't have access to HeinOnline, you can retrieve most of the recent Bound Edition pages from FDsys (covers parts of 1999–2009).

Citations to the Congressional Record by date only are commonly found in some lists and indexes, and they do put the burden on the researcher to obtain the required page numbers for herself. Working with only the date can be onerous, since a single dated issue can be quite lengthy. To get a particular page number, the researcher must usually turn to the internal indexing of the Record, which is, of course, provided separately for the two different print editions.

3.13 CONGRESSIONAL RECORD INDEXING

The Bound Edition includes, in the final book of each volume, an index entitled "History of Bills and Resolutions." This gives, for each bill introduced in that session, the page numbers in the permanent edition where action was taken on that bill. There is also a subject index, in the unlikely case that you are not looking for references to a particular bill. In the Daily Edition, very brief descriptions of the proceedings for that day are grouped in the Daily Digest section under broad rubrics like "Measures Passed," giving the appropriate daily edition page numbers within that issue. While there is no numerical list of bills in the Daily Digest, the descriptions are brief enough that scanning the material for mentions of a particular bill number is quite easy, and certainly more efficient than reading through the whole issue looking for your bill. Page references to the Daily Edition by bill number are given in the History of Bills and Resolutions section of the biweekly *Congressional Record Index.*

3.14 STATE LEGISLATIVE HISTORY

While the same principles apply in state legislative history as in federal, the state legislative historian does face some special problems. The principal problem is that of paucity of raw material. Many states do not publish all or indeed any of the deliberative materials that would provide evidence of legislative intent. The Manz guide, which we already encountered in **Section 2.31** as a good source for information about state bills, is also full of information about other state legislative history documentation. One source that comes up frequently in the state context is the work product of various law reform commissions. Again, individual state legal research manuals will provide more detail (see **Appendix**). As both the state legislatures and the large legal database vendors continue to put additional legislative material online, the situation is changing to one more similar to the federal environment. Using what you know about the federal legislature's documentation of its work, you can search the state website or speak with a state librarian looking for analogous documentation in the state context.

If your state statute's source was a uniform or model act, you can tap into the larger body of legislative history and commentary that pertains to the act in its proposed generic form, and also in other jurisdictions (see **Section 11.2** for more on this). One component of this legislative history is the law itself: the variations between versions from jurisdiction to jurisdiction and between any one jurisdiction and the original uniform version can all be telling. Given the aims of uniform acts, to unify statutory law where inter-jurisdictional need dictates and to replace common law in a rational manner, they are popular subjects for analysis in law reviews, and the commentary that the latter contain (see **Chapter 4**) will provide much grist for the state legislative historian.

3.15   TABLES

TABLE 3.A: SELECTED SOURCES OF COMPILED FEDERAL LEGISLATIVE HISTORIES

1. ProQuest Legislative Insight

   If you have access to this subscription database, you should start here. It includes Legislative Histories (for Public Laws only) with links to .pdf files of the related documents. Coverage begins in 1789 and legislative histories of new laws are regularly added.

2. ProQuest Congressional

   This subscription database has more limited coverage of legislative histories for Public Laws than ProQuest Legislative Insight, but it, unlike PQLI, does include some legislative history documents associated with bills that never became law.

3. Nancy P. Johnson, *Sources of Compiled Legislative Histories.* Buffalo, N. Y.: W. S. Hein, 2014.

   This publication, sponsored by the American Association of Law Libraries, lists in Public Law number order the legislative histories located in government documents, law review articles, books, and microfiche sets. For each compiled legislative history listed, the nature of its contents is noted: i.e., whether it contains citations or full texts, and which legislative history components are covered. Also available on the subscription-based HeinOnline, in the U.S. Federal Legislative History Library.

4. HeinOnline: U.S. Federal Legislative History Library

   In addition to the Johnson bibliography described in number 3, this subscription database includes the U.S. Federal Legislative History Title Collection, a selection of compiled full-text legislative histories organized by publication title, public law number, and popular name.

5. Bernard D. Reams, Jr., *Federal Legislative Histories.* Westport, Conn.: Greenwood Press, 1994.

   This bibliography covers narrower ground, since it only includes legislative histories published by the government, but it includes much more descriptive detail about each one.

6. Congressional Information Service, *CIS Index*. Bethesda, Md.: ProQuest.

    Since its beginning in 1970, this annual publication has pulled together the components of a basic legislative history for each Public Law enacted; since 1984, the annual Legislative Histories volumes have compiled comprehensive lists of legislative history components, including background history from earlier Congresses. This material is also available in the subscription databases ProQuest Congressional and ProQuest Legislative Insight, for documents associated with Public Laws. The CIS Index is also searchable on Lexis Advance (see number 7 of this table).

7. Lexis Advance: Statutes & Legislation > Legislative Histories > US—CIS/Index

    Includes CIS Index material from 1970 to present. Shortcut: type "CISLH" in the home page main search box.

8. *United States Code Congressional and Administrative News*. St. Paul, Minn.: Thomson West.

    This annual contains not only a list of some of the basic legislative history for each Public Law enacted, but also excerpts from what the editors deem to be the most significant Committee Report. Also available on Westlaw (see number 9 of this table).

9. Westlaw:

    Legislative History > Legislative History—United States Code

    Includes legislative history material from *U.S.C.C.A.N.* between 1948 and 1989 and broader coverage of documents tied to bills beginning in 1990, as well as additional material.

    Legislative History > U.S. GAO Federal Legislative Histories

    Includes legislative histories for many public laws enacted between 1921 and 1995, including hyperlinks to .pdf files of underlying documents.

    Legislative History > Arnold & Porter Legislative Histories (under "Tools & Resources" on the right)

    Includes legislative histories compiled by the law firm Arnold & Porter for over 30 pieces of selected major legislation.

TABLE 3.B: SOURCES FOR COMMITTEE REPORTS

1.   ProQuest Legislative Insight

   If you are looking for a Committee Report associated with a Public Law, start with this subscription database. Coverage begins in 1789 and new reports are regularly added.

2.   ProQuest Congressional

   This subscription database includes select Committee Reports tied to both Public Laws and introduced bills, with coverage beginning in 1789.

3.   *United States Code Congressional and Administrative News.* St. Paul, Minn.: Thomson West

   Often, this is all you will need. Reprints the highlights of the principal Committee Reports where the editors deem it potentially significant for the discernment of legislative intent. 1948–Present. Updated with monthly softcover supplements. Also available on Westlaw.

4.   United States Government Publishing Office, FDsys

   http://www.gpo.gov/fdsys/browse/collectiontab.action

   Click on "Congressional Reports including Conference Reports." Coverage begins in 1995, and includes both text and .pdf files.

5.   Library of Congress, Congress.gov

   https://www.congress.gov/

   [Select "Committee Reports" from the drop-down menu left of the search bar, or the "Committee Reports" link under the "Site Content" heading.] Coverage begins in 1995. Offers both text and .pdf files.

6.   Westlaw: Legislative History > Legislative History—United States Code

   Reports from 1948 to 1989 are from U.S.C.C.A.N. (and, therefore, are edited versions); thereafter from the GPO text. Not available as .pdf files.

7.   Lexis Advance: Statutes and Legislation > Legislative Histories > Committee Reports

   Continuous coverage begins in 1989 and is regularly updated. You can also access this content by typing the shortcut CMTRPT in the main search box.

8.   United States, *United States Congressional Serial Set.*
     Washington, D. C.: Government Publishing Office, 1817–

     The Committee Reports and Congressional Documents bound
     in permanent volumes. Note that there is no indexing, and no
     through pagination in this set.

     Subsets of this series have been republished in The U.S.
     Congressional Serial Set, 1817–1994, distributed by Readex as
     part of their "Archive of Americana." It currently covers the
     15th through 103rd Congresses. The Library of Congress has
     also put selected reports from the period 1833–1917 on the web
     in image files as part of its American Memory project at http://
     memory.loc.gov/ammem/amlaw/lwss.html.

9.   Bloomberg Law: Browse All Content > Laws & Regulations >
     Legislative Resources > Official U.S. House & Senate Committee
     Reports

     Coverage includes reports from 104th Congress (1995) to
     present, as copies of authenticated GPO .pdf files.

TABLE 3.C: SOURCES OF COMMITTEE HEARINGS

1. ProQuest Legislative Insight

    If you are looking for a Committee Hearing, published or unpublished, associated with a Public Law, start with this subscription database. Coverage begins in 1867 and new hearings are regularly added.

2. ProQuest Congressional Hearings Digital Collection

    Subscription database available as an add-on module to ProQuest Congressional or as a stand-alone service. Offers indexed .pdf files of hearings from 1824–present.

3. United States Government Publishing Office, FDsys

    http://www.gpo.gov/fdsys/browse/collectiontab.action

    [Click on "Congressional Hearings including House and Senate Appropriations Hearings"]

    Limited coverage begins in 1985, with significantly more, though still limited, coverage beginning in 1997. Text and .pdf files.

4. HeinOnline: U.S. Congressional Documents Library

    This searchable subscription database includes select .pdf files of hearings from the 50th Congress (1889) through the 113rd Congress (2014).

5. Congressional Information Service, *CIS U.S. Congressional Committee Hearings on Microfiche*. Bethesda, Md.: CIS

    Covers published hearings from 1833 through 1969.

6. Individual libraries' holdings of particular hearings as published by the Government Publishing Office, usually best searched in the individual library catalog (or on WorldCat.org) by the title of the hearing.

7. Congressional Information Service, *CIS Unpublished US Senate Committee Hearings on Microfiche*. Bethesda, Md.: CIS

    Covers 1823 through 1984.

8. Congressional Information Service, *CIS Unpublished US House of Representatives Committee Hearings on Microfiche*. Bethesda, Md.: CIS

    Covers 1833 through 1976.

TABLE 3.D: SOURCES OF THE CONGRESSIONAL RECORD AND FLOOR DEBATES

1. HeinOnline. U.S. Congressional Documents

   Includes the Congressional Record, vols. 1–157 (1873–2011) and the Congressional Record, Daily Edition, vols. 126–163 (1980–2017).

2. Library of Congress, Congress.gov

   https://www.congress.gov/

   [Select "Congressional Record" from under "Site Content."] Coverage begins in 1995, available as .pdf files.

3. United States Government Publishing Office, FDsys: Congressional Record

   http://www.gpo.gov/fdsys/browse/collectiontab.action

   [Select "Congressional Record (Bound)"] for coverage from 1999 to 2001 (and isolated later dates) as .pdf files. [Select "Congressional Record (Daily)"] for coverage from 1994 to current issue, text for all and .pdf files starting in 1995.

4. United States Congress, *Congressional Record*. Daily Edition. Washington, D. C.: Government Publishing Office

5. United States Congress, *Congressional Record*. [microform] Bound Edition. Washington, D. C.: Government Publishing Office

6. Westlaw: Legislative History > Congressional Record

   Daily Edition, coverage begins in 1985, html only.

7. Lexis: Statutes & Legislation > Congressional Record > Congressional Record

   Daily Edition, coverage begins in 1989, html.

   Statutes & Legislation > Congressional Record > Congressional Record Retro (1873–1997)

   Bound Edition, coverage from 1873 to 1997, .pdf files. Accessed by search only, not browseable.

8. Library of Congress, American Memory: Debates of Congress

   http://memory.loc.gov/ammem/amlaw/lwdebt.html

   Includes .pdf files of the *Congressional Record* (43rd Congress, 1873–1875 only), *Congressional Globe* (1833–1873), *Register of Debates* (1824–1837), and the *Annals of Congress* (1789–1824).

CHAPTER 4

INTRODUCING SECONDARY SOURCES: LAW REVIEW ARTICLES

■ ■ ■

4.1 LAW REVIEWS AS A TOOL FOR THE LEGAL RESEARCHER

It would be difficult to overstate the utility of secondary sources to the legal researcher. Law review articles in particular can save much time and heartache by offering a jumping off place into an unfamiliar area of the law. Moreover, since law review articles serve both explicative and normative functions with regard to the law, the researcher is doubly bound to take notice of their content and the trends in jurisprudence they indicate.

Law reviews (or, more generally, law journals) are academically-based periodicals, the editorial work for which is provided by law students. Whereas the prestige-conferring journals in other disciplines are typically peer-reviewed, the law reviews that serve this purpose in academic law are edited by the publishing institution's own top students. The typical journal publishes a number of different types of articles, and they vary in their usefulness to the legal researcher. "Lead articles" are the first article or two in an issue, usually written by a prominent law professor. These articles are typically contentious pieces that put forward ideas about how the author thinks the law should develop in a particular area. Lead articles are the most likely type of article to be cited either to or by courts. Other articles follow, written by less prominent academics, by judges, and by practitioners. Since these authors have less clout, their articles may branch off into the merely analytical and explicative, although some articles in this category maintain the prescriptive model of the lead articles. Articles of this type written by law student staffers are usually shorter and are frequently called "comments." The uniquely student-written contribution to law reviews is the type of piece called a "note": a shorter piece going deeply into the background and the likely impact of some recent statutory or case law development. While these student notes (often unsigned in the past—a tradition now all but dead) are unlikely to be cited, the mass of footnotes they contain can still be a legal researcher's best friend.

The conventional structure of most of these articles facilitates their use as a road map for someone using these materials for the first time. You can count on the first few paragraphs, in which the author is setting out the context for his presentation, to be a very rich source of background material on the topic at hand. Typically, the footnotes to these initial paragraphs contain citations to all the primary sources that are central to understanding the article's subject (statutes, cases, regulations, administrative rulings), and also citations to seminal commentary (especially other law review articles). The middle of the article usually includes lots of case citations, along with analysis that helps to determine the significance of the cases cited. By sorting out the important cases in an area and discussing how they interact with relevant statutes, this part of an article helps the researcher identify what is critically important. Finally, these pieces wind up with policy recommendations, which may be interesting, but, except in the case of lead articles by big players in the area, are clearly of limited utility for legal research. The same might be said of the book reviews that usually round out the law review bill of fare.

4.2 FINDING LAW REVIEW ARTICLES

As with so many tasks in legal research, you have two basic choices when it comes to looking for law review articles. You can use an index, or you can search full-text databases of articles. For most purposes, you will be better served by starting off with a legal periodical index, since that way your search results will focus on articles that are devoted to your subject of interest, rather than be diluted with articles where your subject is merely mentioned.

There are two principal general indexes for this purpose. The first is the *Index to Legal Periodicals & Books*, published by EBSCO; it is currently available both in print and in a variety of electronic versions. Its precursor, the *Index to Legal Periodicals*, was first published in 1908 by H.W. Wilson (some catalogs will still make reference to H.W. Wilson in conjunction with this resource). The second is LegalTrac, a database that began as the print *Current Law Index* in 1980, and that appears as Legal Resource Index on Westlaw. Other indexes extend the period of coverage back even further, for those interested in historical legal articles (see **Table 4.A**). For journals and years that are covered, you will want to use the electronic version whenever it is available to you. The electronic versions of these indexes offer the ability to combine multiple search criteria, and eliminate the need to search through multiple volumes and non-cumulative supplements to cover a range of dates. If you have access to the electronic versions of the indexes, the best use remaining for the print index is as a current awareness tool to keep an eye on a particular area of the law and see everything published on that subject. The electronic versions are for the most part taken from the print indexes, so the contents and currency of the different formats of a given index should be the same. The principal exception is the LegalTrac/Legal Resource Index electronic products, which add coverage of legal newspapers, law-related articles from the general press, and other types of material to the law reviews and journals indexed by the paper *Current Law Index* (which ceased publication after the 2016 volume).

If it is important to you to get absolutely every article, as when, for example, you are doing a preemption check to ascertain whether another article has already been written on a topic on which you propose to write, it is worth it to check multiple indexes. Note that searching Legal Resource Index on Westlaw permits you to use refined searching techniques like requiring one term to appear within a certain proximity to another, which can cut down on false drops (results that meet your search criteria but are actually irrelevant). However, the absence of this search flexibility in the stand-alone web versions of the indexes is not too serious, since the documents you are searching, bibliographic records of articles, are already so short.

Another index, the *Current Index to Legal Periodicals*, offers less elaborate indexing of a narrower range of journals with a faster turnaround time than the two primary indexes. Other law review indexes focus on the journal output of particular jurisdictions (e.g., the United Kingdom and Canada). Indexing of law review articles is also provided in various subject-specific treatises and looseleaf services; their advantage is the inclusion of articles from more specialized sources than those covered in the general indexes, and the use of more precise and specialized subject headings.

The other principal method for finding law review articles is by full-text search. The law review article databases on Westlaw, Lexis Advance, and Bloomberg Law offer coverage of a large number of law reviews (although not as many as are indexed in the Index to Legal Periodicals and Books and on LegalTrac); they generally only go back in their coverage to about 1994. For earlier articles and for whenever you need a .pdf version of an article, the principal online source is HeinOnline, a subscription database on the web that offers full-text searchable .pdf files of many law reviews from the beginning of their runs. The searching on HeinOnline is not as flexible as that offered by Lexis Advance and Westlaw, but the benefit of access to .pdf versions of law review articles back to inception cannot be overstated. Particularly for academics, who are the target audience for many law review articles, having .pdf versions of law review articles is invaluable because it allows for proper citation according to *The Bluebook*, and also avoids the constant "hunt" for star pagination you'd face using Lexis Advance or Westlaw.

4.3   LOOKING FOR ARTICLES BY SUBJECT

When you are just starting out, a general subject may be all you have to go on. In order to avoid casual mentions of the terms you are using to describe your subject, you should start off with an index, rather than full-text searching. The subject indexing varies considerably among the three general legal periodical indexes, so searching in all of them might well be fruitful. LegalTrac and the Legal Resources Index use subject headings from the Library of Congress system. The *Index to Legal Periodicals* (ILP) tends to have much more general subject headings, which can be either a blessing or a curse. Some of the subject headings (e.g., constitutional law) are so general as to be almost useless when conducting legal research; fortunately, when searching these indexes electronically you can combine a subject heading with a word from the title or with a second subject heading for much more precise targeting.

The longevity of the *Index to Legal Periodicals and Books* has meant that some subject headings have become obsolete or anachronistic; EBSCO has undertaken to change the subject headings for more consistency with modern usage. Therefore, the electronic version of the Wilson indexing for pre-1981 articles may use different subject headings than the print volumes do. If one or the other is not working out for you, it may be worth trying the other even though the articles indexed are the same.

In general, if your attempts to guess at good subject headings are not panning out, there are two techniques you should use. First, you can usually find an appropriate subject heading by starting off with a reference to just one good article, found by a keyword in the title or subject. While it's a bit backwards, you could also resort to fishing around in the full-text database for that one good article, which you would then look up in an index, for our current purpose. Once you have found the record for that one good article in the index, go down to the very bottom of the record for a list of what subject headings were assigned to that article. Usually one or a combination of those subject headings will get you to other good articles, and possibly even more helpful subject headings. A second method to find good subject headings is to scan a list of all the subject headings used by an index. You can get to this list on EBSCOhost's online Index to Legal Periodicals and Books by clicking on "Thesaurus." On LegalTrac, you cannot scan a full list in the same way, but you can click on Subject Guide Search and type in any concept of interest, paying attention to the Subjects that are fleetingly suggested to you. Both lists provide copious cross-references to the subject headings used in the databases.

4.4   LOOKING FOR ARTICLES BY CASE NAME OR CITATION

If your purpose in looking for law review articles is to investigate the legal penumbra of a particular case, there are numerous ways to zero in on the appropriate articles. When an article is devoted to consideration of a particular case (as is true of many student-written articles in particular), the index record for that article may include the name of the case and its citation, even if that information is not included in the article's title. The decision to add the case name and citation to the article's record is made by the indexer, and while the index entry for an article may get a case name slapped on it in one index, the same may not be true in another index. This is another reason to do your searches for articles in both of the major indexes.

The electronic index entries can all be searched for articles by case name and citation. The Index to Legal Periodicals and Books permits fielded searching by case party name or case citation. In Westlaw's Legal Resource Index the records that you are searching include case name and citation. LegalTrac has added case name and citation to the area searched by a keyword search. While CILP does not offer fielded searching, you can use your web browser's search function to look for the beginning of a case citation. Since the format of the citation may not be what you are expecting, it's probably most efficient to type in only "volume number<space>first letter of the reporter title." The print indexes also offer article lookup by case name.

Since the association of an article with a particular case in the journal indexes is a matter of editorial discretion, you may wish to dispense with the judgment of the editorial middleman and construct a search in a full-text journal database that will retrieve articles about your case. The trick here is to find the articles that are devoted to the case, without getting mired down in every article that ever merely mentioned it. On both Lexis Advance and Westlaw you can use the "atleast" command (e.g., atleast5(discrimination)) and on Bloomberg Law you can use the "ATL" command (e.g., ATL5(discrimination)) to require a certain number of appearances of your search term within the document: this could be pressed into service to find just those articles that mention the name of your case (or a distinctive word from that name) over and over again.

If you are unable to find an article devoted to your case, and are ready to settle for any old article that at least cites to your case, you can use a citator. KeyCite on Westlaw includes references to law review articles in the Secondary Sources category of Citing References to cases. Shepardizing on Lexis Advance puts references to law review articles in a content filter called "Law Reviews" within the overly general "Other Citing Sources." *Shepard's* in print puts citations to law review articles about the case in a group at the end of the citations for that case. This is another instance of how you can enhance your results by using both competing citators. KeyCite sometimes indicates, via use of a headnote signal, which legal point in the case is the subject of discussion in the law review article. KeyCite also includes references in law reviews not covered by Shepard's, but Shepard's (both on Lexis Advance and in print) includes citing articles going further back, before the period of online journal availability. For the most complete coverage, you should check your case in both citators.

4.5   LOOKING FOR ARTICLES
ABOUT A STATUTE

As when looking for articles about a case, you will need to distinguish between articles that are about your statute, and articles that merely mention your statute in passing. All the techniques and sources described above in the section on articles about cases should be pressed into service here as well, but only after checking one very valuable additional source: the annotated code containing your statute. In the *U.S.C.A.*, after a code section that has been the subject of a law review article, there appears in the Library References annotations a listing of "Law Review and Journal Commentaries" pertaining to that section. Similarly, in the *U.S.C.S.*, the Research Guide after such a section will have a list of relevant law review articles. When using the print versions of the codes, more recent article citations will appear in the pocket parts and in the paperback supplements.

4.6   LOOKING FOR AN ARTICLE BY
A PARTICULAR AUTHOR

Occasionally the legal researcher may have call to look for articles by a particular author. A judge or colleague may have remembered a relevant article but only by its author, or the work of a certain writer may be acknowledged as significant in a particular area. In case you do need to find an article by a particular author, you should use electronic means if possible. A good first step is to locate the author's CV online. If an up-to-date CV is not available, you can turn to the same tools you would use to find an article by subject, as discussed above. All of the electronic periodical indexes offer fielded searching by author. Full-text searching on Westlaw, Lexis Advance, and HeinOnline all also provide the ability to limit your search amongst their law review data by author. For additional discussion of author searches in print periodical indexes, please see the 4th edition of *Where the Law Is.*

4.7   EVALUATING THE USEFULNESS
OF LAW REVIEW ARTICLES

Once you have identified a list of law review articles that look helpful, and have even read them, you will still need to evaluate the usefulness of any particular article that you find. Obviously, the content of the article itself will either prove useful or not, in terms of leading you to citeable authority for your legal proposition or in terms of educating and orienting you with respect to a previously unfamiliar area of the law. But the article's content is not the only aspect you need to consider when working with law review articles. Especially if you are considering citing to an article as evidence of the direction in which the law should be moving, you will want to consider the prestige or standing of that article.

The most straightforward indication of the prestige of the article is the status of the person who is named as the author. A roughly descending order of punch is probably packed by the following types of authors: United States Supreme Court Justice, other judge, famous law professor, other law professor, famous practitioner, other practitioner, and student. Of course the identity of the author can be important to you for reasons other than prestige. The different experiences and backgrounds of these different types of author can offer valuably different perspectives on the issue at hand. Useful information on what that perspective might be can be gleaned from the information in the first (usually non-numbered) footnote of the article, which includes the author's place of employment, and acknowledgments of gratitude and intellectual indebtedness. Since these footnotes are part of the full text of the articles, they can be searched and analyzed to follow the influence of a particular individual or coterie. Another subject for reflection with respect to article authorship is whether the article is the author's first, or whether this is the latest of many articles. If the latter, is the repeat author focused on one subject (and, hence, a specialist) or wide-ranging?

Another component in the prestige of an article is the reputation of the law review that published it. One window onto that reputation is provided by online rankings and other quantitative measures of journal impact. More generally, among the different types of student-edited law journals, the school's top journal usually confers more cachet than the other journals. The top journal at a school is the one that gets the top students to work for it, the one that probably is more generously supported financially (either by the school or by alumni, as well as by subscriptions), the one that has more clerical and/or business management support, and (sometimes) the one that offers more academic credit to student staffers. At most schools this publication is a generalist publication, with only the name of the school and either "Law Review," "Law Journal," "Journal of Law," or "Law Quarterly" in its title. This is the publication that tends to attract higher caliber articles, in terms of the authors that publish in it, and in terms of the citedness of those articles by other law reviews and by judicial opinions. In some cases the footnotes are better edited, either because of higher standards imposed by editorial policies, or because of preferential treatment and training by the law librarians working with the student staffers.

By comparison, most law journals devoted to a particular subject are the secondary journals at their school. Some of these publications, particularly at the top schools or if the journal was groundbreaking in introducing scholarship in a new topic, are moderately prestigious, with all that the modifier implies about editing quality and content quality. These journals may be the only place where certain topics are covered, but arguably the best articles about most subjects go to the generalist law reviews at the top schools anyway. If you have lots of articles from which to choose and limited time to review them, you will need to balance these factors in deciding how to allocate your reading time.

Another factor to consider in evaluating the potential value to you of a law review article is its length. Length by itself is clearly not always an indicator of worth: consider that the average law review article is now somewhere over 50 pages long. However, in choosing which to read from an otherwise undifferentiated list of articles, realize that at least a longer one will go into more detail about the topic, and probably have either lots of background, or lots of statistical information, or lots of policy discussion, as well as analysis of the legal issue and its treatment in courts. In accordance with *The Bluebook* Rule 3.2(a), often when you encounter a citation to an article only the number of its first page will be indicated. You can use a periodical index to fill in the final page number, and thus learn for evaluation purposes how long the article is. The *Index to Legal Periodicals* started supplying terminal page numbers for articles in 1973, and *Current Law Index* had them right from its beginning in 1980 and this practice continues in LegalTrac and the Legal Resource Index.

You will probably also be interested in the date of the articles you find. Very recent articles are preferable for the purpose of mining the footnotes for still-current references. Although the major law journal databases, including indexes, bring back results in relevance order by default, they each also allow for ordering by date.

Since 1948, the University of Washington's Marian Gould Gallagher Law Library has published the weekly *Current Index to Legal Periodicals*, providing indexing of law review articles up to 6 weeks earlier than the commercial indexing publications. CILP is available in a variety of formats (see **Table 4.A**) including as an e-mail alert by subscription (SmartCILP). It is most easily searched within HeinOnline, which allows you to search multiple weekly indexes at once. For articles even newer than those listed in CILP, you can seek out articles as yet unindexed by full-text searching with a date restriction in the law review databases of Westlaw and Lexis Advance. Some law reviews put their current issues up on their websites, or at least abstracts of the current issue's contents. Certain law reviews or issues of law reviews not available on Lexis Advance, Westlaw, Bloomberg Law, or HeinOnline may still be available in large combined journal article databases available through university or other research libraries to their affiliates.

For even more recent material, articles that are not only as yet unindexed but as yet unpublished, you can turn to working papers (see **Table 4.B**). Originally physical papers distributed in print by the institution where the authors worked, today working papers (or at least abstracts of them) are more likely to be electronic, distributed by subject-oriented extra-institutional organizations such as the Social Science Research Network (SSRN). When you encounter unpublished material like a working paper you should always check to see if it was subsequently published. Be careful here! Just because something has not yet been published doesn't mean it is fresh and new: the Internet is, among other things, a boneyard of stale research.

At the other end of the spectrum, older articles that are still being cited long after their publication are particularly likely to have good analysis in the text, so determining citedness is another reasonable way to evaluate articles, especially older ones. This can be done to a limited extent (limited in that only articles present in full text can be researched) on Westlaw's KeyCite, and can be done more broadly in Shepard's. HeinOnline, which has the full text of law review articles as .pdf files back to inception, has developed a tool called ScholarCheck that gives information on and links to other articles (and some cases) that cited your original article.

4.8   USING THE FOOTNOTES IN LAW REVIEW ARTICLES

Most legal researchers working with law review articles find their reward in the mass of footnotes they contain. Especially with regard to student writing, the real meat of the articles is the collation of relevant legal authorities and other sources, rather than in the students' opining. While the plenitude of law review footnotes is the butt of many jokes, that same plenitude can be impressive and useful. The footnotes to the best articles are plentiful, detailed, logical, and accurate.

In print law reviews, the footnotes are traditionally at the bottom of the page of text that cites to them, the assumption being that the reader is at least as interested in the footnotes as in the text. This presentation is preserved in the .pdf files of HeinOnline and Bloomberg Law. The html files on Lexis Advance and Westlaw offer various less satisfactory ways of handling footnote display (Westlaw's more graceful than that of Lexis Advance). Those html files, along with HeinOnline's .pdf files, do offer one enormous advantage to the legal researcher over the reading of print: the citations in the footnotes are frequently links to the full text of the documents cited. Again, hard to beat that convenience!

Not all the footnotes will be links, however, and those references you will need to hunt down yourself. The information gathered in footnotes is recorded in the highly standardized forms prescribed by *The Bluebook*. Thus, you may encounter abbreviations that you cannot understand without reference to that indispensable volume. The abbreviations table in the back of *The Bluebook* contains not only the specific abbreviated titles for many publications, but also the accepted "Bluebookese" for many words that commonly come up in the titles of legal publications not specifically listed. Remember, for instance, that "L." means "Law," but that "Law." means "Lawyer"! You are likely to encounter abbreviations in the footnotes of law reviews for which *The Bluebook* offers no guidance. Rule 20 specifies that for foreign legal materials with no abbreviation in *The Bluebook*, you should follow the "respective country's own citation rules for the sources as modified by [the] general rules" that follow in Rule 20. Numerous legal abbreviation dictionaries can rescue you here. See **Table 4.C** for the most important ones.

Footnotes can be used not only as a source of citations, but as a source of information about citations. If you find an ambiguous citation in a reference, or if you are having trouble with an incomplete or erroneous citation from any source, you should check the citations to that material in more than one article. Frequently, looking at the work of the student staffs of several different law reviews will reveal the origin of the problem.

One of the thorniest problems that arises is that of ghost references: an author didn't look at the underlying cited document, but just appropriated someone else's (invalid) citation. Passing along a ghost reference like this is a blot on the law review's escutcheon, and a reminder to the entire research community of the need to maintain the integrity of our common enterprise.

4.9   TABLES

TABLE 4.A: SELECTED LEGAL
PERIODICAL INDEXES

1. EBSCOhost: Index to Legal Periodicals Retrospective: 1908–1981 (H.W. Wilson).

    This subscription database is also available in print.

2. EBSCOhost: Index to Legal Periodicals and Books (H.W. Wilson) (Covers 1981–Present).

    This subscription database is also available in print.

3. LegalTrac

    Coverage of this stand-alone subscription database starts with articles published in 1980. Updated daily. Most of the content is also available in print as *Current Law Index* up through 2016. See also Legal Resource Index on Westlaw below.

4. Westlaw:

    Secondary Sources > Legal Resource Index under "Tools & Resources" on the right.

    Coverage begins in 1980.

5. Leonard A. Jones (vols. 1–2) and Frank E. Chipman (vols. 3–6), *An Index to Legal Periodical Literature*. Various publishers. This series, known as the "Jones-Chipman index," was published between 1888 and 1939, and covers articles published between 1770 and 1937.

6. University of Washington, Marian Gould Gallagher Law Library, *Current Index to Legal Periodicals*. This electronic publication is available by subscription from the University of Washington and in .pdf files on HeinOnline within the Law Journal Library. The most recent eight weeks are also available on Westlaw.

TABLE 4.B: EXAMPLES OF SOURCES FOR WORKING PAPERS IN LAW

1. Legal Scholarship Network. A component part of the Social Science Research Network (SSRN), which also embraces research in accounting, economics, and finance.

    https://www.ssrn.com/en/index.cfm/lsn/

2. NELLCO Legal Scholarship Repository. Maintained by the New England Law Library Consortium.

    http://lsr.nellco.org/

3. American Bar Foundation. An example of a different sort of source of working papers, the ABF is a research institute that develops a research program, and funds and publishes research.

    http://www.americanbarfoundation.org/research/project/index. html

TABLE 4.C: SELECTED DICTIONARIES
OF LEGAL ABBREVIATIONS

1. Mary Miles Prince, *Prince's Bieber Dictionary of Legal Abbreviations*. 7th ed. Getzville, N. Y.: W. S. Hein, 2017.

    The first two editions of this indispensable companion to law reviews were written by Doris M. Bieber.

2. *World Dictionary of Legal Abbreviations*. Igor I. Kavass and Mary Miles Prince, general editors. Buffalo, N. Y.: W. S. Hein, 1991–

    Multi-volume looseleaf set.

3. Cardiff Index to Legal Abbreviations

    http://www.legalabbrevs.cardiff.ac.uk/

    Dealing primarily with English-language publications from nearly 300 jurisdictions, this resource allows you to search by abbreviation to identify a source, providing both the full title and the jurisdiction of publication. This can be especially helpful when, as is often the case, one particular abbreviation is used by multiple publications around the world.

4. *Guide to Foreign and International Legal Citations*. New York University School of Law. 2nd ed. New York, N. Y.: Aspen Publishers, 2009.

CHAPTER 5

CASES

■ ■ ■

5.1   THE CORE OF OUR ENTERPRISE

Despite the primacy of statutes in our research scheme of things, case law research is the *sine qua non* of the lawyer's art. "Finding out the law" in a statute book is something a diligent lay person with a real interest can manage. Ascertaining the law from the vast array of possibly relevant cases, however, requires a legal education. Knowledge of substantive law, experience in issue spotting, and familiarity with legal analysis and synthesis all contribute to successful case law research. Thus, the finer points of working with cases are better appreciated in an advanced legal research course than in the initial whirlwind exposure to the subject. Hence we begin this discussion of case law research with a general overview of how to do it. As an advanced student, you need to become comfortable not only with finding all of the cases that have to be found, but also with determining their significance by analysis and by investigation of their background and of both their progeny and commentary.

5.2   FINDING ALL THE RIGHT CASES

The first year of law school frequently offers research experiences that bear little resemblance to research in the larger worlds of scholarship and practice. Scavenger hunt library exercises are devised to see whether the student can find a known item. Moot court problems, often the first-year student's principal research experience, are usually purposely composed of live legal issues in areas rife with recent judicial developments. Again, there is definitely something out there, by design, for the student to find.

By contrast, when a student begins to work outside the academic walls, she may well find the whole enterprise transformed: all of a sudden there don't seem to be any answers out there anymore. Research assignments seem more often than not to lead to a dead end, or a huge question mark. This is only natural, given the structure of the legal workplace: the research assignment is given by a more experienced lawyer who has a real problem; that lawyer's questions about the law will tend to cluster around unconventional or unlikely points of interpretation. The saving grace, for the novice researcher, is that their law school spent a lot of time teaching them to think like a lawyer. In order, however, for that lawyerly thinking to have the proper grist on which to work, the researcher must have found all the necessary cases to form a correct and defensible view of the law.

We have already explored, in **Chapter 2**, how to find the cases that interpret a particular statute. Given the structure of our legal system, that has to be the starting place for most legal research. However, pure case law research still has a role to play: there may be no controlling statute, the matter may be in an area governed by common law, you may want to compare the case law of many jurisdictions subject to different statutes without initial reference to those statutes, or you may be checking your statute-based work by reference to case law generally to make sure you found the right statutes.

The researcher in search of cases without reference to a statute has three basic options. The first option, and often the best for the non-expert, is to start off by finding a secondary source that has identified principal cases and work from those. **Chapter 4** explored how to do this by using journal articles, and **Chapter 6** will do the same with treatises. The second option is to employ the highly-developed tools of case indexing that categorize and organize the enormous body of decisional law by a number of different criteria. The third option is to dive directly into full-text searching of case law databases.

Beginning researchers engage most often (at their peril) in this third option, full-text searching. We say "at their peril" because of the twin dangers of the full-text researcher becoming either overwhelmed by the amount of decisional law, or overly charmed by the apparent suitability of a retrieved case for the purpose at hand (or both). While these pitfalls can certainly threaten the index-employing researcher as well, they sit more squarely in the path of the researcher who relies on the Way of Full Text. That said, the allure and convenience of full-text searching is such that we open our discussion of how to find cases with a rundown of its dos and don'ts.

5.3　FULL-TEXT SEARCHING OF CASE LAW DATABASES

Full-text searching is actually an index of almost every word in the case. While an index produced by a human indexer brings with it the limitations of that person's wisdom and abilities, with full text you are avoiding possible errors in judgment by the editorial middleman because you can look up every actual word in the case (except common stop words— e.g., "the" or "a"). However, by the same token, with pure full text you are constricted by ONLY being able to look up those words that actually appeared in the case (with certain structural variants). The full-text researcher, therefore, must leave no plausible synonym unturned. The principal case law databases have supplemented the full text of the cases with added descriptive terms in order to make this easier, thereby reinserting the human editorial eye, either directly or via the application of an algorithm, into the process.

The legal landscape is dominated by two competing online information vendors, Westlaw and Lexis Advance. Other players (including, currently, Bloomberg Law and Fastcase) provide specialty information or niche pricing of a subset of similar information, but the big two provide the most legal content and the most sophisticated mechanisms for using it. Their competition has prompted a stream of constant changes and improvements, including completely new platforms for both vendors within the last decade. Due to the frequency of these changes, it would be futile to try to capture here the details of how to search optimally in either system. Instead, our discussion will focus on the broader principles of how to engage in full-text searching, in the hopes that those principles will usefully inform how you go about using both Westlaw and Lexis Advance, as well as any other full-text system you encounter.

After identifying the relevant jurisdiction, your first choice involves picking a search method. The two most common options are "Terms and Connectors" searching and "Natural Language" searching. Terms and Connectors adds operators to traditional "Boolean" searching, and is what many search engines, websites, and databases will deliver if you go to any available "Advanced Search" option. Strictly speaking, Boolean searching only makes use of the traditional Boolean operators ("And," "Or," "Not"), whereas Terms and Connectors searching includes those options plus many other database-specific connectors (e.g., within a certain number of words; or located in certain parts of the text). In practice, the two terms (Boolean and Terms and Connectors) are often used interchangeably. Choosing whether to use Terms and Connectors or Natural Language searching will depend on the degree of precision with which you wish to control the terms of the search, and on how you wish to have the results presented to you. In Terms and Connectors searching, you have the ability to specify the exact criteria for documents to be returned to you, in accordance with a defined list of conditions that you can apply. This kind of control is essential when you are dealing with concepts that you understand very well, where the vocabulary, terms of art, and turns of phrase you can anticipate in the case language are both significant and familiar to you. This kind of searching enables you to specify, via the connectors, exactly what relationship the search terms must have to each other in the retrieved documents. Terms and Connectors searching is also necessary when you wish to require many different variables and then swap them in and out to control for different ones.

By contrast, Natural Language searching algorithmically infers a relationship between your search terms by their identity and the order in which you entered them. Note especially that some of the criteria you enter in your search may not be present in the results, even toward the top of the list, depending on how the relevance ranking operated on your search terms. Think of how you can get some weird stuff toward the top of a list of Google results and you'll be thinking along the right lines. This process takes you out of the driver's seat, to a large extent, and for that reason *should never be used exclusively* in any legal research project. Natural Language searching can be great, however, if you are searching, for content reasons, in the service that you use less often, since it can let you at least get started without getting mired in command errors.

Choosing search terms to use calls upon all your legal training, and then some. When you receive a research assignment in an unfamiliar area, assume that the language used in describing the problem to you contains terms of art. Using the Advanced Search function, enclose in quotation marks any phrases that were used, or employ appropriate proximity connectors, to ensure that you retrieve cases where the phrase is used in the precise form that you heard it. Later, when your initial results have given you some idea of what kind of concepts are in play, you can start thinking up lists of synonyms to expand your search.

There are several important search components that are common to Terms and Connectors searching in both Westlaw and Lexis Advance. You will want to be fully versed in the connectors available to specify maximum and minimum proximity of search terms to each other, to truncate search terms or substitute unspecified characters at any point in the term, and to specify the order or placement of terms within the document. Arm yourself with an actual list of connectors, printed out and sitting on the desk next to your keyboard, since otherwise you will be tempted to stick with only those connectors that you happen to remember from frequent use.

More specific to case law research is the ability to locate your search terms within fields of data particular to case law documents. The case is divided into portions (called "fields" or "segments") that can be searched separately, and the significance of a search term's appearance in one field versus another should be taken into account. Thus, one field in a case document is restricted to the name of the judge who wrote the opinion. Another consists of the editorially-produced summary (headnote) of a specific point of law touched upon in the case. Another is the court-produced summary of the entire case (e.g., the Syllabus in U. S. Supreme Court cases). The ability to search these fields separately contributes enormously to the efficiency of full-text searching. Searching the headnotes or summary of a case for a combination of search terms is much more likely to avoid cases that only mention those terms peripherally. This principle is presumably reflected in the proprietary relevance algorithms used by the systems, but the exact details of how those algorithms work is not publicly known. You can, however, bring the same principle into play yourself through the informed use of fielded searching. Note that each type of document (e.g., case, statute, treatise) on Westlaw and Lexis Advance offers different fields that can be searched, and a list of such fields is available from the advanced search screen.

5.4   USING SUBJECT INDEXES TO CASE LAW: DIGESTS AND THE KEY NUMBER SYSTEM ON WESTLAW

As with statutes, subject access to cases is paramount to the legal researcher. The chronological order in which cases appear is of minimal importance: even the reporters, so seemingly sequential in their long marches down the shelves, are not arranged in strict chronological order (a case published in one volume may actually have been decided prior to cases published in an earlier volume). Subject access is all important, and although full-text searching is one important way to find cases by subject, there are other ways that are powerful and more organized. The paradigm of these methods is that embodied in the Key Number System created by West in its American Digest System, and carried over to and further developed in Westlaw.

Long the foundation of American legal case research, West's American Digest System continues today as the principal print subject index to published American case law (as well as the "unpublished" cases printed in the *Federal Appendix*). Once the starting point for virtually all legal research, the West digests have been pushed increasingly into the shadows by both the advent of case-law databases and the ascendancy of statutes. But researchers raised in the era of full-text searching are frequently thrilled when they become aware of the structure, clarity, helpfulness, and ergonomic pleasure provided by these print tools. As you explore West's American Digest System, note the different kinds of access to case law that its different features provide: access by subject, by name, and by reference to a hierarchically arranged set of subject rubrics (the Key Numbers). These same types of access are offered by many case-indexing tools, and when you encounter any such tool for the first time, you should remember to look for each of these features (see, e.g., **Chapter 9** on looseleaf services).

West's American Digest System indexes case law: for the federal jurisdiction, for states by region, for individual states, for the whole country by historical period, and for different specialized subjects (see **Table 5.A**). The heart of this system is an index of subject headings (called Topics) and sub-headings (called Key Numbers) that is used across all jurisdictions covered by the system. Even though you will hear people refer to "Key Numbers," they almost always actually mean a "Topic and Key Number," since a Key Number needs to be identified in relation to the Topic under which it exists. Referencing merely a Key Number (without Topic) is no more helpful than referencing a page number without identifying a book. For example, "Key Number 93" is meaningless; Animals 93, however, signifies "What constitutes a trespass" (for an animal) and Trusts 93 signifies "Mistake in conveyance." These Topics and Key Numbers can be used on Westlaw as well: every current digest volume contains a list of the numerical equivalents for the Topics. These can, with their associated Key Numbers, be used to search for cases on Westlaw. Alternatively, you can drill down in the Key Number system to a known Key Number to identify cases related to your subject.

This move to electronic format does, however, come with a potentially significant limitation. State-specific West digests can include some cases that were published in non-West reporters (e.g., in the Pennsylvania District and County Reports), and those cases are assigned Topics and Key Numbers based on their subject just like any other. For such cases, in the move to the electronic Key Number System, this information is lost, so looking at the same Topic and Key Number that led you to the case in print cannot locate the same case in electronic format. Further, if you instead retrieve that case through another means (e.g., citation or party name), it will appear on Westlaw without any headnotes. Some such cases, which are present in a print digest from West but are not available in the electronic Key Number System and are missing the corresponding headnotes in Westlaw, will have Lexis Topics and Headnotes assigned on Lexis Advance (see, e.g., *Packer v. Imboden*, 37 Pa. D. & C.3d 13).

5.5   FINDING A TOPIC AND KEY NUMBER

The West system aims to encompass all American case law (although not all American cases!) within its approximately 400 Topics and the 100,000 or so specific Key Numbers that they contain. In the print digests, the Topics are arranged alphabetically (Abandoned and Lost Property in the first volume to Zoning and Planning in the last) in a series of volumes that make up the bulk of each set. Within each Topic, however, the indexing scheme changes from alphabetical to hierarchical.

The researcher unfamiliar with either the system or the legal topic being investigated will need to start by finding appropriate Topics and Key Numbers. On Westlaw this can be done most directly via the "Search for Key Numbers relevant to your issue" box that appears when you click on "Key Numbers" on the initial Westlaw screen. Entering legal concepts, fact elements, or both will get you started with a list of some suitable Topics and Key Numbers. Note, however, the system artificially limits this result list without indicating such: no matter how broad the term you search (e.g., "liability," "law"), you will be cut off after 10 results, with no real explanation of why those 10 (out of the many others that fit the search) were chosen. A "Title Search" at the bottom of the page alleviates the problem somewhat, retrieving up to 500 results that include your search term anywhere in the topical hierarchy.

Another way to get to a good Topic and Key Number on Westlaw is simply to do a full-text search that uses whatever terms you know, in order to find some case, any case, that includes discussion of your topic. Perusal of the Topics and Key Numbers assigned to the headnotes of the case will identify at least some relevant ones, and you can proceed from there to branch out to other related parts of the hierarchical Key Number tree. You can focus your preliminary search for that "jumping-off point" case by limiting your search to the headnotes of the cases, so you have a greater chance of landing in the right subject area. Another good way to head for the right ballpark is to identify one of the "Practice Areas" and search cases within that limited universe. The analogous search on Lexis Advance uses "Practice Area or Industry" and works the same way as an entry point into its topical organization.

Despite all the ways you can enter into the Key Number system on Westlaw, the classic tool for this task, the print-only Descriptive Word Index, is still, in some ways, the most extensive finding aid for Key Numbers. Each digest includes several volumes of Descriptive Word Index—a subject index that enables you to look up a legal term or a fact setting in a single alphabetical index and be referred to a Topic and Key Number. Thus, entries under the legal concept "Consideration" include key numbers under the Topics of Health, Public Contracts, and Taxation; entries under the fact component "Dogs" include Key Numbers under the Topics of Animals, Divorce, and Public Amusement and Entertainment. The Descriptive Word Indexes are not related to actual cases indexed in that particular digest edition, but rather are virtually identical from digest to digest at any one time, and embody a set of rules about where cases with that characteristic would be (or, probably, have been, in at least one of the many digests) categorized within the Key Number System. If you look up "Treason," for instance, in the *Pacific Digest* (a digest that includes no federal cases), the descriptive word index includes the same detailed entries as does the *Federal Practice Digest*, even though almost all of the entries lead to Key Numbers under the Topic "Treason," under which no cases appear in the current *Pacific Digest*, nor ever have.

At the beginning of each Topic is printed a valuable explanation of what subjects are included under that Topic and what subjects are excluded but covered by other Topics. This scope note can be reached on Westlaw by checking on the "i" icon (only visible when you mouse over the name) next to each Topic in the Key Number list. Also at the beginning of each Topic in the print digests is the complete outline of subtopics and Key Numbers under that Topic. Come here if you want to try a "top down" analytical approach akin to that of using the table of contents at the beginning of a statutory code chapter. Looking at the hierarchical arrangement of subtopics and Key Numbers under a Topic can clarify for you the importance of always checking overarching Key Numbers, such as "—in general," at the beginning of a Topic (or subtopic), in addition to focusing in on the Key Numbers more specifically related to your issue.

On Westlaw, this subject outline can be viewed by expanding each level of Topics and subtopics in the Key Number hierarchy. The online presentation is graphically less graceful than is the print outline, and of course it can tempt you to skip over possibly relevant subtopics by requiring you to click on them to see what Key Numbers they harbor. On the other hand, at this exploratory stage the convenience of not having to assemble a bunch of different volumes off the shelf to investigate the contents of a variety of plausible-looking Topics can be very appealing.

5.6 CHANGES TO THE TOPICS AND KEY NUMBERS

The infrequent changes to the classification and numbering scheme can also be traced only in the print digests. Such changes are, by design, infrequent: the Topic "Dueling" was only dropped in the early 1990s. In order to maintain the alphabetical order of the Topics, new introductions generally get shoehorned into the existing lineup (when a place had to be made for Automobiles and Aviation they became Topics 48A and 48B in between number 48 Audita Querela and number 49 Bail).

When renumbering of Key Numbers within a Topic does have to occur, the digest volume involved is reprinted (with a pair of tables going back and forth between the old and new numbers); on Westlaw, searches on the old number will retrieve results with the new number. The best place to see how the whole system works together is in a separate annual volume called *West's Analysis of American Law*, which sets out all the material from the head of each Topic in one sequence. This volume also lists all the Topics, including the ones that have been dropped from use, and contains a brief but highly detailed "Explanation of Key Number Analysis."

5.7 WORKING WITH KEY NUMBERS

Once you have found at least some Key Numbers that seem appropriate, the next step is to try them out and see what kind of cases they retrieve. As mentioned in **Section 5.4**, in Westlaw, the numerical formulation (e.g., 156k9) for the Topic and Key Number can be used as a search term or you can drill down through the Key Number hierarchy until you get to your Key Number, and then either formulate a search or browse the cases under that Key Number. The benefit of the latter method is that it also allows for the opportunity to note adjacent headings or even Key Numbers, and perhaps to be struck by their possible usefulness or even superiority to that which you originally sought. In the print digests, the process is somewhat different. For a more in-depth discussion of that process, see earlier editions of this book.

What the Key Number System allows you to do quite efficiently is to compare the headnotes summarizing the legal content of individual points made within many cases. The beauty and strength of the West Key Number System lies in the continuity with which it has largely been maintained for over 100 years, permitting comparison of judicial discussion of a single legal concept across jurisdictions and throughout that period.

Looking for cases using this method on Westlaw offers the obvious advantage of convenience when compared with the print digests of yesteryear. Once you find references to cases that look promising, you need only click through to a particular case and read it. This does, however, bring with it added risks as well. It can be all too easy for the online researcher using the Key Number System to head down blind alley after blind alley clicking through case law without a firm grasp of context. It is far better to establish at the outset a plan of which Key Numbers seem relevant before diving into the full text of opinions. That way, once you've begun down a particular path (or multiple paths), you can use your plan to remind you of all the places you originally wanted to go.

5.8   OTHER SUBJECT-BASED SEARCHING FOR CASES

As the old joke has it, if the West editors were not in the forest when the tree fell, would it have made a sound? Other indexing and subject-finding aids to case law research have indeed been produced by different editorial hands, and can be used as supplements to the West system. On Lexis Advance, organization is done within the Topic system. Lexis Advance headnotes, assigned by Lexis Advance editors to cases on their platform, are drawn from the language of the cases on selected legal points. Working through both the Lexis Advance and Westlaw headnote indexing systems will often get you quite different results in terms of which cases you retrieve. For some research projects the greater specificity of West's Key Number System (about 100,000 subjects compared almost 22,000 on Lexis Advance) will be a decisive advantage. Also, the historical development of the Key Number system in the successive editions of the print digests offers a perspective over time that cannot be gleaned from the recently-created headnotes on Lexis Advance.

One potential strength of the Lexis Advance Topical organization, when compared directly against West's Key Number System, is the inclusion in the former of material besides merely case law. Statutes and treatises, for example, are often also placed within the Topic arrangement. When it works perfectly for a particular legal issue (and it doesn't always), the Lexis Advance Topic system can then outshine the Key Number

System. Still, it is still in its (relative) infancy and cannot generally go toe-to-toe with the Key Number System when looking only at case law. In any event, the value of having two completely different editorial assignments of subject headings is that if one of the systems is not well-suited to uncovering cases on your particular issue, the other one might be.

Other resources are also available. For example, the *United States Supreme Court Digest*, a publication tied to a family of titles published by LexisNexis, combines the features of a typical digest (subject and name indexing of cases) with additional research references. Specialized finding aids abound for cases published in topically specific reporters or databases, either as part of those publications or as freestanding indexes (see **Table 5.B**).

Citators also provide highly targeted subject-based searching for cases. Even though any given case can discuss many legal issues, the principle behind using a citator as a case finding tool is that a case that cites to an earlier case for a particular legal issue must logically discuss that same legal issue. By following the citations of a case for a particular point, therefore, you can find other cases on that point. KeyCite on Westlaw and Shepard's on Lexis Advance both provide the case names of the citing cases, signals about the substantiality of the citation, and complete citation information. Both Shepard's and KeyCite also often provide information about which portion of the earlier case is the reason for the subsequent citation, based on headnote numbers. In order to retrieve the maximum number of cases, you should consider conducting your research in both KeyCite and Shepard's (when both are available to you), since they return overlapping but not identical lists of cases.

Both Shepard's and KeyCite also indicate the treatment of the original case by the subsequent case, but it is vital to note that there is human judgment involved in characterizing that treatment, and it often varies from one citator to the other. Think of the citator in this respect as offering you a heads up that something is worth looking into, without being dispositive of how you should interpret or analyze it. The rules that the citators apply in order to arrive at these characterizations have led to individual choices with which few researchers would agree. Notoriously, *Shepard's United States Citations* indicated online at least as late as 1993 that the 1954 landmark case *Brown v. Board of Education* merely "questioned" the 1896 *Plessy v. Ferguson*, rather than overruled it. The print *Shepard's* had changed the characterization of *Brown* only in 1987. Less outlandish instances also illustrate the value of dual perspectives when determining how a particular case treated an earlier one. Consider *Roe v. Wade* and the creation of a trimester system in evaluating restrictions on abortion procedures. Did the subsequent case of *Planned Parenthood v. Casey* overrule in part *Roe* (as indicated by Shepard's) or did it merely *modify* the holding (as indicated by KeyCite)? Functionally, is there really a difference? Scholars on the subject can form reasoned argument on either side, but the citators in both instances serve to make you, the researcher, aware of the need for careful analysis.

5.9   FINDING CASES BY NAME

In the course of your case law research, you may encounter a case name without a citation. Realistically, there is little reason to take the initial step of identifying the proper citation in a paid database. A simple free web search will often yield information about the case—specifically the citation—that you can then use to go directly to the case in Westlaw or Lexis Advance, skipping over the potentially costly search step. This is also true if you don't actually have any party names but instead only a nickname for the case (e.g., "the Sick Chicken Case").

5.10   FINDING CASES BY CITATION

Most case citations follow the straightforward and easy to use format of volume number followed by reporter abbreviation followed by initial page number. But beyond these most common citations, you are sure to encounter some others that require more interpretation. In order to follow your research trails where they ought to go, you will have to learn to work with these more unfamiliar citations. Do not write them off as unimportant! One of these might well turn out to be the most significant case on your point.

Most standard citations to American cases follow fairly predictable patterns. A reporter name given simply as an abbreviated or full name of a jurisdiction will be the official reporter for the cases of the jurisdiction's highest court (e.g., ___ U.S. ___, ___ Mich. ___, etc.). A citation to a state's name followed by the word "Reporter" usually indicates a commercially published set of reports, which may include cases from lower courts as well as the state's highest court. Where the reporter name is the last name of a person, you are usually dealing with early reports published in what are called "nominative reporters" (or, in England, "nominate" reporters).

5.11   NOMINATIVE AND OTHER UNFAMILIAR REPORTERS

Nominative reporters bear the names of their court reporters or editors rather than the jurisdictional names that later became standard. Pre-1874 United States Supreme Court cases, for example, were published in series known as Dallas, Wheaton, etc. (abbreviated Dall., Wheat., and so forth). When a citation includes only this nominative reporter name, you may need to get the equivalent citation in the standard set (such as the *United States Reports*) into which these early volumes were later incorporated. Typing the nominative citation into the function that retrieves by citation in an electronic case law database will bring up all the parallel citations in the standard reporters.

If you are working non-electronically with a nominative citation, you can ascertain the jurisdiction involved by looking up the abbreviation in a dictionary of legal abbreviations. Then, consult *The Bluebook* section for that jurisdiction to see if a modern citation should also exist for that case, and if so, what the volume equivalents in the modern set will be. This same approach can be used wherever you do not recognize the abbreviation comprising the middle element in a case citation. Specialized case reporters exist to cover particular subject areas, and while some of these may be included in Westlaw and Lexis Advance, and therefore be directly retrievable by citation without knowing the actual name of the reporter, some may not. For these, resort to a legal abbreviation dictionary (see **Table 4.C**) is your best bet.

5.12 DOCKETS

Sometimes the problem is not an odd reporter name, but no reporter name. Probably the most common type of non-reporter citation is reference to a particular docket. When an opinion has not been published, it may be cited by the identifying information that the court has assigned it within its own record keeping system. Typically, a docket number is used to identify the docket sheet (a basic listing of all the documents filed in a particular legal matter) and can be recognized because it includes a date component and then a sequential number assigned to the case as it was received into the court's workload. This number usually remains the same from the start of the court's involvement with the case. Individual docket items are then added sequentially to a docket sheet in chronological order of filing (so for example, a complaint—the document that initiates most legal proceedings—will be marked as entry one on the docket sheet of a case).

The most familiar docket numbers are probably those for the United States Supreme Court, since the high level of interest in Supreme Court cases from their outset means that people want to find information about their progress through the Court long before they are eventually published. However, while a docket number in a Supreme Court citation means only that at the time of citation the case had not yet been published (and quite possibly not even decided yet), a docket number citation for a lower court case (especially a citation long after the date of the case) may mean that the case was never published.

The first step in tracking down a case cited by docket number is to ascertain whether the case was in fact eventually published. The easiest way to do this is to run a name search in Westlaw or Lexis Advance. The name used in the docketed version of the case may vary from the name in the published version, so if the fielded name search comes up empty, you should try both whatever names you have and the docket number itself as search terms in the appropriate full-text case law or docket databases.

For more recent cases, you can try to locate the docket itself in electronic format. The best source available for locating dockets is Bloomberg Law. At the federal level, Bloomberg Law pulls docket materials directly from the Public Access to Court Electronic Records (PACER) system, but instead of retrieval generating additional fees (as it does in PACER itself), retrieval from the Bloomberg Law system is part of the subscription cost. The search interface of Bloomberg Law is also much more user-friendly and powerful than that of PACER, which is designed merely for document retrieval, rather than for docket searching. Bloomberg Law also has additional coverage from state courts, which will not be available via PACER. Coverage is not comprehensive on Bloomberg Law (not every state court is available) but, importantly, it does cover some documents from some courts that were not filed electronically. For those documents, most often initial complaints, Bloomberg Law actually sends runners (sometimes for an extra fee) to collect the document and then it is scanned into the Bloomberg Law system.

Beyond merely unpublished cases, however, docket numbers and docket searches can lead to a wealth of information in the form of the filings (most often the briefs) that preceded the opinion. Later in the chapter we will make references to collections of briefs available from particular courts, but you should always keep in mind the availability of docket filings as another method of access. In many cases, going directly to the docket will be the most efficient means of accessing that material, particularly if you are looking for a brief filed in a specific case. This can be particularly powerful if you have identified a highly relevant decided case through some other means, because you can then check to see whether the brief that was so persuasive in that case can aid you in crafting a brief in your own matter. If all else fails, you can call the court to see if you can obtain a copy of the case documents from the court's records (see **Table 15.A**).

5.13 OTHER CITATION WRINKLES

Non-reporter citations that you may encounter include generic Westlaw or Lexis Advance citations, and medium-neutral citations, all of which are designed to identify materials without respect to where they appeared in print. You can work directly with the former only in the database for which they were devised, though the text of the opinion can often, though not always, be retrieved in the other database by using an advanced search for the relevant party names. The medium-neutral citations should be retrievable in both systems, and also on the court's own website.

If a citation is faulty or incomplete, Terms and Connectors searching usually will enable you to overcome the deficiency. If some component of the citation is missing, use what you have as a full-text search term, in conjunction with any other information you have about the case. One common error in citation is transposition of the numbers, so if you don't have anything except a string of numbers, try them in differing positions. Also, check to see if all elements of the citation are consistent (e.g., volume number with date, reporter with jurisdiction).

5.14   USING INDEXED AND FULL-TEXT SEARCHING TOGETHER: THE HEART OF THE CASE RESEARCH PROCESS

The single most common mistake in the case law research process is the failure to pursue leads from one search method into another. Optimal case law research will involve going back and forth repeatedly between full-text searching and the use of subject indexes. When you first start out and have no idea what indexing terms apply to your situation, a fishing expedition in full text is a reasonable (although possibly costly) way to get started. Use a subject-targeted subset of the case law database, if you know enough to select the appropriate one.

Once you have found a good case, via any method, you should examine its subject headings (the Key Numbers or Topics assigned to it) and look at other cases under those headings. Those cases are likely to have additional subject headings, some of which may be relevant, and should be pursued in turn. For some sources that are indexed by more than one publisher (e.g., the *Supreme Court Digest* and the *United States Supreme Court Digest Lawyers' Edition*), you can proceed within one system from a subject heading to a case with that subject heading, and then jump to that same case in another system, and follow up on the different subject headings it has been assigned in the second system. Within the cases that you find, you will learn of other terms and phrases that you should use as new full-text search terms. And for every case that you find during this multi-stage process, you can proceed to look both at the cases that it cites and at the cases that cite to it.

In discussing full-text searching at the very beginning of this book, we mentioned that one useful application would be to combine keywords pertaining to the facts or issues of interest to you with the names of the attorneys involved in the current matter, since they may well have previously been involved in similar legal issues. This type of search has been facilitated on Westlaw by Litigation History Reports (part of a Westlaw tool called "Profiler"), a resource that assembles cases involving particular counsel or particular judges and arranges them by subject area. Many of these cases will have some docket filings available, either in

Westlaw, Lexis Advance, or Bloomberg Law, that could allow you to read briefs filed in those earlier cases. These briefs can then lead you to paths of research it would be prudent to investigate.

Throughout the process you should use one method as a way to enlarge upon and to verify the completeness of the work done via the other method. When you do a full-text search, are you coming up with the same (and *only* the same) indexing terms in the cases that you retrieve? When you do an indexed search, are you coming across new language to use as search terms in full-text searching? Remember that indexing takes some time, so to ensure the currency of your research you should, as a final step, do a date limited full-text search, based on everything you have learned, since it will include as yet unindexed material. The multitude of ways that you can find cases, and the myriad trails that can lead out from any case as a starting point, can confuse you mightily unless you keep track of where you've been. A research plan and log are more vital here than anywhere else in the research process!

5.15   RESEARCHING THE AUTHORITY FOR WHAT SEEMS LIKE A HOARY OR EVEN SELF-EVIDENT WELL-ESTABLISHED PRINCIPLE

Seeking authority for a legal chestnut can sometimes be challenging, because of the sheer volume of cases relying on the principle or because the origins of the doctrine are shrouded in the mists of legal time. One way to address this problem is to find an early Supreme Court or a landmark Court of Appeals case, plus a recent case: this puts you into a position to say that the doctrine has been upheld ". . . at least from [old case] to [recent case]. . . ." Full-text searching should include the exact phrase in which the well-established doctrine is optimally expressed.

Other ways to approach this task are to resort to secondary sources that offer summaries of the law, backed up with case authority. Restatements, treatises, and encyclopedias (see **Chapter 6**) will be helpful here, as collections of maxims may be. *Black's Law Dictionary* supports some of its legal definitions with case citations. When, on the other hand, it falls to you to argue *against* such a well-established principle you will need first to establish the authority for the principle (in order to delimit it), and then to distinguish it. Your goal will be to find multiple cases that resemble your facts, and where the judge decided that the hoary principle does not apply.

5.16   PROVING THE NEGATIVE

The person in charge of evaluating a potential case, advising a client prospectively, or devising a defense needs to know what is *not* out there. Background defensive research, for instance, *always* needs to be thorough.

When proving a negative, the research log (in conjunction with your professional analysis and conclusion) is your main contribution to the enterprise. It enables you to convey concisely and logically where you looked and for what, which provides the building blocks for proving the negative. Merely stating that nothing relevant was found leaves open the possibility that the lack of results were based on some failing of yours as a researcher. Identifying the steps you took, the resources you used, and the cases you found (and subsequently discounted) establish much more strongly the likelihood that your conclusions are well grounded. As you proceed with your research, be sure to maintain a list of cases distinguished, and the grounds on which you distinguished them.

5.17 WHEN TO STOP

As you approach the completion of your case law research, you should feel like you are at a cocktail party, scanning the crowd for new faces. You should keep at it until all the case names you meet that are still pertinent to your situation in terms of fact or law are like old friends (or enemies). Actually, coming yet again upon cases that you've known about for a long time through their mention in a fresh case can also be illuminating, as when a new acquaintance tries to introduce one of your own old friends to you. It's always interesting to compare others' perceptions against your own. Of course, once you have tested your familiar case against the new idea, you may end up even more confident in your hard won understanding. Once you find that each new case you are turning up is too remote from your research problem to be considered relevant, you should review your research log and your research plan, to make sure that all the paths you planned to go down have been thoroughly explored. Only then is it time to evaluate and work with what you have found.

5.18 RESEARCHING THE DIFFERENT LEVELS OF FEDERAL CASE LAW

Our federal system, with all its layers of courts and its different claims to jurisdiction, makes working with case law uniquely complex. All the different types and layers of judicial expression have their uses, and the legal researcher needs to keep in mind when to focus on what. In the remainder of this chapter, we will focus on the federal court system as an example, with remarks on state case law only as significant differences make it necessary to do so.

5.19 SUPREME COURT CASES

Since the decisions of the Supreme Court of the United States are definitive and binding on all federal courts, every researcher must ascertain the very latest position taken by the Court on all issues pertaining to the subject of the research. Old Supreme Court cases are also vitally important, even where they vary from the current position, since they show trends in the development of the Court's doctrine over time, providing fodder for analysis and for predictions of further future developments.

Sometimes old cases are all there is to find. Many subject areas of the law rarely reach the Supreme Court level of deliberation, e.g., commercial sub-areas that typically involve small monetary stakes, the kinds of cases that are too time-sensitive to wait for Supreme Court action, or areas that rely only on well-settled legal principles. For these areas (as well as for very narrowly defined issues that do not come up often), the leading Supreme Court case can be a century old. The problem for the researcher in these areas is to work with the huge body of progeny engendered by old but still valid Supreme Court cases. As mentioned in **Section 5.16**, one solution is to start at both ends and meet up in the middle, i.e., use that old Supreme Court case and a new local case relying on it, without necessarily referring to much or anything in between.

The Supreme Court's position of authority makes any indication of its thinking useful to the researcher. The Court's opinions are most important, of course, since they trigger *stare decisis* as well as provide evidence of the court's thinking (see **Table 5.C**). The best support you could possibly find for your proposition is a unanimous Supreme Court opinion in your favor from a currently valid case. Second best would be a majority opinion. An opinion joined by a plurality of the justices is pretty good, too! You can still make some hay from a concurring opinion, and even (depending on the identity of the dissenter and the subsequent development of jurisprudence on the matter) from a dissenting opinion. *Per curiam* decisions, unsigned and usually short (although not always unanimous) appear in the same places that publish full dress opinions and are useful as, if nothing else, a full stop to the appellate controversy below, as is also true of denials of certiorari and other unsigned memorandum orders.

In the *United States Reports* and in Lexis Advance, the text of each opinion is preceded by a Syllabus (a summation of the majority opinion and the court's decision) prepared for the convenience of researchers by the Court's Reporter of Decisions. Commercially edited versions of the Court's opinions are preceded by an editorially-produced summary and headnotes. The *United States Supreme Court Reports (Lawyers' Edition)* and the Lexis Advance version of the opinions based on it include summaries of each concurring and dissenting opinion, as well as of the opinion of the Court. Westlaw merely notes at this point the existence and authorship of these minority opinions.

The headnotes, next in the prefatory material, are consecutively numbered editorial summaries of legal points discussed in the case, couched to a great extent in the language of the opinion itself; their numbers are inserted into the case to permit location within the opinion of each point discussed. Each headnote is assigned a subject heading (e.g., a West Key Number in the *Supreme Court Reporter*) and the headnotes then constitute the basis for the subject indexing of the case. As with the Syllabi and summaries, the condensed nature of the headnotes makes them an excellent field for online searching for legal concepts.

The opinion itself begins with the opinion adopted by the court. This opinion is the only one that receives headnotes in the commercially edited versions of the reports; neither concurring nor dissenting opinions receive any subject indexing. Looking for treatment of a topic in these minority opinions requires doing a fielded full-text search restricted to concurring or dissenting opinions.

Because of the broad significance of Supreme Court jurisprudence, materials other than the Court's actual judicial opinions are quite widely available. The records and briefs filed with the Court (see **Table 5.D**) may be significant to the legal researcher for a number of reasons. The information they contain may illuminate the Court's decision or its reasoning, and thus be helpful in interpreting the significance of a particular opinion. The same could be said of the oral arguments heard by the Court (see **Table 5.E**). More fundamentally, the record filed with the Court may contain the only version of the trial court's opinion outside the unpublished courthouse records of the court below.

The legal researcher will also want to ensure that she understands the jurisprudential context of any Supreme Court case, e.g., what circuit splits preceded Supreme Court action, or what other reasons prompted the Court to take the case. Other background information to particular cases that would be of interest to the legal researcher would include the political background to the case (think of the Nixon cases, the Election 2000 case, or the Guantanamo detention cases), and where the case fits in to the personal background of individual justices. A wealth of such information is available, e.g., in books about individual justices and on the websites of various watchdog groups, but it does start to exit the realm of legal research.

5.20   THE UNITED STATES COURTS OF APPEALS

At the next level down from the United States Supreme Court, the cases are more numerous and less authoritative. Since there can be disagreements between courts at this level, the researcher needs to be prepared to argue on various levels for the correctness of one court versus another. You will want to take into account that not all circuits are created equal for all purposes. Some circuits possess expertise respected above that of other circuits in a given legal area. For example, the Fifth Circuit, which includes prominent maritime ports and industries, takes a more prominent role in the definition of admiralty law than does the Tenth Circuit. There are also powerhouse circuits, whose general volume and level of work enhances the level of jurisprudential prestige attached to its decisions (the Second Circuit comes to mind). Note also that the Federal Circuit, created in 1982, has subject-defined jurisdiction, combining the jurisdiction of the former U.S. Court of Customs and Patent Appeals and the appeals part of the U.S. Court of Claims with authorization to hear appeals of patent cases tried in the federal District Courts and appeals from certain federal administrative boards.

Moreover, neither are all types of decisions created equal. While the Supreme Court justices all weigh in on each case for which an opinion is issued, most cases in the Courts of Appeals are heard only by a three judge panel. Occasionally a case is brought before a larger conclave of judges (in most circuits, all court of appeals judges for that circuit) for hearing or rehearing *en banc*, and that fact should be indicated parenthetically (see *The Bluebook* Rule 10.6.1. for other factors that structurally affect the weight of a decision's authority). And, of course, different judges have different judicial histories, making for different reputations and different levels of prestige and influence.

The opinions of the Courts of Appeals are widely available (see **Table 5.F**), but not to the duplicative extent that Supreme Court opinions are available. In print, they are published unofficially only, by West. The courts select less than 25 percent of their opinions for publication; those cases selected currently appear in the *Federal Reporter, Third Series*. These published cases are the ones singled out by the courts as cases that can be cited unreservedly as precedential. Other opinions released by the Courts of Appeals but not so selected, which in earlier years would have been unpublished, are now "reported" by West (though still unpublished by the courts) in their *Federal Appendix*, and appear on Westlaw and Lexis Advance. They are covered by the citators of these services as well. The *Federal Appendix* cases, like the published cases, get Headnotes and Key Numbers assigned to them, and appear in *West's Federal Practice Digest 5th*. While in 2006, the Supreme Court promulgated Federal Rule of Appellate Procedure 32.1 obliging all federal appeals courts to permit *citation* of future (i.e., those issued on or after January 1, 2007) unpublished opinions, the precedential value accorded these cases varies by circuit. In fact, the Advisory Committee Notes to this rule specifically says that the rule "says nothing about what effect a court must give to one of its unpublished opinions or to the unpublished opinions of another court." If you find such a case to be significant to your situation, you will need to research what weight (if any) is given to such opinions in your jurisdiction.

Court of Appeals opinions, since they generally review a lower court action, usually accompany a decision to uphold, reverse, or remand that lower court action. Even more often than with the Supreme Court, a published Court of Appeals case can involve review of a case below that was not itself selected for publication. For that reason, as well as for explicative background, you may wish to obtain the records and briefs filed with the Court of Appeals. However, those records and briefs (see **Table 5.G**) at this level of the court system from before the national rollout of the federal Case Management/Electronic Case Files system in 2005 are nowhere nearly as readily available as are Supreme Court records and briefs. For these earlier materials, you may be just as well off going back to the trial court for a copy of the opinion below as seeking it out via the Court of Appeals record. Since 2005, and at this point almost universally, your best bet for these filings is via the electronic docket in either PACER or Bloomberg Law (see **Section 5.13**).

Other relevant background information would include circuit splits over the issue at hand. Bloomberg BNA's *United States Law Week* offers a helpful feature in the first issue of each month titled "Circuit Splits." This roundup of circuit splits appears both in the Case Alert and Legal News section of the print edition and in the electronic version of Law Week, available on Bloomberg Law. For progeny of a Court of Appeals case, refer to KeyCite on Westlaw, or Shepard's on Lexis Advance.

5.21 UNITED STATES DISTRICT COURTS

When we get down to the trial level of the federal District Courts, the cases' greater abundance and lesser authority both contribute to a much smaller proportion of them being published compared with the decisions of higher courts (see **Table 5.H**). District Court opinions chosen by the court for publication are currently published unofficially in the *Federal Supplement, Third Series*, and select opinions not chosen by the court for publication are collected in the *Federal Appendix*. Because of the multiplicity of judges and cases, you may well have to limit your search by criteria other than subject and jurisdiction at the outset. Ideally, you would like to find decisions by a particular judge, *your* judge. This can readily be done on Westlaw and Lexis Advance by including a name limitation in the judge field.

Many case reporters devoted to specialized subjects include District Court opinions that are unreported in the Federal Supplement. These include some reporters that appear online as well, such as Bloomberg BNA's United States Patents Quarterly on Bloomberg Law. As with unreported decisions from the Courts of Appeals, direct docket retrieval (for filed opinions) is often the best available option (see **Section 5.13**).

Even if you can't find an appropriate opinion written by the judge assigned to your case, you can pick out a case from that judge's pool of colleagues, by narrowing your results by jurisdictional facets not evident from the reporter title (e.g., individual districts, in the federal District Courts). This facet limiting is available on both Westlaw and Lexis Advance and allows for incredibly efficient refinement.

Your interest may focus on trying to find cases by your judge (or one of her near colleagues) that concerned a procedural posture similar to your own. A recitation of the case's procedural posture usually occurs toward the beginning of the opinion, so doing a proximity search requiring a maximum distance between a key word or phrase from the posture (e.g., summary judgment) and a key word from the citation (e.g., a distinctive word from the name field) should do the trick. Since a field may have been added at the beginning of the case specifying the procedural posture (e.g., a Key Number on Westlaw or a Topic or Headnote on Lexis Advance), you should also do a search across that type of field.

Another way to narrow down your selection of cases is to consider the subject expertise of individual judges. This can be determined by, for example, their contributions to the secondary literature, and by their citation as an expert by the Court of Appeals, both of which can also readily be determined by electronic searching. Sometimes you may be able to obtain statistical information about a judge's affirmance rates on a particular issue. You may also wish to consider whether an opinion was written by a Senior Judge, or a judge in some other way not in the mainstream of the district's judicial activity.

The volume of cases produced by the federal District Courts means that you will want to try to find a case that's ideal on your very particular set of facts. In the fact-rich set of data that comprises the output of the federal District Courts, you can begin to look by executing a Terms and Connectors search with key words from your fact pattern (e.g. "banana peel" and "grocery store" and "slipped"); you don't even have to supply the legal term "negligence," but will learn it from reading the cases this search brings up. As with all case law searching, you will want to select distinctive words, especially terms of art, once you get to the point of including legal concepts in your search. Keep in mind, of course, that you will often have to resort to drawing analogies between cases dealing with a particular legal issue and your own factual scenario (e.g., when the case law talks about slipping on a banana peel and your client slipped on a watermelon rind).

Even though there is a general reporter for federal District Court cases (currently the *Federal Supplement, Third Series*, published by West), subject-specific reporters play a larger role in the reporting of District Court cases than they do for higher courts. Inclusion in specialized reporters permits the publication of cases involving many different fact patterns within that special area, even with little variation in the legal concepts expounded.

5.22   STATE CASE LAW

For the most part, the states mirror the federal court system in having more elaborate reporting available of the output of the highest courts, and less coverage of the lower courts. With 50 state jurisdictions (and the District of Columbia), some sort of road map to the structure of the state courts will prove invaluable in research into the case law of unfamiliar states. Not only can the names of the courts vary wildly between states (e.g., in New York the "Supreme Court" is partly a trial level court), but the court system structures vary as well (e.g., some jurisdictions have appellate courts of limited jurisdiction, such as criminal appeals). Useful comparative sketches of those structures are available in print reference guides (such as the annual *Federal-State Court Directory* or *BNA's Directory of State and Federal Courts, Judges, and Clerks*), on the Court Structure Charts page of the National Center for State Courts' Court Statistics Project (www.courtstatistics.org), and often from the website of the relevant state's judiciary branch. *The Bluebook* itself is a handy source for information about the reports of different states, and research guides for individual states can offer more detail than you are likely to need (see **Appendix**).

One aspect of state case law research that occasionally requires attention is to discern which reporter amongst the several that may be available enjoys "official" status for *The Bluebook* purposes. The current edition of *The Bluebook* (20th) mandates different rules on state case law citation for practitioners citing state cases to courts in the cases' state of origin than it does for all other legal writers. The former group are referred to local citation rules, which may require a parallel citation to the state's official reporter. The latter group is obliged to cite to the regional reporter, and to a medium-neutral citation (a citation based on court of origin and filing order, rather than on publication in a reporter) if available in either of those. If not, the researcher is to follow the detailed order of preference set out in Rule 10.3.1 and in Table T.1, which usually gives preference to official sources in those instances where neither a medium-neutral nor a regional citation is available.

Some jurisdictions publish their own case reports, especially for the state's top court. Others contract this job to a private publisher, designating that publication as official. In some cases, where the state has designated the West reporter as official, this means that the West regional reporter is the only physically published source for a state's case law. As more states turn to medium-neutral citation and publish their own cases on their websites, the same issue that we saw in connection with physical distribution of session laws comes to mind. Without wide distribution of a physically fixed text, how can the authenticity and reliability of the cited text be assured? For some jurisdictions, the move has been toward authenticated .pdf documents that are formatted just as they would be if a print publication was being produced, but this is far from universal. It will be interesting to see how this concern plays out as medium-neutral citation becomes more widespread.

For state cases that fly below the radar of the official reporters and the National Reporter System (West's system of federal, regional, and state reporters), a variety of local publications sometimes step in to fill the breach. Typically, by virtue of the nature of the courts generating these cases, these will often not appear in the general state case law databases on Westlaw and Lexis Advance unless specifically selected for publication by the courts. Legal newspapers in the major markets often publish cases deemed of local interest only; these are sometimes indexed in separate digests and are sometimes accessible via the newspaper's website. Specialized local reporters have also emerged in some high volume or highly remunerative areas of practice, such as New York City residential real estate. See individual state research guides for details (see **Appendix**).

As with the federal trial level courts, you can find some additional state trial level decisions by searching dockets. Electronic access to dockets at the state level, however, is generally far more limited than at the federal level. Many state court websites that provide this sort of information online are listed at the Public Access to Court Records page of the National Center for State Courts (http://www.ncsc.org/Topics/Access-and-Fairness/Privacy-Public-Access-to-Court-Records/State-Links.aspx). In addition to dockets, full-text searching of some specific filings is available on Westlaw under Trial Court Orders and Trial Court Documents and on Lexis Advance under Briefs, Pleadings & Motions. Also worth noting, unlike in the federal courts, where citing to the unpublished case is permitted by rule (though its weight is variable), some state courts still adhere to the old rule that unpublished decisions cannot be cited at all. The specific rules of the jurisdiction should be investigated if you are interested in citing such a case.

5.23 UPDATING CASE LAW RESEARCH

The text of a case is not dynamic, but its significance is. As with statutes, you must make sure that no development subsequent to the issuance of an authority upon which you are relying has undercut that authority. In the statutory context, that means repeal, amendment, or replacement. In the case law context you are required to ascertain whether your case is still good law. This involves not only the direct subsequent history of your case, but also what developments in the case's subject matter are going on around it. Subsequent developments affecting your case can emanate from the legislature, the executive, or the judiciary, and the legal researcher should investigate each of these.

The most overt judicial action would be for a superior court to overrule or uphold the case. This kind of direct history is readily researched by using a citator (e.g., KeyCite on Westlaw or Shepard's on Lexis Advance). Less overtly, the case could be either criticized, cited, or ignored. This group of less-directed actions covers a broad spectrum, which can be discerned but not necessarily pinned down precisely by the citators. The case could have been cited a lot—but with what level of enthusiasm? The case could have been left behind, remaining uncited as case law goes off in another direction—but that could merely indicate some factual anomaly that made it an inconvenient vehicle for a doctrine on a roll. On the other hand, a check of the cases on which your case relied (check the Table of Authorities within KeyCite or Shepard's) may show that your case's jurisprudential foundations have been eaten away. The citators are indispensable, but they only get you to where your hard labor of skimming the citing (and cited) cases begins.

The legislature's most overt act would be to countermand the case by statute. This could have come up in the course of the statutory research with which you began your work. Less overtly, the statutory landscape in which the case originally was born may have changed so much that the facts giving rise to the doctrine that the case announced are no longer likely to occur. This lessens the persuasiveness of the case for modern purposes, and is one reason that recent cases are generally to be preferred.

The executive branch of the government can undercut the effectiveness of a case by not complying with it, or not carrying out the actions it mandates. While in principle these executive actions would be illegal, they are sometimes used as the basis of arguments that the case result is untenable. If there is a case that undercuts your position, research into the real life consequences of that case may cast doubt on that case's vitality as authority.

Your initial indication of a problem with your case (or, on the contrary, its robust good health) could be the status indicator previewing the citator information on Westlaw (colored flags) and Lexis Advance (colored shapes, most notably yellow triangles and red octagons). These status indicators on Westlaw and Lexis Advance are dynamic, changing with the advent of new cases or statutes affecting the significance of your case.

Some of the citing cases are listed with specific information about the nature of their citation to your case (see also the discussion of citators as subject research tools in **Section 5.9**). Labels conveying this information are variously assigned by programmed language analysis or by a human reader, and in all cases should not be relied upon. They can be helpful as a starting place for deciding which cases to look at first, but thorough research will have to encompass all cases cited. Some of the labels denote the length of discussion of your case in the citing reference, and some denote the purpose or treatment of the citing reference. Here again, facet limiting can be extremely helpful, allowing you to see, for example, all of the cases that cited your treatment negatively from a particular jurisdiction.

For some cases, there can be hundreds or thousands of cases that have not been given treatment analysis by the citator, instead being identified merely by the generic "Citing References" in KeyCite or "Cited by" in Lexis Advance. Your time is obviously not well spent reading those hundreds or thousands of cases, but it is worth a quick moment to combine use of the facets and the "Search within results" functionality to see whether any subsequent case from your jurisdiction cited to the case you were checking on and involved similar factual circumstances. It is best to look at any such cases earlier in your research process, before your thinking has started to calcify.

Other limiting criteria available include date of the citing case, the particular headnote/topic that the citing and cited case share (when one has been identified), and the publication status of the citing case. Pay close attention to the available "Narrow/Narrow by" facets that are available on Westlaw and Lexis Advance—this is an area where the power of doing legal research in electronic format is most effectively brought to bear.

Citators do cover a wide range of courts and cases, but where your case is not covered by a citator (e.g., a case from a foreign jurisdiction) you can do a full-text search for its citation in the appropriate case law databases. This search should be done in Terms and Connectors mode rather than via a Natural Language search whenever possible. Searching full-text case law using a citation as a search term can also be used as a double-check on citator results, especially with regard to date-limited searches for very recent citations that may not yet have been added to the citator.

5.24   TABLES

TABLE 5.A: PRINCIPAL COMPONENTS OF WEST'S AMERICAN DIGEST SYSTEM

1. Federal digests:

   West's Federal Practice Digest 5th, and its predecessors

   United States Supreme Court Digest, a subset of the *West's Federal Practice Digest*

   West's Bankruptcy Digest

2. Regional digests:

   West's Atlantic Digest, 2d, and its predecessor

   North Eastern Digest, discontinued in 1969

   West's North Western Digest, 2d, and its predecessor

   West's Pacific Digest, Beginning 585 P.2d, and its predecessors

   West's South Eastern Digest, 2d, and its predecessors

   West's Southern Digest, discontinued in 1988

   South Western Digest, discontinued in 1958

3. State digests:

   Many states have West digests devoted to those cases from their state and federal courts published in West reporters.

4. Comprehensive digests:

   West's General Digest, 12th Series

   Twelfth Decennial Digest, and its predecessors

   Century Edition of The American Digest: A Complete Digest of All Reported American Cases From the Earliest Times to 1896 (a pre-Key Number digest)

TABLE 5.B: SOME EXAMPLES OF NON-WEST SUBJECT INDEXES TO CASES

Subject indexing of cases can be found not only in the standard digests, but also in many treatises, looseleaf services, and indexes to specialized reporters.

1. *U.S. Supreme Court Digest, Lawyers' Edition*, Charlottesville, Va.: LexisNexis

   The companion digest to *United States Supreme Court Reports, Lawyers' Edition*, long a part of the Lawyers' Cooperative Publishing family of interconnected publications, uses a different system of subject headings.

2. *Housing Court Reporter Index*, Johnson City, N. Y.: Treiman-Roody Publications

   Highly specialized subject indexing to a set of case reports concerned with a practice local to New York City.

3. *PUR Digest, 4th Series*, Reston, Va.: Public Utilities Reports, Inc.

   Subject indexing to the *Public Utilities Reports, Fourth Series* in a familiar digest format, but with a specialized subject classification system developed continually since 1915 to cover this particular area of the law.

4. James H. Pannabecker, *Banking Law Digest*, New York, N. Y.: LexisNexis A. S. Pratt

   Another specialized index to cases, covering decisions appearing in *The Banking Law Journal* and some important ones published elsewhere. Looseleaf format.

TABLE 5.C: SELECTED SOURCES OF SCOTUS OPINIONS

As befits their importance as a seminal source of the law, SCOTUS output is readily available from a variety of sources.

Normally cited report series:

1. *United States Reports.* Washington, D. C.: U.S. Government Publishing Office

    The official reports, citation to which is required (if case appears therein) by *The Bluebook* T.1. All recent volumes are available as .pdf files in HeinOnline's U.S. Supreme Court Library (subscription only). The Supreme Court's own website http://www.supremecourt.gov/opinions/boundvolumes.aspx has .pdf files of the bound volumes from volume 502 (1991) to the most recently published volume.

2. *Supreme Court Reporter.* St. Paul, Minn.: Thomson West

    The reports with Key Numbers, tied into West's American Digest System. Content also on Westlaw in html and .pdf.

3. *United States Supreme Court Reports, Lawyers' Edition.* Charlottesville, Va.: LexisNexis

    Content also available on Lexis Advance.

4. *United States Law Week.* Washington, D. C.: Bloomberg BNA

    In addition to the complete text of opinions (often the first print version to appear), has docket information and status reporting on pending cases. Content also on Bloomberg Law.

Other access:

5. Supreme Court of the United States, Opinions.

    https://www.supremecourt.gov/opinions/opinions.aspx

    This web page also has a link to a page entitled "Where to Obtain Supreme Court Opinions," which gives additional sources. The Court does not consider its electronic opinions official.

6. Google Scholar (full text of U.S. Supreme Court cases back to 1791)

    https://scholar.google.com

    Google Scholar also includes select case law from other courts.

TABLE 5.D: SELECTED SOURCES FOR
SCOTUS RECORDS AND BRIEFS

1. Westlaw: Briefs > Briefs (below U.S. Supreme Court) then click Advanced to search using the document fields, but note that *citation* is, perhaps counterintuitively, the Westlaw specific citation of the brief, rather than the citation of the case the brief is connected to. The earliest brief in this selected collection is from 1870.

2. Lexis Advance: Briefs, Pleadings and Motions > Federal > U.S. Supreme Court Briefs

    The earliest brief in this selected collection is from 1936.

3. Bloomberg Law: browse All Content Legal Search > expand U.S. Courts > expand Court Briefs > expand Federal Court Briefs > select U.S. Supreme Court to add the source and then search within it.

    The earliest brief in this selected collection is from 1936.

4. The Making of Modern Law: U.S. Supreme Court Records and Briefs, 1832–1978.

    Fully-searchable text and image database, produced by Gale Cengage Learning, distributed by subscription to research libraries.

5. *Landmark Briefs and Arguments of the Supreme Court of the United States: Constitutional Law.* Philip B. Kurland and Gerhard Casper, editors. Washington, D. C.]: University Publications of America.

    The earliest brief in this selected collection is from 1793.

6. United States Department of Justice, Office of the Solicitor General.

    Browse at https://www.justice.gov/osg/supreme-court-briefs

    Search at https://www.justice.gov/osg/search-osg-brief-pdfs

    Briefs filed by the Solicitor General in the Supreme Court since 1985.

7. Supreme Court of the United States Blog

    http://www.scotusblog.com/

    Search by case name in the upper right search box or browse by term under Merits Cases to identify case pages, which include hyperlinks to .pdf files of filed briefs since the October Term 2007.

8. Findlaw: Supreme Court Briefs. Select coverage runs from 1999 to 2007.

http://supreme.findlaw.com/supreme_court/briefs.html

Additionally, many large law libraries have collections of Supreme Court Records and Briefs on microfiche, and some may have bound collections in hard copy. Consult library catalogs for details.

9. The Supreme Court announced, just prior to this publication, that it is creating an electronic filing system that will be accessible via a quick link on the Court's webpage. See their Press Release (http://www.scotusblog.com/wp-content/uploads/2017/08/2017-08.03.17-Press-Release-Electronic-Filing.pdf) for more information.

TABLE 5.E: SELECTED SOURCES
FOR SCOTUS ORAL ARGUMENTS

1. The Oyez Project. Audio files and transcripts of oral arguments before the United States Supreme Court, starting in 1955.

   http://www.oyez.org

2. United States Supreme Court. Transcript coverage begins with October Term 2000. Audio recording coverage begins with October Term 2010.

   https://www.supremecourt.gov/

   [Select "Oral Arguments" and click on "Argument Transcripts" or "Argument Audio."]

3. Westlaw: Trial Transcripts & Oral Arguments > U.S. Supreme Court

   Coverage begins in October Term 1990.

4. Lexis Advance:

   [Type "United States Supreme Court Transcripts" into the primary search bar and then select the source from the drop-down menu.]

   Coverage begins in October Term 1979.

5. *Landmark Briefs and Arguments of the Supreme Court of the United States: Constitutional Law*. Philip B. Kurland and Gerhard Casper, editors. [Washington, D. C.]: University Publications of America.

   Coverage begins in 1793.

6. Oral Arguments of the U.S. Supreme Court on Microfiche (1953–2010)

   Microfiche set of transcripts, sold by ProQuest. Coverage is comprehensive from 2010 back to the 1969–70 term, and includes all arguments that were transcribed from the 1953–54 term through the 1968–69 term.

7. Supreme Court of the United States Blog

   http://www.scotusblog.com/

   Search by case name in the upper right search box or browse by term under Merits Cases to identify case pages, which include hyperlinks to .pdf files of oral argument transcripts since October Term 2007 and audio files since October Term 2010 under the "Argument" heading at the top.

TABLE 5.F: SELECTED SOURCES FOR FEDERAL COURTS OF APPEALS CASES

1. *West's Federal Reporter, Third Series*, and its predecessors (see *The Bluebook*). St. Paul, Minn.: Thomson West.

2. *West's Federal Appendix*. St. Paul, Minn.: Thomson West

   Select cases not selected for publication by the courts, beginning in 2001.

3. Westlaw: Cases > U.S. Courts of Appeals

   Coverage goes back to 1891.

4. Lexis Advance: Cases > United States Courts of Appeals

   Coverage goes back to 1891.

5. Bloomberg Law: From the Browse menu—Litigation & Dockets > Court Opinions Search > Select Courts > expand Federal Court Opinions > check box next to U.S. Circuit Courts of Appeals Coverage goes back to 1891.

6. Courts of Appeals websites

   Varies from one circuit to the next, but generally available from a simple Google search or at www.ca[x].uscourts.gov where [x] is the number of a given circuit (e.g., www.ca3.uscourts.gov). From there, look for either Opinions or Decisions. Starting coverage varies, but new opinions are added to each as they are decided.

   A complete collection of direct links to Courts of Appeals websites is available from the Administrative Office of the U.S. Courts at http://www.uscourts.gov/about-federal-courts/federal-courts-public/court-website-links

TABLE 5.G: SELECTED SOURCES OF COURT OF APPEALS RECORDS AND BRIEFS

1. Westlaw: Briefs > U.S. Courts of Appeals

    Coverage varies between circuits.

2. Lexis Advance: Briefs, Pleadings and Motions > Federal > [select particular] Circuit

    Coverage varies between circuits.

3. Bloomberg Law: Not searchable as separate material, but for matters that were filed electronically (varies, but generally ~2007 to present) briefs can often be retrieved via individual docket sheets (see **Section 5.12**).

4. Michael Whiteman and Peter Scott Campbell, *A Union List of Appellate Court Records and Briefs: Federal and State.* Littleton, Colo.: F. B. Rothman, 1999.

5. PACER: Public Access to Court Electronic Records.

    https://www.pacer.gov/

    Pay-as-you-go access to the electronic records systems of individual federal appellate, district, and bankruptcy courts.

TABLE 5.H: SELECTED SOURCES OF FEDERAL DISTRICT COURT CASES

1. *West's Federal Supplement, Third Series*, and its predecessors (see *The Bluebook*). St. Paul, Minn.: Thomson West.

   Note that before the inception of the first *West's Federal Supplement*, District Court cases were published in *West's Federal Reporter*.

2. *West's Federal Rules Decisions*. St. Paul, Minn.: Thomson West.

3. Westlaw: Cases > Federal District Courts.

   You can then choose a particular state or run a search and narrow by filters such as specific court, reported/unreported, date, topic, judge, etc. Those decisions included in the *West's Federal Supplement* and *West's Federal Rules Decisions* are available as .pdf files.

4. Lexis Advance: Cases > Federal District Courts.

   You can then either choose a state or run a search and then narrow by reported/unreported, date, topic, judge, etc. If you want to narrow to a particular court after conducting a search, first narrow to the relevant circuit and then narrow further to the individual court.

5. Bloomberg Law: Court Opinions Search > Select Courts > [expand] Federal Court Opinions > [expand] U.S. District Courts.

   You can then select a particular state in which to search or search across all District Courts, then limit to a particular Circuit, state, or court, and narrow by topic, judge, or date.

6. District Court websites

   Direct links to District Court websites are available from the Administrative Office of the U.S. Courts at http://www.uscourts.gov/about-federal-courts/federal-courts-public/court-website-links or via a simple web search; once there look for either Opinions or Decisions. Opinions or decisions are not made available for every court, and tend to be from only relatively recent cases.

7. PACER: Public Access to Court Electronic Records

   http://pacer.psc.uscourts.gov/

   Pay-as-you-go access to the electronic records systems (some including opinions) of individual federal appellate, district, and bankruptcy courts.

CHAPTER 6

INTRODUCING SECONDARY SOURCES: TREATISES AND OTHER OVERVIEWS

■ ■ ■

6.1 TREATISES

Legal treatises offer narrative exposition and analysis of a whole area of law. While this sounds like (and can indeed often prove to be) a gift from the legal gods, the use of treatises comes with at least a small price. That price is the particular authorial stance of the analysis, an explicit feature of many treatises. Treatises proper are usually the product of an individual, a group of individuals, or a series of individuals, and they generally eschew neutrality about the subjects whose mastery they display in their work. However, the marketplace abounds in treatises and if you don't appreciate or can't use the dominant treatise in your area, you can always look for another one. Unlike relevant primary sources like statutes or cases, you are under no obligation to cite to a treatise. That said, treatises can be an exception to the general rule that secondary sources are (usually) not the best sources to cite to the court. There are some treatises that are so well respected that they will be cited regularly. *Nimmer on Copyright*, for example, boasts thousands of citations in case law. Be aware that, if a preeminent treatise author has argued against your point, simply ignoring it isn't wise, since your opponent certainly will not!

The usefulness of treatises resides in the combination of broad scope and scholarly detail that they provide. While law review articles explore a narrow legal topic in depth, treatises cover the field within a substantial area from the most fundamental principles through the most complex and troublesome problems. Many important treatises track a major statute, combining textual and historical analysis of the statute itself with discussion of case law interpretation of each section. Others cover a broad common law subject, typically including analytical comparisons of the law in different jurisdictions (see **Table 6.A**). Still others hold a special place in practice, in that they are the definitive go-to source for questions within a particular jurisdiction. Siegel's *New York Practice*, for instance, is ubiquitous on the bookcases, or even the desks, of attorneys dealing with civil litigation (especially motion practice) in New York State. Interestingly, this valuable West publication is not uniformly accessible via Westlaw (it traditionally is not included in academic plans).

While some treatises include auxiliary practice features such as forms or reprinted selections of primary materials, the main body of the treatise concerns legal researchers in a different way, since it can itself be cited to and by a court. The only way to determine if a treatise has been cited by the courts is via a search of the full-text case law databases. To evaluate the esteem in which the courts hold a particular treatise, search on the author's last name (perhaps in proximity to a principal word from the treatise title) to see how many times the work in question has been cited, and by which courts, and in what fashion. Did the court refer to the treatise as authoritative or otherwise rely on its statement of the law? Add a search term pertaining to your legal issue to see if a court has actually cited the treatise on a point pertinent to the subject of your research.

Westlaw and Lexis Advance offer numerous treatises online, including some of the biggies, e.g., *Williston on Contracts* and *Nimmer on Copyright*, respectively. One of the great assets of the Westlaw and Lexis Advance treatise collections is the ability to click through to many of the cited sources. That said, however, print treatises, like so many print sources, make it much easier to see a particular treatise section in its surrounding context. Occasionally an older treatise may be useful, and many thousands of them have been digitized in a fully searchable text and image database called The Making of Modern Law: Legal Treatises, 1800–1926, produced and distributed on a web subscription basis to libraries by Gale Cengage Learning. Another subscription database of old treatises that may prove useful is the Legal Classics Library on HeinOnline.

Print treatises take a number of forms, with particular formats enjoying bursts of popularity at different times. Huge multi-volume treatises tend to be either looseleaf format or hardback with pocket part supplementation. When an individual volume becomes substantially outdated before the others do, it gets replaced. When the whole treatise undergoes a major revision, volumes of the new edition are frequently issued piecemeal, often with completely renumbered contents and volume numbers. As with digests (see **Section 5.6**), you will need to find the tables provided by the publisher that convert old citations to the new numbering scheme.

Shorter multi-volume treatises are increasingly published in looseleaf format, and single volume treatises can be either looseleaf, hardback with pocket part, or (especially those with institutional authorship) an annually-revised soft cover book. Each of these formats has its good and bad points from the researcher's point of view. The looseleaf format, for instance, is a problem for someone wanting to investigate what the prevailing view of the law was at some earlier date, a date for which the relevant looseleaf page has already been replaced and tossed in the garbage. Since each update can include changes to the text as well as citations to new cases on old points, looseleaf supplementation makes it all but impossible to track the evolution of this commentary.

The electronic treatises generally offer table of contents access as well as full-text searching, and some offer indexes as separate browseable documents. Use of these online indexes involves the same problem with the use of online statutory indexes discussed in **Chapter 2**: you have to click on entries to see their sub-entries, rather than sweeping your eyes over everything at once as in a print index. As a result you might miss something important because you failed to click on one of the headings to open it up.

The print treatises also have tables of contents, of course, and indexes that unfortunately vary quite a bit in their quality. Nonetheless, using a print index, especially one that includes subheadings under index entries, can let you pick your treatise section on the basis of more information than if you had to examine each section that came up in response to a full-text search.

6.2   RESTATEMENTS OF THE LAW

The Restatements of the Law, introduced to every first-year law student via at least the Restatement of the Law of Contracts, and available through both Westlaw and Lexis Advance as well as in print, might be described as quasi-institutionally authored treatises. They combine the prestige of their individual editor (the "Reporter") with the legwork and peer-reviewed imprimatur of the American Law Institute. Restatements all contain narrative text synthesizing black letter formulation of the law from the best cases nationally. However, they vary in the degree to which they aim to be normative. In the beginning, way back in 1923, the first Restatements started out to be plain old descriptive of "what the law was." The original undertaking was to be descriptive of the actual prevailing judicial consensus on the matters covered. Subsequent Restatement Second and Third projects, however, have embraced a more prescriptive intention by focusing on those cases considered by the Institute to reflect the "best" interpretation of the law.

Restatements were designed to be persuasive authority: court citations to them can be found in the Appendices to each of the Restatements (and in the predecessor publication to the Appendices, the *Restatement in the Courts*), and in *Shepard's Restatement of the Law Citations*. Since the courts of a particular jurisdiction may have adopted the doctrine announced in an earlier Restatement and then not followed up later by adopting the subsequent Restatement's different doctrine on that point, you should not regard the earlier series as necessarily being superseded. One note on finding Restatements: since the titles vary quite a bit, we recommend always doing a keyword search rather than a straight title search whenever you are looking for a Restatement in a library catalog or database.

As with any joint legal utterance, the adopted texts of the Restatement were preceded by deliberations; these tentative drafts and other historical underpinnings are available in a variety of formats (including an extensive collection in HeinOnline's American Law Institute Library), and can be used after the fashion of legislative history.

6.3   ENCYCLOPEDIAS

Like treatises, encyclopedias offer narrative exposition and analysis of the law, replete with a full arsenal of statutory and case citations. Unlike treatises, however, they are not the product of a recognized or budding authority, flowing instead from the anonymous editorial staff of a commercial publisher. Thus, encyclopedias are not accorded the same position or regard as are treatises in most circles. Encyclopedias do not offer the extensive coverage of any subject that a treatise can, because their scope is broader. Although they point with pride to the number of times they have been cited in judicial opinions, you should not think of the encyclopedias as citeable, but as tools to help you find citeable material. One important benefit of most legal encyclopedias, when compared with treatises, is that they require a less thorough understanding of an area of law at the start. Treatises, by virtue of their extensive coverage, often presume a certain level of substantive knowledge on the part of the researcher; encyclopedias, on the other hand, are generally more accessible to the non-expert with respect to the language used and the knowledge assumed.

As with treatises, encyclopedias are produced on a number of different scales. The enormous multivolume general legal encyclopedia, a tremendously popular format in the pre-electronic past, is represented today by two titles: *Corpus Juris Secundum* ("CJS") and *American Jurisprudence, 2d edition* ("AmJur2d"), both of which are available on Westlaw as well as in print. AmJur2d is also available on Lexis Advance, but sometimes there has been a delay in its updating. Each of these two encyclopedias contains articles on legal topics, covered nationally, studded with footnotes, and updated annually with additional references.

Historically, one difference between these two encyclopedias was that AmJur2d tended to be more selective in its case coverage, while CJS aimed at being more generous with its citations. On the other hand, AmJur2d has been known for more focused attention to statutes than CJS, with the former including a helpful table of statutes cited right at the beginning of each article. The relationship between the two has changed recently, however, since they are now both published by West, and it remains to be seen whether these distinctions will continue to hold true. Previously, and throughout most of their run to date, the two sets were produced by rival publishers. That historic rivalry still has consequences for today's legal researcher: prior to 1996, when the owner of AmJur2d's publisher merged with the publisher of CJS, cross-references in many legal materials to secondary sources like these encyclopedias were limited to citations to that publisher's own products. The *U.S.C.A.*, a West product, would follow a code provision with a section of Library References that included only other West products, like CJS. The *U.S.C.S.*, similarly, would cite to AmJur2d but not to any West products. Even though the ownership picture has shifted dramatically over the last thirty years of American legal publishing, the researcher who wants a full spectrum of secondary cross-references, or one who prefers to use a particular secondary source, needs to be aware of who publishes what. When the interrelationships between the different publications is understood, you will have a clearer picture of where to look for citations to which research tools.

Look (e.g., in the sources listed in the **Appendix**) to see if a local encyclopedia exists for the jurisdiction whose law you are researching. Like the national encyclopedias, these multivolume publications offer narrative expositions of state law, integrating discussion of statutory and case law. Some local encyclopedias specialize in a particular area of practice.

When starting to use an encyclopedia unfamiliar to you, you should take a moment to evaluate the nature of its editorial stance. Pick a legal subject about which you know a fair amount, and see how you would characterize the way the encyclopedia handles its treatment of that subject. Would you call the treatment simplified? Cautious? Bear your observations in mind when you turn to read what the encyclopedia has to say about matters where you are relying on it for your initial orientation.

6.4   AMERICAN LAW REPORTS: THE ALR

Despite its title, the hybrid *American Law Reports* series ("ALR"), available both in print from West and on Westlaw and Lexis Advance, is more like an encyclopedia than it is a case reporter. You might think of it as an encyclopedia published in chronological order, as issues arise, rather than in an alphabetical arrangement as are CJS and AmJur2d. Since 1919, ALR (and before that, its predecessor *Lawyers' Reports, Annotated*) has selected recent cases of significant legal interest and published them each in connection with an essay (by a journeyman author) surveying the law in the area raised by the case.

The ALR essays, called Annotations, usually go into considerable depth in their presentation of the decisional law on the topics covered. For example, an Annotation on the subject of Recovery of Damages for Emotional Distress Due to Treatment of Pets and Animals covered dozens of pages and over 80 case citations (see 91 A.L.R.5th 545). By contrast, a comparable entry in Am Jur (4 Am. Jur. 2d Animals § 116: Liability for Injuries to Animals—Damages Recoverable—Damages for emotional distress and punitive damages) is a dozen sentences and includes roughly ¼ as many case citations; a related CJS entry (3B C.J.S. Animals § 500: Injuries to or Killing of Animals—Civil Liability—Actions and Proceedings—Damages—For dogs) was four sentences long and had 13 case citations. It is worth noting, however, that both the AmJur2d entry and the CJS entry included citations or references to this more in-depth ALR Annotation. If you can find a recent ALR Annotation that touches on (or, best of all possible worlds, is devoted to) the topic of your research, it can save you a lot of time and definitely get you pointed in the right direction. Subject access to the essays is gained by full-text searching (on Westlaw and Lexis Advance), by an elaborate system of index volumes in the print sets, or by mining related references in one of the more general resources like legal encyclopedias.

The Annotations do get updated regularly with new case citations and statutes. On Westlaw and Lexis Advance the new materials are added to the existing list of sources cited. In the print ALR the new cases and statutes are of necessity (and more logically) segregated from the Annotations: they are provided via pocket part supplementation in those parts of the series that are currently being updated.

The problem with this updating is that the new material, especially new case law, is being cited to support an idea that might have become beside the point. Annotations go stale, even if they sport updating cases from last week. Each Annotation's text is like a snapshot of the current state of decisional law, and, like all snapshots, their freshness starts to fade away immediately. Find out just when the Annotation you are reading first appeared. Since an ALR Annotation, like any secondary source, is only used to get you started on what must eventually become your own professional investigation of the primary legal sources, even a faded Annotation can sometimes still give you a good head start. The problem arises when the law has veered sufficiently away from what it was at the time the Annotation was written to make the whole thrust of the analysis dated. You are generally better off starting off with a fresher viewpoint, either a newer ALR Annotation, a recent law review article, or a regularly updated treatise.

6.5   TABLE

TABLE 6.A: SOURCES FOR LISTS OF PROMINENT TREATISES

1. Kendall F. Svengalis, *Legal Information Buyer's Guide and Reference Manual*. Annual. Guilford, Conn.: New England LawPress.

   Available to search, but not browse, on Lexis Advance under the title Legal Information Buyer's Guide.

   After a 2-year embargo period, available on HeinOnline (as .pdf files) as part of Spinelli's Law Library Reference Shelf.

   Chapter 27, "Legal Treatises & Other Subject Specialty Materials," includes an excellent introduction to the different kinds of treatises, followed by more than 400 pages of evaluative descriptions of treatises grouped under 61 different legal subjects. Includes detailed information on pricing and supplementation, as well as suggestions for alternative ways to update the information in many of the treatises.

2. Kent C. Olson, *Legal Information: How to Find It, How to Use It*. Phoenix, Ariz.: Oryx Press, 1999.

   Chapter 4, "Law Books," has a section on treatises that starts out with an engaging history and overview of the world of treatise publication, and goes on (in Table 4–1) to list the real multivolume superstars in the treatise heavens. Highly selective list that truly hits the high points as of 1999, still very helpful for names, even if not for editions, in 2017. These are the treatises you will almost certainly be asked if you have checked. No descriptions.

   The same author has an updated and wider selection of treatises, with very useful notes on online availability, in the Appendix to his *Principles of Legal Research*, 2nd ed., St. Paul, Minn.: West Academic Publishing, 2015.

3. Harvard Law School Library, "Legal Treatises by Subject."

   http://guides.library.harvard.edu/legaltreatises

   Part of a series of research guides, this is another selective list of legal treatises, arranged under nearly 50 major subject headings with general descriptions.

4.   Georgetown Law Library, "Treatise Finders"

https://www.law.georgetown.edu/library/research/treatise-finders/

This guide organizes treatises within over 60 subject headings, including brief descriptions and indicating when a treatise is available on Lexis Advance, Westlaw, or Bloomberg Law.

CHAPTER 7

INTRODUCING SECONDARY SOURCES: FORM BOOKS AND JURY INSTRUCTIONS

■ ■ ■

7.1 FORM BOOKS

In the practice of law, it is often necessary to draft certain kinds of documents over and over again during the course of one's career. If, for example, a real estate lawyer wants to work with maximum efficiency, he or she develops a collection of forms that can be reused in different but similar transactions. One can reuse the standard organizational structures and much of the standard or boilerplate language, modifying the text with the specifics of each individual transaction. This saves the lawyer a great deal of tedious labor. For an inexperienced lawyer, using a standard form drafted by a more senior lawyer makes mistakes less likely. Because of the elimination of repetitive work and the confidence that comes from working with a document already successful in another transaction, form books have become an indispensable part of the lawyer's arsenal, and a resource with which every law student should become familiar. Moreover, they can alert the newcomer to some of the legal issues that need to be researched in an unfamiliar category of transaction or proceeding.

The publication of legal forms has a long and venerable history in Anglo-American law. In English law, one can find centuries-old examples of legal forms. By the time of the reign of the Tudors, the publication of books of forms, or of the inclusion of forms in legal treatises, was widespread and common. Lawyers practicing as, for example, conveyancers of land or drafters of wills relied heavily on form books to obviate the need to begin anew for each transaction or document. In America, even during the colonial era, lawyers, justices of the peace, sheriffs, and others used printed legal forms for a wide variety of transactions and pleadings.

Today, there are many different ways to find and use forms. As we will discuss below, there are a few standard, multi-volume form books in print that cover every aspect of legal practice imaginable, although in a very general way. There are also commercially available electronic collections of forms that serve as word processing templates for the practitioner. Law firms often collect a selection of forms and pleadings their lawyers have drafted over the years. In addition, the web is increasingly becoming a good resource for locating forms, although as with anything found on the web, you have to be very careful to check the reliability of your source.

7.2   A WORD OF CAUTION ABOUT FORMS

Although forms are, and always have been, a great boon and an important labor-saving device for lawyers, a word of caution is in order. Remember that forms are written in response to the requirements of the law in a specific transactional, jurisdictional, or procedural setting. No matter how seemingly official is the source of a form on which you want to rely, you must always check to see that the form comports with all of the requirements of the jurisdiction in which you are practicing. Moreover, you must always investigate to ensure that the form you plan to use is still current. In other words: laws change, rules change, and you have to be certain that the form you intend to use satisfies the requirements of the current version of that law or rule.

No matter the source, you can never substitute reliance on forms for your own research and investigation. Even in a law firm setting, where senior lawyers have drafted the pleadings or forms you want to use, it is incumbent upon you to make sure that you are satisfying the subject matter, currency, and procedural requirements of the situation you currently face.

7.3   GENERAL COLLECTIONS OF FORMS

While it is possible to find collections of forms on even the narrowest of topics, many lawyers prefer to consult the handful of general form sets. These often contain dozens of volumes and may be kept current with pocket parts. Forms found in these sets will usually be annotated with citations to cases construing the actual language or situation addressed by that form. Most law libraries of any size own one or more of the large sets described below. Most sets focus on either transactional forms (wills, leases, sales of real property, etc.) or on procedural forms (complaints, interrogatories, motions, and other pleadings), and a few of the major sets maintain this distinction, publishing two different collections, divided into a transactional set and a procedural set.

For example, the encyclopedia *American Jurisprudence 2d (AmJur2d)* (see **Section 6.3**), has spun off a number of complementary titles, including two large collections of forms. *American Jurisprudence, Legal Forms, 2d*, is the *AmJur2d* transactional collection of forms. This set covers a wide variety of transactional topics in a collection of over 60 books. The *AmJur2d* procedural collection is called *American Jurisprudence Pleading and Practice Forms Annotated*. Even more voluminous, this set checks in at more than 80 books, and contains examples of all manner of pleadings and motions forms. Both sets are carefully indexed and annotated, and are available in electronic format via Westlaw.

A competitor collection, also published by West, is commonly known overall as Nichols Forms. Again consisting of a transactional title and a procedural title, forms in Nichols are annotated, kept current with pocket parts, and attempt general coverage of all common legal forms. The procedural set, *Nichols Cyclopedia of Federal Procedure Forms*, contains annotated forms for motions and pleadings according to the rules of procedure for federal courts. The transactional form set, called *Nichols Cyclopedia of Legal Forms Annotated*, is probably the better known of the two. This set, which dates back to the 1930s, contains a wide variety of forms for common legal transactions such as wills, deeds, leases, and so on. It is also available on Westlaw.

A newer entrant to the field is *West's Legal Forms*. This set of mainly transactional forms contains nearly 70 books, is annotated (by West, and therefore coordinated with other West primary and secondary sources), thoroughly indexed, and supplemented with pocket parts. Again there is an associated procedural set, *West's Federal Forms,* covering both federal civil and criminal procedure. Unsurprisingly, both of these are also available on Westlaw.

On the web, there is a burgeoning list of free sites where one can find general legal forms. Again, it is absolutely vital to make sure that you can trust the source from which you are getting your forms, and that you conduct independent research sufficient to ensure that the form you intend to use is appropriate for your specific intended use. One of the better known is Findlaw Forms, at http://forms.findlaw.com. This is a portal site, hosting some forms available for purchase and linking out to free state and federal forms provided by the courts for both procedural and transactional subjects. A number of law school and university libraries have also begun to collect links to forms, from both official and unofficial sources, often with a focus on a particular jurisdiction. Two good examples are the Legal Forms page of the University of Denver's Colorado Law Project, at http://www.law.du.edu/index.php/the-colorado-law-project/legal-forms, and the Legal Forms page maintained by the Arizona State University law library at https://web.law.asu.edu/library/RossBlakleyLawLibrary/ResearchNow/ResearchGuides/LegalForms.aspx. Both link to a variety of government and open web resources that contain downloadable forms, with even more available for Colorado and Arizona, respectively. Courts, too, have begun to provide a greater wealth of electronic legal forms via the internet.

7.4   SUBJECT-SPECIFIC COLLECTIONS OF FORMS

In addition to the collections of general forms described above, there are many specialized form books containing forms for use by practitioners in areas as diverse as elder law (*ElderLaw Forms Manual*), securities (*Securities Regulations Forms*), and environmental law (*Environmental Law Forms Guide*). There are dozens more like this, in nearly every area of practice you can imagine. The reliability, currency and authority of these forms is, of course, always a question on which you will have to satisfy yourself before using any of these resources.

Do note that there are also forms included in many legal treatises. Often, a scholarly treatise will contain an appendix with representative forms. Examples include *International Child Abductions: A Guide to Applying the Hague Convention, with Forms* and *Land Use Practice and Forms: Handling the Land Use Cases*. There are, of course, hundreds of other examples in a wide variety of subjects. Often, treatises containing forms will say so in the title, but not always. It is wise, when examining treatises in an area of the law in which you need to conduct research, to note which ones contain forms that might prove useful to you later.

7.5   JURISDICTION-SPECIFIC COLLECTIONS OF FORMS

Many specific jurisdictions, usually at the state level, have collections of forms tailored to that jurisdiction's law. Most common are state-specific collections of procedural forms. Among the leading examples are *Carmody-Wait 2d Cyclopedia of New York Practice, With Forms*, a very important encyclopedia of New York procedural practice, and *West's Texas Forms, 2d*, widely used by Texas practitioners. Both of these titles are available in print and on Westlaw. Lexis also publishes a wealth of state-specific form collections, most under the Matthew Bender imprint. *Bender's Forms for the Consolidated Laws of New York*, for example, is an excellent resource that includes forms connected to particular New York statutes, and is available on Lexis Advance. There are others, even for these two specific jurisdictions, that are available in print, on Lexis Advance and/or Westlaw, and on the web via subscription. The point here is that reliable and useful collections of forms are readily available in a variety of formats.

There is also a selection of comprehensive collections of forms specifically focused on federal procedure. These form books track the federal court rules described in **Chapter 10** of this book. Many lawyers rely on these form books to help in drafting motions and pleadings when appearing before federal courts.

7.6   PATTERN JURY INSTRUCTIONS

One last category of form book merits a mention here. In civil and criminal jury trials, part of the judge's task is to instruct the jury on the applicable law before the jury retires to deliberate. It is often the case that the lawyers submit suggested jury instructions to the judge, from which he or she may fashion the instructions to be read. To help facilitate this process, collections of instructions that have already met with judicial approval have been published for many decades. It is now the case that there are pattern jury instruction sets for federal civil and criminal trials, as well as for virtually every state.

These pattern jury instructions can help lawyers and judges craft acceptable and appeal-proof jury instructions. It is the wise litigator who is familiar with the pattern jury instructions in the relevant jurisdiction and subject matter before beginning case preparation. In some sense, the outcome of trials often depends upon how the judge instructs the jury, and the careful lawyer prepares for this phase of the trial from the beginning.

Federal civil and criminal pattern or model jury instructions are readily available in print and online. Print sources include *Federal Jury Practice and Instructions* (also available on Westlaw) and *Modern Federal Jury Instructions* (also available on Lexis Advance). There are other print sources, including the *Model Jury Instructions* series produced by the American Bar Association, that contain jury instructions for specific areas of practice, such as patent litigation, civil antitrust, federal employment law, and so on. At the state level, practices vary, but a good starting place is the website of the National Center for State Courts, which maintains a portal at http://www.ncsc.org/Topics/Jury/Jury-Management/State-Links.aspx?cat=Model%20Jury%20Instructions with links to many model jury instructions provided by state courts.

CHAPTER 8

ADMINISTRATIVE LAW RESEARCH

• • •

8.1 INTRODUCTION TO ADMINISTRATIVE LAW RESEARCH

Traditionally, administrative law has been considered a highly complex field, one presenting special difficulties for the researcher. In this chapter we will discuss the sources of administrative law, the publication patterns of regulations and other documents related to the act of regulating, and show the ways in which lawyers practicing in heavily regulated areas conduct research and stay current with recent developments. Despite its reputation, research in administrative law is not especially difficult; it does, however, require mastery of techniques not usually taught in the typical first year legal research curriculum.

Broadly speaking, Congress is empowered to do two different things, make laws and delegate lawmaking power to other bodies. That delegated lawmaking is regulation. And to whom is this lawmaking (or, more properly, rulemaking) delegated? Congress delegates this power to executive branch agencies. In fact, several hundred of these agencies are empowered to make regulations. Some agencies are familiar, such as the Internal Revenue Service, the Food and Drug Administration, and the Department of Agriculture. Others are rather more obscure: the Local Television Loan Guarantee Board, for example.

Congress grants to each of these agencies the power to make and enforce rules on specific and limited topics. As we begin looking at the primary sources of regulation, notice that each unit of regulation contains something called an authority note, a citation to the particular place in the *United States Code* or *United States Statutes at Large* where that agency's authority to regulate on that specific topic was authorized by Congress. This will be discussed more fully in **Section 8.13**.

Agencies are not free to regulate as they please. It may seem strange to think of representatives of the executive branch performing what is essentially a legislative function. Surely, you might think, our general principle of separation of powers prohibits the executive branch from taking action that is, to all outward appearances, legislative. Constitutional problems, however, are avoided by the fact that Congress retains the power to approve, reject, or amend any regulation put forward by the regulating agency. In that way the agency is acting as the proxy of Congress, and Congress adopts and approves, usually tacitly, the regulation as if it had passed through the normal congressional lawmaking process. It may be a strange state of affairs, but this arrangement is a practical solution to an increasingly complex world in need of more oversight and detailed regulation than Congress can provide by itself.

What kinds of rulemaking does Congress delegate to executive branch agencies? What is the difference between the subject matter of federal laws and federal regulations? Can you tell whether a specific subject will be treated in the *United States Code* or the *Code of Federal Regulations*? These questions have no simple answers. In theory, Congress passes laws outlining principles, desired outcomes, general prohibitions and the like, and delegates to agencies the power to make rules to help implement Congressional will. In practice, the division is not so neat. In fact, it is not too much to say that there is no way to know with certainty whether any given topic will be dealt with by Congress, by an agency, or both. There are a variety of political, practical, economic, and other reasons why Congress makes the choices it does. For the researcher, it is enough to know that in order to thoroughly research any area of federal law it is necessary to look for both federal statutes and federal regulations.

In the following pages we will examine the *Federal Register*, the *Code of Federal Regulations* (or *CFR*), and other related publications that make up the primary sources of the administrative law world. The patterns of publication in this field should be familiar to you by now. First, there is a publication that tracks the developments of the field in chronological order. In administrative law this chronological publication is the *Federal Register*. Next, owing to the difficulty for the researcher in using the publication of record (with its chronological rather than topical arrangement) to determine what regulations exist on any topic, someone has to come along to rearrange that chronological material into subject order. In administrative law that subject arrangement is the *Code of Federal Regulations*. Next, there are judicial or quasi-judicial proceedings used to determine the meaning or application of the regulations in specific factual situations and/or cases in controversy. Hundreds of executive branch agencies hold such administrative hearings, and the federal courts can review their decisions in certain circumstances. Finally, there is a wealth of secondary sources used to explain the primary sources, advocate for particular interpretations or changes, serve as student or researcher aids, and so on. Thus, the materials the researcher has at his or her disposal in this field are roughly parallel to the materials used in the legal research subjects we have discussed up to this point. In fact, there are only a small number of ways to arrange and present legal information no matter what the subject matter may be. Administrative law materials, although facially different from more familiar federal statutes and cases, follow these same publication patterns.

With that short introduction as background, let's look at administrative law sources and their use in more detail. First, we will examine the primary sources themselves, paying particular attention to those specifics that experienced researchers seek out when faced with previously unfamiliar sources. Next, we'll discuss the methods of using those sources to determine what regulations exist, what they mean, how they fit together, and what impact they have on the research at hand. Finally, we will discuss how experienced practitioners in heavily regulated fields actually conduct legal research in their areas of administrative law, how they keep current, and what sources exist to help. That final topic of discussion will introduce you to the looseleaf, the subject of the following chapter, arguably the crowning achievement of the legal publishing world. By the time you've worked through this chapter's primary sources and the methods of their use, you will understand how critically important looseleaf publications are and why they arose in the form they did.

8.2   SOURCES OF ADMINISTRATIVE LAW: THE *FEDERAL REGISTER*

Regulations have been part of the legal landscape from the country's earliest days. Recognizing the need to enlist the executive branch in some aspects of rulemaking, Congress delegated certain rulemaking to its sister branch as far back as the 18th century. Until the early decades of the 20th century, however, the publication of executive agency regulations was haphazard and irregular. While this had been no more than a small inconvenience before the New Deal era, at that point the lack of reliable, timely, and accurate publication of regulations quickly escalated into an intolerable situation. In several oft-told stories of outrageous lack of governmental oversight, the government itself was mistaken as to the current state of regulation in particular areas. For a discussion of this sorry state of affairs, read *Government in Ignorance of the Law—A Plea for Better Publication of Executive Legislation*, 48 HARV. L. REV. 198 (1934). As currently with the issuers of much municipal regulation (e.g., most city and county building codes), federal agencies before the middle 1930s were under no obligation to publish their own regulations. Often, the only accurate copies of regulations then in force were held at the agency offices themselves.

When it eventually became apparent that this state of affairs could not be allowed to persist, Congress passed the first of several acts intended to make the texts of all federal regulations readily available and the patterns of publication transparent to all. The first legislative response to the need for publication of rules, the Federal Register Act, c. 417, 49 Stat. 500 (1935), required, among other things, the timely publication of all federal regulations.

The resulting publication, the *Federal Register*, has slowly evolved into the publication of today as the government worked out the details of just what should be published, in what format, and according to what arrangement. The story of this development has been told elsewhere, and is in any case not entirely pertinent to our purpose here, so we will jump ahead a few decades to what might be considered the modern era of the *Federal Register*. Researchers who find themselves conducting research in older regulations can consult Richard J. McKinney's web page "A Research Guide to the Federal Register and the Code of Federal Regulations," at http://www.llsdc.org/fr-cfr-research-guide. There is nothing particularly difficult about researching older regulations, but one must be prepared to commit a little time to becoming familiar with older usages and patterns.

The form of the *Federal Register* of today reflects its beginnings and a number of important evolutionary steps along the way. Several other federal laws, aimed, in part, at increasing the transparency of the regulatory process, have changed the substance and methodology of the *Federal Register*. Probably the most important piece of legislation in the area of administrative law is the Administrative Procedure Act, c. 324, 80 Stat. 237 (1946). This milestone legislation established the framework for modern administrative practice. The effect of this statute on the publication of federal regulations was profound; most notably, this law required agencies to publish notices of proposed rules in the *Federal Register* in order to give citizens a clearer understanding of the actions of agencies and a better opportunity to participate in the rulemaking itself. The Freedom of Information Act, P.L. 84–487, 80 Stat. 237 (1966), required agencies to publish much more detail about their structures, their activities, their rulemaking, and other information. The Sunshine Act, P.L. 94–409, 90 Stat. 1241 (1976), required agencies to hold open meetings and to publish notices about those meetings. Together, these Congressional acts and the resulting practices of agencies, lawyers, and the citizenry at large have led to today's *Federal Register*.

The *Federal Register* is published every business day of the year. In it, every federal agency empowered by Congress to make rules of general application must list every action they take, or plan to take, that might add, remove, or change regulations. As we will see, this description is only partial because a number of things find their way into the *Federal Register* apart from those described above. We will look at the constituent parts of each day's issue in order to fully understand this most important publication.

In recent years, the publication of the *Federal Register* has been overseen by the Office of the Federal Register, part of the National Archives and Records Administration. Early in the morning of each business day, that current day's *Federal Register* is made available electronically via FDsys at http://www.gpo.gov/fdsys/browse/collection.action?collection Code=FR. (For information on where else the *Federal Register* can be found, see **Table 8.A**). Note that federal law specifically states that this electronic version is as official as the printed version. Only in a very few select locations is the current day's printed *Federal Register* available (think of mailing times, for one thing) so for most researchers, the *Federal Register* for the current day is only available online. The official website of the online *Federal Register* contains a number of other useful features as well, including the full text (in .pdf files) of the *Federal Register* from 1990 (Volume 55) forward. The site also offers a number of different ways to search for specific citations or terms. Recently added is an email service for each day's Table of Contents, which some practitioners might find useful. Later in this section we will discuss the *Unified Agenda*. It, too, can be found online at FDsys.

Each day's *Federal Register* contains several different parts. It is critically important to understand the purpose of each section and the related finding aids and other user aids. It is our belief that it is very difficult, if not impossible, to effectively use the online versions of administrative law sources without achieving some fluency with the printed versions from which the electronic versions were derived. With that in mind, what follows is a short overview of the basic structure of the *Federal Register*, with an emphasis on the uses to which each section can be put.

The first thing to examine is the cover itself. Note the date and volume number. Each year begins a new volume, starting with the first business day of the year. In 2017, for example, the *Federal Register's* first issue of the year was January 3, which is Volume 82, Number 1. The page numbering is also worth noting. Each volume is through-paginated, meaning that each year (or each volume, which amounts to the same thing) the page numbering begins with issue number 1 and continues until the last page of the last issue of the year. In 2016, for example, the *Federal Register* ran all the way up to page 96,702. Why bother telling you about page numbering? The reason is that most finding aids (indexes, cross-references from other sources, and so on) will cite to a specific page of the *Federal Register*. But since the *Federal Register* is published in daily pamphlets, it is natural when standing in front of a shelf of printed *Federal Registers*, or browsing through the online versions, to think in terms of dates, not page numbers. We will see in **Section 8.17** that there are a number of aids to help you easily translate pages numbers into dates, and vice versa.

Each day's *Federal Register* contains a Table of Contents. The *Federal Register* prints information from a variety of executive branch agencies;

sometimes any one issue contains submissions from dozens of different agencies. The Table of Contents, in alphabetical order by agency, allows the researcher to quickly scan to see whether the agency he or she is concerned with has included any information of any sort in that day's *Federal Register*. To facilitate this current awareness use of the *Federal Register*, the Government Publishing Office has instituted an email listserv that each morning distributes that day's Table of Contents to subscribers (you can subscribe at https://public.govdelivery.com/accounts/USGPOOFR/subscriber/new). Presumably, the vast majority of these subscribers are lawyers, legislators, researchers, non-profit organizations, and others who need to stay current with the doings of one or more agency. There are also other ways to keep current with the rapidly changing world of federal regulation, methods to be discussed later in this chapter.

Near the beginning of each day's *Federal Register* is a chart titled "CFR Parts affected in this issue." The "parts" referred to are divisions of the *Code of Federal Regulations*. Although this concept, and the particulars of how to use lists of parts and sections affected, will be discussed fully in the section on the *Code of Federal Regulations* that follows, it is important to note here that this section exists. The reason is fairly obvious; if a practitioner is concerned with a narrow area of regulation as found in a particular part of the *CFR*, one way that practitioner might keep himself or herself current on any changes made or contemplated by the regulating agency would be to scan the list of parts affected each day to see if there is anything in that issue that pertains to the matter in which the practitioner is interested. At the back of every day's *Federal Register* there is a similar table listing the parts affected during the current month. This list is cumulative, building each day of the month until starting over on the first day of the next month. The use of this table should also be clear: that same practitioner can quickly determine if anything has been issued so far this month that might affect the issue or issues with which the practitioner is concerned. This cumulative list of parts affected is also a useful tool for the all-important task of updating sections of the *Code of Federal Regulations*, which will be discussed in more detail in the *CFR* section that follows.

After the preliminaries and Presidential Documents (such as new Executive Orders) when appropriate, the main body of each issue consists of agency information, divided into the different kinds of texts the agencies produce. A web of federal laws establishes the reporting obligations of rulemaking agencies, and it is these obligations that give the *Federal Register* its form.

8.3   RULES AND REGULATIONS SECTION OF THE *FEDERAL REGISTER*

The most significant section in each day's *Federal Register* contains the texts of new regulations, and is titled "Rules and Regulations." In the typical scenario, these new regulations have been proposed by the agency, undergone the public comment period, and been the subject of one or more open meetings or hearings to discuss public opinion about the regulation. With that process complete, the regulation is printed in its final form, complete with its effective date, its *CFR* citation, and other pertinent information. Final regulations are usually printed well in advance of their effective date.

Note that final regulations (as well as proposed regulations, discussed next) are written with reference to the *CFR*. They either contain a new *CFR* section number (if an entirely new section is being added) or the citation of an existing *CFR* section that is being altered or amended. Contrast this practice with the far less orderly practice of internal numbering within Congressional session laws, discussed in **Section 2.23**. Acts amending code sections in Titles that have been enacted into positive law cite code section numbers just as new and proposed regulations do. However, in acts affecting code sections in Titles not enacted into positive law, the practice is quite varied. Sometimes a bill is written with reference to the code section that may be affected, but often this is not the case. It is frequently the case that the text of the bill is numbered in outline form with no reference to the code structure at all, leaving it to the Office of the Law Revision Counsel to determine the impact on the code should that bill become law. The fact that new and proposed regulations are always written reflecting the *CFR* arrangement into which they will fit makes it easier for the researcher to evaluate the impact of a new or proposed regulation on the language currently in force.

The importance of this codification structure in the electronic era should be readily apparent. If every new regulation has as part of its language the place in the *Code of Federal Regulations* it will occupy as well as its effect on existing sections, it becomes easy to keep a constantly updated version of any particular *CFR* section. There is never any doubt about or interpretation of the current subject arrangement of regulations in any area. In fact, Westlaw, Lexis Advance, and the Office of the Federal Register itself now all offer versions of the *CFR* that are updated continuously. In **Section 8.18** we will take up the advantages and potential pitfalls of online versions of the *CFR* that are updated daily and do not match the official version in print. For now it is enough to know that such practice exists, and that it is the structure of new and proposed regulations in the *Federal Register* that makes it possible.

In the Rules and Regulations section of each day's *Federal Register*, it is the text of these rules that is, obviously, of paramount importance. However, be sure to note any other items of useful information published along with the new regulations. First, be sure to read the preamble to any group of regulations, if there is one. The preamble may contain a statement of the intended scope or interpretation of the entire section, definitions to be used throughout, or other textual clues that may help the researcher. In this sense it might be said that the preambles often serve as a kind of legislative history for regulations. One danger in regulatory research is that the preambles occasionally are not reproduced in the *CFR* and thus the researcher can miss them. Similarly, it is easy when searching through online versions of the *CFR* to retrieve a particular provision and not realize that there is a preamble associated with it, a preamble one needs to read in order to fully understand the specific section retrieved. Each *CFR* part will contain a source note directing the researcher back to the original publication of the regulation in the *Federal Register*, but it is not always evident that there is any reason to double check the *CFR* text by looking up what may prove to be identical language in the *Federal Register*. Looking for a preamble is one good reason to do so.

8.4   PROPOSED REGULATIONS SECTION OF THE *FEDERAL REGISTER*

The section containing new regulations is followed by the Proposed Rules section. Proposed rules are put forward constantly by agencies. Usually, there is an open comment period, during which members of the public, corporations, organizations, or anyone else can comment on the proposed rule. Even the smallest and seemingly least consequential amendment to a rule is treated as a proposed rule, as are, of course, entirely new regulations.

Proposed rules are always published in a stable and recognizable format. After the agency's name comes the citation of the *CFR* part or parts that will be added or changed if the rule becomes final. Then come parallel citations to other places the proposed regulation's text has been published, often an official publication of the agency itself. After that, one finds the title of the proposed rule, an identification of the type of action (e.g., "Notice of proposed rulemaking," "Notification; extension of comment period," "Proposed rule"), and then a short summary of its provisions. After the summary, the dates for submission of comments are listed, and then the address to which comments can be sent. One interesting recent development is that the government has established a website, at http://www.regulations.gov, where comments on proposed regulations can be submitted electronically. Previously, one had to send paper copies of comments to a specific address. The government has recently begun making most submitted comments available for viewing over the internet, but all comments can be viewed at one or more agency locations, which are listed in this part of the proposed regulation. Following the section related to comments are contact names, addresses, phone numbers and occasionally an email address to use when requesting further information. Finally, there may be special or supplementary information designed to aid the reader in understanding the proposed regulation or the process of its adoption and approval.

8.5   NOTICES SECTION OF THE *FEDERAL REGISTER*

The Proposed Regulations section is followed by the Notices section. There are a variety of notices one can find here. Various federal laws require publication of notices for open meetings to discuss proposed regulations (called Sunshine Act meetings in the *Federal Register*). In addition, this is the section in which one can find notices of expiring or expired regulations, technical corrections or amendments to previously published regulations, announcements of a general nature, and so on. It is difficult to categorize the many types of notices found here, but it is enough to know that most of these notices are of only ephemeral interest, and thus usually have little enduring value for the researcher.

8.6   READER AIDS SECTION OF THE *FEDERAL REGISTER*

At the end of each day's *Federal Register* appears the Reader Aids Section, which contains many of the most useful finding aids for the administrative law researcher. After a short listing of contact information for various services provided by the Office of the Federal Register and the Government Publishing Office, the researcher can find the two most important reader aids in the *Federal Register*: the *Federal Register* Pages and Date Table and the cumulative table of CFR Parts Affected this month.

The Pages and Dates Table allows the researcher to quickly translate *Federal Register* page numbers into dates. This makes retrieval of specific passages easier because, although pinpoint citations are always made to page numbers, it is easier to find issues by date, both in print and online, since the *Federal Register* is published each business day. You should note that in each day's *Federal Register* the table that appears contains only page numbers and dates from the current month. Sometimes the researcher armed with a page from previous months needs to determine the date on which that page number appears. To go back in time to before the first day of the current month, there is a cumulative annual table in every month's *List of Sections Affected* pamphlet, discussed in more detail in **Section 8.17**.

The table of CFR Parts Affected lists all of the *CFR* parts affected or even potentially affected by developments contained in the *Federal Register* issues produced in the current month. This table is the quickest way to see whether a particular *CFR* part has been changed recently or whether there is any recent proposed rule or other agency action that would affect that *CFR* part. The *List of Sections Affected* pamphlets (or the electronic equivalent) help a researcher update the *CFR* from the last time that Title was recodified and reprinted up to the date of the last *LSA* pamphlet, but from there the researcher needs to rely on this cumulative table in order to update the *CFR* language to the current day.

8.7 HOW THE *FEDERAL REGISTER* IS ACTUALLY USED IN LEGAL RESEARCH

Now that we have dissected and described the *Federal Register*, how does one use it? What do lawyers, law students, and others really do with the *Federal Register*? One obvious answer is that, like all chronological legal publications, the *Federal Register* serves as the publication of record. The *United States Statutes at Large* contains the exact texts of new public laws in chronological order as passed. So, too, with the *Federal Register*. Like other chronological publications, the *Federal Register* is used primarily for retrieval purposes. When one needs to see the text of, say, a final rule as it appeared when first adopted a decade ago, the *Federal Register* is the only option. Because the *CFR* is constantly updated and amended and rearranged into subject order, just like the *United States Code*, the *Federal Register* is usually the only place to find the original text in its original form. This retrieval function is useful more often than might be supposed. Many times cross-references from other primary or secondary sources are to *Federal Register* pages, not to *CFR* parts or sections. As noted above, preambles to new regulations occasionally are found only in the *Federal Register* version, not in the *CFR* section to which it gets codified. The administrative law researcher will need to know how to find *Federal Register* provisions in order to conduct effective research.

Another use researchers make of the *Federal Register* is as a current awareness tool. As mentioned above, there are several ways to keep current on specific topics by viewing each day's table of contents, the monthly index, or the *List of Sections Affected*. Many lawyers make use of one or more of these techniques to help monitor developments in a particular field. In the discussion of looseleaf services in **Chapter 9**, we will examine another, and potentially more powerful, way to do this.

A final feature of the *Federal Register* one should bear in mind is the twice-yearly publication of the *Unified Agenda*. Recent federal law (and a related Executive Order) mandated that each rulemaking agency publish twice each year a description of the regulations it is developing or has recently completed. These descriptions are published in the *Federal Register*, usually in April and October, and are known as the *Unified Agenda of Regulatory and Deregulatory Actions* (or *Unified Agenda*, for short.) The *Unified Agenda*, though not binding on the agencies, is a useful and generally quite accurate description of the next six months of regulatory action by each agency. This is a very important publication, and lawyers and other researchers often consult the most recent *Unified Agenda* to determine if the agency has any plans in the immediate future to alter specific regulations.

As might be apparent from the preceding paragraphs, the *Federal Register*, even though it is a critical primary source, is of limited utility for the administrative law researcher. Most regular research is conducted using the *Federal Register*'s cognate publication, the *Code of Federal Regulations*.

8.8   SOURCES OF ADMINISTRATIVE LAW: THE *CODE OF FEDERAL REGULATIONS*

The *Code of Federal Regulations* is the subject arrangement of regulations first printed chronologically in the *Federal Register*. This pattern should be very familiar to you by now; first chronological, then by subject. In this case, only a part of what appears in the *Federal Register* makes it into the *CFR*. Why is this the case? What appears in the *Federal Register* but is not included in each year's *CFR*?

If you will recall the discussion of the several sections of the *Federal Register* from the preceding pages, the answer will be relatively obvious. First, of course, there is no need to reprint the tables of contents, reader aids and such, as these are of only ephemeral importance. The daily and cumulative monthly lists of parts and sections affected are not reprinted in the *CFR*, but rather appear separately (in a slightly different format which we will discuss in **Section 8.17**) in monthly *List of Sections Affected* pamphlets. The Notices section, too, is of merely temporary interest since by the time the *CFR* is reprinted the dates and other items in the Notices section will be moot. Less obvious is that proposed regulations make no appearance in the *CFR*. This makes perfect sense on reflection, however. Unless the proposed regulation becomes final it has no legal force, so there is no need to codify it.

That leaves for inclusion in the *CFR* the final, new regulations published in the Rules and Regulations section of the *Federal Register*. All of the final rules except those of temporary duration (those that expire before the *CFR* Title in which they would otherwise appear is reprinted) are considered of general and permanent application. This is not to say that they apply to everyone or that they will not soon be superseded, mooted or eliminated, but only that these regulations will remain in force until some affirmative act in the future changes their status. It is these final regulations that get arranged into subject order, added to the appropriate section or part, then reprinted the next time the Title containing that section or part gets recodified. For information on where the *CFR* can be found, see **Table 8.B.**

8.9   *CFR* BASICS

The *CFR* is similar in form to other codes you have examined. It is divided into Titles, corresponding to broad subjects, then further subdivided into more manageable subcategories. There is an index that helps researchers find specific sections or topics. Tables of contents and a variety of other tables help the researcher access information in different ways. Each Title has a table of contents, many Titles have their own indexes, and the internal structure of each Title carries intellectual content. In all these ways, the *CFR* should remind you of other codes, but there are some important features to note that are unique to the *CFR*.

Specifically, the entire *CFR* is reprinted each year, according to a rolling schedule. Also, unlike many other codes, there is currently no annotated, commercially published complete version of the *CFR*, although there are several commercially published versions of the index, owing to the execrable and largely useless one volume index published with the official set. (The tables in that index volume, on the other hand, are quite useful, as discussed in **Section 8.15**.) The *CFR* is bound in paper, with a different color spine for each year, rather than being hardbound and updated with pocket parts or other supplements.

There are a few key concepts to understand before we turn to a discussion of how to use the *CFR*. We noted above the peculiar publication pattern of the Titles of the *CFR*. The entire code is reprinted each year, but roughly one fourth of the Titles are reprinted each quarter, in accordance with the schedule found in **Table 8.C**. This means that it is vitally important to check the cover of any *CFR* volume containing a relevant regulation. The cover will tell you the date when that particular volume was last recodified and reprinted. Updating (which we will discuss in subsequent paragraphs) must proceed from the date on the cover.

A related issue is that each year the *CFR* is given a new cover color; perhaps blue one year, red the next, green the year after that. It can be distressing for a novice researcher to approach the 250 or so volumes of the *CFR*, only to see that the spines are, for example, half red and half blue. On further inspection, the red spines have one year printed on them, the blue the previous year. What's gone wrong? Nothing. An illustration should help make things clear. Let's say that last year's *CFR* set had blue covers. Once the last of the reprinting is done, which would be after October 1 (see **Table 8.C**), the entire current set on the shelves is blue, every volume.

Then comes January 1, and the first revisions of the new year arrive in the library, with the new year's red covers. Now the first sixteen Titles have red covers and the rest, from last year but still current, have blue. After April 1, the next eleven Titles get reprinted with their red covers, and now the set, which consists of the most recently published volumes, is roughly half red and half blue. And so on throughout the year. To make it more complicated, the new volumes tend to be published and delivered to libraries a few at a time, so it is often the case that volumes even within any single Title have covers of different colors. This presents no problem for the updating tools, which track cumulative changes since the last time each particular section was reprinted.

Another peculiarity of the *CFR* is Title 3, which contains Presidential documents. (Given that the *CFR* is the place where executive branch agencies publish their regulations, it should not be surprising that at least some space should be given over to documents from the President, the chief executive.) Title 3 always has a white cover to set it apart from the other Titles. It is not cumulative as are the other Titles. Title 3 reprints in full the texts of all Presidential Proclamations, Executive Orders and other Presidential Documents (which include Administrative Orders, Reorganization Plans, Designations, and so on). There are also several parts that cover rules of the Executive Office of the President. Finally, Title 3 contains a number of tables that serve as finding aids to Presidential Documents. Note that all of this material is available in a variety of other locations, including the *Daily Compilation of Presidential Documents*, the *Weekly Compilation of Presidential Documents*, the *United States Statutes at Large*, the White House website (http://www.whitehouse.gov), commercial online services, and so on, but that *The Bluebook's* preferred source is Title 3 of the *CFR*.

8.10   STRUCTURE OF THE *CFR*

It is important to understand exactly how the *CFR* is arranged in order to be able to use this code effectively and efficiently. It is slightly different from other codes and other subject arrangements you have seen up to this point. One major difference is the way Titles are subdivided by issuing agency (more on that in the next few paragraphs.) Another difference is how the user updates a specific *CFR* section, which will be discussed in **Section 8.16**. On the whole, though, the arrangement, the indexing, the tables, and most other features will be familiar to users who have gained some fluency with the major statutory codes, such as the *United States Code*, one of its commercially annotated versions, or with a state code. Let's take a look at the *CFR* and its divisions: Titles, chapters, parts and sections.

8.11 TITLES OF THE *CFR*

Just like the *United States Code*, the *CFR* is divided into forty-nine major subjects, called Titles. It would be logical to assume that the 50 *CFR* Titles track wherever possible the subject matter of the 53 Titles of the *United States Code*, making a neatly parallel set of related subjects. It would be logical to assume that, but it would be wrong. Not completely wrong, maddeningly, but mostly wrong. For it is true that a few Titles of the *CFR* (Title 26, for instance, where regulations concerning taxation are found) match up with the *United States Code* (Title 26 is the Internal Revenue Code Title). There are a handful of other examples (see **Table 8.D**).

It should come as no surprise after a little reflection that the Titles don't track exactly. After all, Congress legislates and agencies regulate in some very different areas, and the Titles emanating from them reflect the differing ranges of subjects they each cover.

Remember from the above that each of the Titles is reprinted once per year according to a rolling schedule (see **Table 8.C**). How does this process work? It is actually simpler than one might guess, given that each year's *CFR* numbers well over 200 volumes. An illustration should help clarify this process.

Take Title 23—Highways, as an example. It is revised and reprinted on April 1 of each year. As of this writing, the current edition is the 2017 version, which was revised as of April 1, 2017. This softbound volume is, if you will, a snapshot of the regulations in force on one particular day, April 1, 2017. Understand that a new regulation may have gone into effect on April 2 (or any date in the year thereafter) that materially changed one section or another. In fact, part of the process of learning how to use the *CFR* has to do with updating a relevant section from the date of its last revision and republishing (the procedure for which is laid out in **Section 8.16**).

What will happen on April 1, 2018? Title 23 will be revised and republished. The compilers of the *CFR* will start from the text from the last printing, then revise it by taking into account any changes in the regulations made at any point during the intervening year. (These changes, of course, will have been noted in the *Federal Register* during the year). The compilers will add any new language and remove any repealed or expired language necessitated by agency (or Congressional or court) action. The resulting revision will then be printed. Remember that the April 1, 2018 revision will just be a snapshot view of the state of these regulations on that one day. On April 1 of the next year, the process will start all over again.

The only exception to the process described above is, you should recall, Title 3. This Title reprints Presidential Documents, including Presidential Proclamations, Executive Orders, and the like. It is not cumulative, a completely new Title 3 is begun each year. Since Title 3 is printed each January 1, it stands to reason that the Presidential Documents included are always from the previous calendar year.

8.12   CHAPTERS OF THE *CFR*

Each Title is divided into chapters, which represent different subjects addressed within the Title. In some cases, the result of this is that each of the agencies empowered to make regulations on that Title's subject matter has its own chapter. For example, in Title 20—Employees' Benefits, Chapter I contains regulations from the Office of Workers' Compensation Programs, Chapter II contains regulations of the Railroad Retirement Board, Chapter III has the Social Security Administration's regulations on the subject, and so on. Of course, it is not always so simple (no surprise there, right?), but that is the basic pattern. Notice that chapters are designated with roman numerals, not arabic numbers. This graphically differentiates the chapters encountered in this context from the two kinds of "chapter" rubrics used in the statutory context (see **Section 2.22**). As with statutes, very few of the finding aids that you will use actually cite to the chapters. They are really there to help organize the *CFR*, and to make clear to you the organization of each Title.

8.13   PARTS OF THE *CFR*

The chapters are further divided into parts. According to the *CFR* itself, the parts are subdivisions of the chapters and cover specific regulatory areas. It is probably useful to ignore chapters when thinking about the structure of the *CFR* and instead focus on Titles, subdivided into parts, then into sections. Each part has a descriptive name, then a table of contents-style listing of all the sections within that part, then the authority and source notes.

The authority note contains a citation (or series of citations) to the federal law or other action that gave that particular agency the authority to regulate on the specific subject matter with which the part is concerned. Usually, the citation is to a section of the *United States Code* or a provision of the *United States Statutes at Large*, but many other kinds of things can serve as authority. As an example, it is quite common for another *CFR* part or section to be listed in the authority note in addition to the more typical federal statute. This happens because one agency has deferred to another's authority, or delegated the rulemaking authority to another, or merely incorporated part of one agency's regulation into another.

The *CFR* index volume, which is not available on FDsys, contains a section called Parallel Tables of Authorities and Rules. The first three tables in the section contain cumulative lists of authorities for *CFR* parts from three different parallel citations: authorities in *United States Code* section order, *United States Statutes at Large* order, and finally, Public Law number order. By using these tables, the researcher can quickly determine if a specific code section or session law authorizes any current regulations. It is important for the researcher to be able to trace the development of a given *CFR* part in some cases, and the authority note is the place to begin.

The source note is the same concept as the source note after each section of the *United States Code*. The source note refers back to the source of the language contained in that *CFR* part. In almost every case the source cites the *Federal Register*, which is logical. Just as the source for a section of the *United States Code* is one or more public laws, so it is that the source for a *CFR* section is a new regulation printed in an issue of the *Federal Register*. The source citation, of course, allows the researcher to retrieve the original text of the language as printed in the *Federal Register* when it was first adopted. It is common for the source note to cite a *Federal Register* issue, then say "unless otherwise noted." That simply means that one or more sections within that part came from a different source (it was added later, for instance) than the rest of the part. The differing source will be noted after the individual section to which it applies.

8.14 SECTIONS OF THE *CFR*

Finally, we arrive at the section, the basic unit of regulation. In theory, the section represents one discrete topic, one indivisible idea or command. Researchers used to the general (or occasionally even vague) language of federal statutes are surprised by the specificity and granularity of the *CFR* section. It is sometimes hard to believe the level of detail. Regulations concerning drawbridges, for example, list each drawbridge under federal jurisdiction in a separate section, complete with information specific to that bridge. For those dying to know, the drawbridge over the Tuckahoe River will open on signal if at least 24 hours notice is given (33 C.F.R. § 117.758). It is in the sections that the researcher will find the answers to most research questions in administrative law.

8.15 HOW TO USE THE *CFR*

How, then, to use the *CFR*? Beginning researchers may find it a little daunting, but the truth is that after mastering a few concepts and techniques even a relative novice should be able to conduct effective research using the *CFR*. The steps are really quite simple.

The first thing a researcher must do is locate relevant *CFR* citations. There are a variety of ways to do this. This is relatively simple when the researcher sets out to discover whether there are any regulations on a specific topic. In that case, the *CFR* index is probably the place to start. The *CFR* index, as discussed above, is not without its problems, but a persistent researcher willing to spend a little time with the index can usually find what he or she seeks.

It is not unlikely that the researcher began by identifying a federal statute on point. If there is one, one approach for finding associated regulations would be to look in the Parallel Tables of Authorities and Rules in the *CFR* index. Annotations to statutory code sections often contain references to associated *CFR* sections. Or, if the researcher feels a full-text search might be effective, he or she can conduct a full-text search in the online *CFR*s available through Lexis Advance, Westlaw, Bloomberg Law, HeinOnline, or on the web via FDsys or the e-CFR (see **Section 8.18**).

When relying on full-text searches, researchers must take care that they don't commit a common error; the error of false precision. The danger is that one might find a section with language that seems to address the question, but because browsing is difficult online, the researcher doesn't take the time to determine where that section fits in the scheme of the entire part or chapter. One runs the risk of ignoring other sections whose meaning bears on the interpretation or application of the one found with the online search. It seems like a small risk, but that's deceptive. It is more common than most researchers think that two or more sections must be read together to completely understand the full meaning of the rule. This is not an exhortation never to use online *CFR*s, only a warning to take care. In statutory or regulatory interpretation and research, context is critical.

Once the specific section has been identified, its context examined, and the other textual clues and references followed, the researcher must then update the section from the date of the last revision. It is possible to update any section to the current day.

8.16 UPDATING A *CFR* SECTION

As discussed above, *CFR* sections are revised and reprinted each year, and the date of the last revision is printed on the cover of every individual *CFR* volume. If the researcher is interested in, say, 23 CFR 751.11, he or she should note that (as of this writing) the current print version was published on April 1, 2017. This section is:

Title 23—Highways

    Part 751—Junkyard Control and Acquisition

        Section 751.11—Nonconforming junkyards

Note also that this section is part of Chapter I—Federal Highway Administration, Department of Transportation, and Subchapter H—Right-of-Way and Environment. Remember, though, that chapters and subchapters are ordinarily contextual clues, and rarely are included in citations.

The process for updating 23 CFR 751.11 from its last publication, April 1, 2017, until today, is mechanical and simple, but takes a little explanation. If you recall from the discussion above, in each issue of the *Federal Register* there is published a list of parts affected, cumulative for the month to date. One could update our *CFR* section by looking at the list of parts affected every day from April 1, 2017 until today. A little further thought will suggest a shortcut; since each day's list is cumulative, one could look at the parts affected list in the last issue of each month since April. Why would this work? By looking at the table in the last April issue, you can see whether anything that appeared in the *Federal Register* that month had any impact on Title 23, Part 751. Then one could check the table in the last May issue for all of May's potential changes to this part, then June, and so on. Arduous, but ultimately effective.

8.17   A BETTER WAY: THE *LIST OF SECTIONS AFFECTED*

Fortunately, there is a far easier way. Each month, the government publishes a thin pamphlet called the *List of Sections Affected* (*LSA*). This pamphlet contains a table with citations to every *Federal Register* issue that affected any individual section of the *CFR* since the last time it was published. Thus, the October *LSA* contains citations to every *Federal Register* issue that affected any section in Title 5 since January 1 (when it was last published), that affected any section in Title 23 since April 1 (when it was last published), and so on for all forty-nine Titles. (*LSAs* from 1997 until the present are also available at http://www.gpo.gov/fdsys/browse/collection.action?collectionCode=LSA).

This means that to update 23 CFR 751.11 from April 1 until the last day of last month (when the last pamphlet was issued), all the researcher needs to do is check last month's LSA. If this section isn't listed as having been affected, the regulation was still in force at the end of last month. That leaves the problem of updating from the last day of last month until today. But that's easy. All that is necessary is a check of the cumulative list of parts affected in the back of today's issue of the *Federal Register*. That will show if anything this month has affected this part.

Note that the *LSA* tracks changes to sections, and the cumulative daily list in the *Federal Register* only tracks to the level of the part. Thus the daily table is a slightly blunter instrument than the *LSA*. This usually doesn't present a serious problem since the researcher rarely has to consult multiple issues in the current month. Remember, too, that the citations in the *LSA* and in the cumulative daily tables are citations to page numbers in the *Federal Register*. One must take the additional step of translating the page numbers to dates, but there is a table to allow just this on the same page as the daily parts affected table, and inside the cover of every *LSA*. When searching online, this presents less of a problem since it is easy to retrieve any particular page or range of pages.

What does one do if, when updating, it becomes clear that one or more days of the *Federal Register* must be consulted because the *LSA* has indicated that your section has been affected? First, obviously, you must retrieve the cited issues of the *Federal Register* and read the relevant language. If, for example, the citation was only to a proposed regulation that was never made final, the *CFR* section was not really changed, so the researcher can probably ignore the proposed regulation and simply rely on the language in the *CFR*. What to do, though, if sometime after April 1, say in the January 3 issue of the *Federal Register*, a new regulation became final, and that regulation made important changes to 23 CFR 751.11? If that is the case, the researcher has to revise the language himself or herself. What was amended, deleted, replaced, or altered? This can sometimes present issues of interpretation, but the updating language will always make clear exactly what changes have been made to the existing regulation.

In the online environment, there are electronic versions of all of these publications: the Parallel Tables, the *LSA*s, and the *Federal Register* and the *CFR*. On Lexis Advance, Westlaw, and at the FDsys website, one can update the *CFR* electronically in precisely the same way as one would with the print equivalents. Lexis Advance and Westlaw also have "current" versions of the CFR available in their platforms. Current in the previous sentence is in quotes intentionally, as the actual currency of the products varies, but often is not updated daily. Both products occasionally have a day or multiple-day lag, though Lexis Advance seems to be slightly more current than Westlaw. There is, however, a free alternative that simplifies the entire process.

8.18   e-CFR WITH ROLLING UPDATES

Because of the way that new regulations are written, with specific citations to the existing *CFR* language into which they will fit, it is possible to maintain a constantly updated *CFR*. Each day the compiler of the e-*CFR* can take the new regulations from that day's issue of the *Federal Register*, and directly revise the affected *CFR* section without awaiting the next publication according to the rolling schedule of publication of print Titles.

The benefits of this arrangement are obvious. Manually updating a printed *CFR* section is simple and mechanical, but it does involve a few steps and requires the researcher to consult several different publications. With the e-*CFR*, there is no need to update at all, as long as the researcher checks carefully how currently updated that version is. It is even possible for researchers who prefer to conduct research (and read the results) in the print *CFR* to update that section online by retrieving the relevant section to see if the text has changed since the print volume was revised and reprinted.

There are a few potential pitfalls to be aware of. First, there is the problem of accuracy. It may be that this updating, unofficial as it is, may not be as accurately or carefully performed as one would like. Second, there is the problem of currency. Has the compiler of the rolling updates kept current? The GPO's e-*CFR* boasts that the Office of the Federal Register updates the material in the e-CFR on a daily basis. Some days, however, there is still a day lag before material from the Federal Register is fully incorporated. Third, it should be noted that, because of the rolling updates, a *CFR* section that one finds may appear in a form that doesn't match any official version of the *CFR*. The print version and the .pdf version of the *CFR* available at the FDsys website are official, but any other version, especially one that features commercially prepared updates, is unofficial. That's not necessarily a problem, but one must keep it in mind.

8.19 ADMINISTRATIVE HEARINGS AND OTHER QUASI-JUDICIAL PROCEEDINGS

In addition to making regulations, administrative agencies are often empowered to hold adjudicative hearings. The hearings may be as informal as a consultation with a member of agency staff, or may be as formal as any court proceeding, with a judge or panel of judges, witnesses, depositions, briefs, evidentiary standards, and all of the trappings familiar from federal court litigation. In very general terms, there are two different hearing systems commonly employed by executive branch agencies.

In one system, of which employment discrimination hearings are an example, the agency itself is the first arbiter of claims that one or another of its regulations has been violated. In the case of employment discrimination, there is a multi-layered series of hearings prescribed by the regulations. These hearings can be investigatory or adjudicative, punishments can be meted out, settlements approved, and all of the other kinds of actions more traditional courts can undertake. After the parties have progressed through all of the layers of review (called "exhausting one's administrative remedies" by courts and commentators), parties have the right to appeal the findings to the appropriate federal court. This system is most commonly found in areas where the agency itself is unlikely to be one of the parties.

The other system, of which tax litigation is an example, provides a roughly co-equal forum along with federal courts for litigating disputes between a citizen and the government, usually the agency itself. This is far less common, as you might imagine. In the case of tax litigation, in certain circumstances, the citizen can choose to bring suit in the United States Tax Court, in the local federal District Court, or in the United States Court of Federal Claims.

Publication of administrative decisions is irregular at best. Generally speaking, there are three different ways that agency decisions are made available to researchers: on the agency's website, in official publications of the agency, or in commercial publications. It is increasingly common for agencies to make hearing decisions available on their websites. You should know, however, that often these decisions are reproduced with no indexes or finding aids, and are usually arranged only by date or party name. There is rarely any kind of subject access to these decisions. A few agencies publish their decisions in official reporters or other publications of that agency. These publications often have better finding aids than web versions. When agency decisions are published commercially, often in looseleaf form, they usually have good indexes and other finding aids.

There is no comprehensive list of which agencies hold administrative hearings and where to find the resulting decisions. For researchers interested in a particular agency, by far the best first step is to examine that agency's website. Failing that, specialized legal research publications can often help. One helpful place to begin an investigation into whether an agency conducts its own judicial or quasi-judicial hearings, and where the results of those hearings are reported, is *Specialized Legal Research*, edited by Penny Hazelton, published by the Gallagher Law Library at the University of Washington School of Law, which describes and provides citations to the official and commercial publications in a variety of heavily regulated legal fields. Westlaw, Lexis Advance, and Bloomberg Law also have reports of decisions from a variety of agencies, and can be useful places to search. Law librarians, of course, also have experience finding these publications and can usually help.

Why would these decisions be so hard to locate? And why are researchers so ill-served by the kind of indexing and other subject access tools that would make them easy to use? In part, the answer stems from the nature of administrative hearings. Unlike courts, administrative agencies generally are not bound by prior decisions. Lawyers doing a thorough job of researching will examine past decisions, however, and urge the agency to follow this or that line of decisions, or depart from it, as the case may be. Agencies have shown a marked tendency to consider their own decisions to be fact-specific and limited in scope to the case and the parties involved in that hearing. They are, therefore, less willing to take pains to ensure that every decision is published and made available to researchers.

Since lawyers make use of this material anyway, it is wise for the researcher to be aware that the agency issuing any particular regulation may well have considered its application or interpretation in a quasi-judicial opinion and released an opinion on the subject. Thorough administrative law research requires a search of these decisions.

8.20 STATE ADMINISTRATIVE LAW RESEARCH

Just as every state has its own legislature, session laws, and code, each state also has its own regulatory agencies with their resulting publications. It is often necessary for the researcher with a state law problem to consult state administrative registers and codes. The publication patterns are very similar to the federal system, but there are some important differences to know about.

State legislatures delegate rulemaking to state agencies the same way Congress delegates to federal agencies. In the state systems, the pace of regulation is slower, and one finds markedly less commitment to publishing absolutely everything. A few words are in order, then, about what the state administrative researcher will have available with which to complete his or her research.

There are state registers that serve the same function as the *Federal Register*. Often published monthly, these state registers typically contain the texts of new regulations along with some notices and other information. Almost every state makes their registers available at the state government website, so finding them is quite easy. They are not, unfortunately, thorough or timely enough to be very useful to the researcher.

States also take the final regulations from their registers and publish them in subject arrangement. These administrative codes, which different states call by a bewildering variety of names, serve the same purpose as the *CFR*. Some are published without any indexing at all, some are published only irregularly, some are available on the state government website, some are not; every possible practice seems to have at least one adherent. The administrative codes of many states are now commercially published, which has helped regularize the publication schedule and has improved the indexes and finding aids. Keeping in mind the need to check currency, there are state administrative codes for each state available on Lexis Advance, Westlaw, and Bloomberg Law.

The point is that once you understand federal administrative research, you can conduct state administrative research even though the tools at your disposal are not as current, thorough, or well indexed. A researcher typically approaches the state administrative code with a topic or a state law in hand. Using the index (if there is one) or table of contents or whatever aid comes with the set, the researcher finds the relevant regulation. Updating is done by checking the state administrative register, which in most cases has nothing like the *LSA* to help. It is common for state administrative codes to contain contact information with each chapter or Title. In order to be confident that you have thoroughly updated your section, it might be necessary to call or otherwise contact the person or office listed. This seeming informality is typical of administrative law practice in many states.

There are state administrative topics that are covered in much greater detail; most notably, taxation. State tax laws are covered by looseleafs and other publications, and it is therefore possible to conduct research very similar in scope and depth to federal tax research, without having to rely on state primary source publication.

Even though states do not expend as much time or energy publishing each day's administrative activity, it is still possible to conduct effective research in state administrative law. The researcher needs to be a little creative and a little diligent, but the tools are there, and they bear a strong resemblance to the more familiar tools of federal research.

8.21 TABLES

TABLE 8.A: WHERE TO FIND
THE FEDERAL REGISTER

1. *Federal Register*, Government Publishing Office (1936–)

   Available in microfiche as well as paper.

2. FDsys:

   http://www.gpo.gov/fdsys/browse/collection.action?collection Code=FR (1990–) (Available in .pdf, .xml, and plain text files. Indexes are not included.)

3. Westlaw:

   Proposed & Adopted Regulations > Proposed & Adopted Regulations—All under "Tools & Resources" on the right > Federal Register

   (Files are in star-paginated text format. The *Federal Register* indexes are not included.)

4. Lexis Advance:

   Federal > Federal Register

   (1980–) (Files are in star-paginated text format. The *Federal Register* indexes are not included. You can also access this by typing "fedreg" as a shortcut in the main search box.)

5. HeinOnline:

   Federal Register Library (1936–) (Subscription-based database, with .pdf files. Includes all *Federal Register* indexes.)

6. Bloomberg Law:

   Browse All Content > Laws & Regulations > Regulatory Resources > Search Federal Register

   (1964–) (Subscription-based database, with .pdf files.)

TABLE 8.B: WHERE TO FIND THE
CODE OF FEDERAL REGULATIONS

1. *Code of Federal Regulations*, Government Publishing Office (1938–)

    In addition to the print edition, the GPO also republishes the *CFR* in a microfiche set.

2. FDsys:

    http://www.gpo.gov/fdsys/browse/collectionCfr.action?
    collectionCode=CFR (1996–) Available in .pdf, .xml, and plain text files. Tables and LSA pamphlets are available, indexes are not.

3. Westlaw:

    Regulations > Code of Federal Regulations (CFR) > Code of Federal Regulations—Historical (1984–)

    Files are in star-paginated html format, with each year searchable separately. The current year's *CFR* is updated on a rolling basis, prior years follow the printed version. *LSA* pamphlets are not included.

4. Lexis Advance:

    Federal > CFR—Code of Federal Regulations

    The current year's *CFR* is updated on a rolling basis. *LSA* pamphlets are not included.

    Archives > Archived Code Search > Administrative Codes

    Coverage begins with 1981. LSA pamphlets are not included.

5. E-CFR:

    https://www.ecfr.gov

    Current year only. It is updated on a rolling basis, and is not official. *LSA* pamphlets are not included.

6. HeinOnline, Code of Federal Regulations Library (1938–)

    Subscription-based database, with .pdf files. *LSA* is included from 1958 to present year.

7. Bloomberg Law:

    Browse All Content > Laws & Regulations > Code of Federal Regulations (Current year only) Subscription-based database with text only.

TABLE 8.C: DATES OF ANNUAL REVISION OF *CFR* TITLES

CFR Titles	Dates of Annual Revision
Titles 1–16	January 1
Titles 17–27	April 1
Titles 28–41	July 1
Titles 42–50	October 1

TABLE 8.D: TITLES OF *U.S.C.* AND *CFR* COMPARED

	United States Code	Code of Federal Regulations
Title 1	General Provisions	General Provisions
Title 2	The Congress	Grants and Agreements
Title 3	The President	The President
Title 4	Flag and Seal, Seat of Government, and the States	Accounts
Title 5	Government Organization and Employees	Administrative Personnel
Title 6	Domestic Security	Domestic Security
Title 7	Agriculture	Agriculture
Title 8	Aliens and Nationality	Aliens and Nationality
Title 9	Arbitration	Animals and Animal Products
Title 10	Armed Forces	Energy
Title 11	Bankruptcy	Federal Elections
Title 12	Banks and Banking	Banks and Banking
Title 13	Census	Business Credit and Assistance
Title 14	Coast Guard	Aeronautics and Space
Title 15	Commerce and Trade	Commerce and Foreign Trade
Title 16	Conservation	Commercial Practices
Title 17	Copyrights	Commodity and Securities Exchanges
Title 18	Crimes and Criminal Procedure	Conservation of Power and Water Resources
Title 19	Customs Duties	Customs Duties
Title 20	Education	Employees' Benefits
Title 21	Food and Drugs	Food and Drugs
Title 22	Foreign Relations and Intercourse	Foreign Relations
Title 23	Highways	Highways
Title 24	Hospitals and Asylums	Housing and Urban Development

	United States Code	**Code of Federal Regulations**
Title 25	Indians	Indians
Title 26	Internal Revenue Code	Internal Revenue
Title 27	Intoxicating Liquors	Alcohol, Tobacco Products and Firearms
Title 28	Judiciary and Judicial Procedure	Judicial Administration
Title 29	Labor	Labor
Title 30	Mineral Lands and Mining	Mineral Resources
Title 31	Money and Finance	Money and Finance: Treasury
Title 32	National Guard	National Defense
Title 33	Navigation and Navigable Waters	Navigation and Navigable Waters
Title 34	Crime Control and Law Enforcement	Education
Title 35	Patents	[Reserved][*Formerly* Panama Canal]
Title 36	Patriotic and National Observances, Ceremonies, and Organizations	Parks, Forests, and Public Property
Title 37	Pay and Allowances of the Uniformed Services	Patents, Trademarks, and Copyrights
Title 38	Veterans' Benefits	Pensions, Bonuses, and Veterans' Relief
Title 39	Postal Service	Postal Service
Title 40	Public Buildings, Property, and Works	Protection of Environment
Title 41	Public Contracts	Public Contracts and Property Management
Title 42	The Public Health and Welfare	Public Health
Title 43	Public Lands	Public Lands: Interior
Title 44	Public Printing and Documents	Emergency Management and Assistance
Title 45	Railroads	Public Welfare
Title 46	Shipping	Shipping

	United States Code	**Code of Federal Regulations**
Title 47	Telecommunications	Telecommunication
Title 48	Territories and Insular Possessions	Federal Acquisition Regulations System
Title 49	Transportation	Transportation
Title 50	War and National Defense	Wildlife and Fisheries
Title 51	National and Commercial Space Programs	
Title 52	Voting and Elections	
Title 53	[Reserved]	
Title 54	National Park Service and Related Programs	

CHAPTER 9

INTRODUCING SECONDARY SOURCES: LOOSELEAF SERVICES

▪ ▪ ▪

9.1 INTRODUCTION: WHAT THIS CHAPTER IS ABOUT

Why devote an entire chapter to looseleaf services? Are they still relevant in the digital age? Why do many practitioners rely on them so heavily? Why are they so large, complex, and hideously expensive? What kinds of legal subjects are covered by looseleafs? Good questions, all.

Looseleafs merit an entire chapter because they dominate legal research in the areas they cover. An extremely clever innovation, looseleafs gather primary and secondary sources together, arrange them in a useful way, add editorial commentary, and, unlike many other secondary sources, update the material frequently, all of which saves the researcher or practitioner a great deal of time and effort. And, at least for now, they are still an important part of legal research, even as more resources move online. While some looseleaf publications now have an electronic equivalent, there are still certain publications that exist only in print, and most electronic looseleaf interfaces leave much to be desired.

Arguably the biggest difference between looseleafs and other secondary sources is the inclusion of fully reprinted relevant primary sources. For those researchers who grew up with the internet, it may be tough to imagine a time when one piece of material did not link directly to another. But once upon a time, treatises, for instance, didn't include hyperlinks to the statutes they cited. It took more than a simple mouse click to move from the journal article about a case to the full text of that case. In most areas, before the migration to electronic sources, research involved reading a secondary source, writing down the citation of a relevant primary source (e.g., case, statute, regulation) referenced in that secondary source, and then going to a different set of books to read the primary source in its entirety. That same process is still followed today, except that steps two and three happen with a click of the mouse.

Conceptually, looseleafs were the precursor to this electronic format because they sought to streamline the research process by including the full text of relevant primary sources within the looseleaf itself. The full text of that statute or case wasn't a mouse click away, but instead a mere flip of the page. Acting as a portal to all of the relevant information on a given subject, looseleafs carved out a devoted following and quickly became a favorite resource among practitioners who prized efficiency. Even today, when researchers can quickly move back and forth between secondary and primary materials online, the looseleaf has another feature that allows its value in print to remain significant—the index.

While any secondary source worth its salt will include a good index, the indexes of looseleafs have traditionally been a cut above the rest. This may be in part because they were born of the desire to create a single comprehensive resource. If the practitioner has learned that whatever is sought exists somewhere in this large set, it behooves the publisher to create an index that allows the looseleaf to be of maximum usefulness as a first—and last—stop. Whatever the reason, the index accompanying a print looseleaf offers a greater level of detail and granularity than most other common resources. Unfortunately, at least at the time of this writing, publishers have been exceedingly reluctant to include the excellent indexes as part of their electronic products. The result, of course, is that the researcher has to rely solely on keyword searching within the full text of the looseleaf.

If you are an expert in the field or have a term of art that is relevant in one and only one possible instance, the lack of an index may be a modest inconvenience; you'll still get to the material you need, with only small inefficiencies. If, however, you have only general language as possible search terms or you are not intimately familiar with the looseleaf or the subject matter, then the lack of an index poses a much bigger problem. Because the looseleaf material is designed to be as close to comprehensive as possible, it means a keyword search is likely to generate a large volume of hits; the answer you are seeking is in there somewhere, but there's a lot to wade through to find it. Though the relevancy algorithms used in the electronic format are impressive in their own right, they are not yet near the same level as the human indexer familiar with the subject matter. If you forgo the use of the index, you're either uncritically accepting the top results returned by the algorithm or spending time going through multiple pages of results and thereby losing the efficiency benefit of the looseleaf—its primary purpose for existing.

Having said that, print looseleafs can be a little tricky to use at first for the uninitiated, and many students find themselves a little overwhelmed when faced with a twenty volume set of looseleaf binders. We will try to demystify these publications, and will argue that a few minutes spent familiarizing yourself with a new looseleaf can save you a great deal of research time later.

Practitioners rely on looseleaf services for a number of reasons and in a variety of ways. First, lawyers use the frequent (often weekly print or daily online) updates to stay current with developments in their field. Second, this frequent updating means that the lawyer need not spend time worrying about the currency of every statute, every case, or every paragraph of commentary he or she finds. The publisher of the looseleaf takes care of the currency issues. Third, as mentioned above, the looseleaf service draws together relevant material from a great variety of sources, which is something the average lawyer has no time to do in a busy practice. Fourth, the looseleaf's collocation and topical arrangement of related material from a variety of sources gives the lawyer a contextual framework from which to proceed. It would be a very foolish lawyer who would substitute a looseleaf editor's judgment for his or her own, but the looseleaf service at least provides the background and context within which to work, imposing some order on the vast universe of primary and secondary sources on any given subject.

Looseleafs are so large, complicated, and expensive because of the labor-intensive manner of their production. In order to achieve all of the benefits described in this chapter, the publisher has to commit vast resources to the retrieval, arrangement, publication, distribution, etc., of new material, often on a daily or weekly schedule. In the print version of an interfiled looseleaf, described below, the publisher sends replacement pages, typically each week, updating the entire set with new developments since the last release. That might include new cases, new statutes, new regulations, new editorial commentary, new index entries, new finding aid entries, and so on. It must all be typeset, new pages printed, instructions for filing produced, and then arranged, packaged, and shipped as a single unit. Every week. If looseleafs weren't so thorough, so complete, so timely, and so useful, no one would be willing to pay the high price of production. Looseleafs are usually the most expensive titles in the law library, and for those who know how to use them, their cost is fully justified.

Not all legal subjects are covered by looseleafs. Indeed, most are not. Why not, if they're so useful? The answer has to do with the particular strengths of the looseleaf: currency and the gathering of a wide variety of primary and secondary sources. Looseleafs tend to flourish in heavily regulated legal subjects such as taxation, labor and employment law, environmental law, securities law, and the like. The previous chapter's discussion of administrative law should have made plain how time-consuming this research can be. The *CFR* and *Federal Register* are not especially difficult to use, but neither are they particularly simple or quick. Administrative hearings can be difficult to locate and often are published without finding aids. Statutes and regulations interact in unpredictable and odd ways, and the relationship between the administrative hearing process and the state and federal courts can be hard to figure out. In just these areas of law are looseleafs powerful antidotes to the complex and unwieldy nature of the underlying sources. Practitioners and other researchers rely on looseleafs to help ease the burden of complex research.

All of this is not to say that looseleafs exist in only the heavily regulated areas of law. Many legal topics have at least one publication in looseleaf format. State jury instructions, for example, are often published in looseleaf form. These looseleafs, and others like them, don't really require weekly updating, are not compiled from a dozen different primary sources, and are not fifteen or twenty volumes in length. Many looseleaf publications are in that form for the simple convenience of replacing old pages with new, without having to discard volumes or pocket parts or supplement pamphlets. There are easy ways to find looseleafs by title, publisher, subject, or means of access, which we will discuss later in this chapter.

9.2   WHAT ARE LOOSELEAFS USED FOR?

There are several situations in which a looseleaf can save the researcher an enormous amount of time. In fact, it is not too much to say that there are certain types of research in specific areas of law that would be so unwieldy and time-consuming to complete using only primary sources as to be almost impracticable. This may seem at first glance to be an extreme claim, but these examples are not as uncommon as you might suppose.

Looseleafs are used in situations where the particular advantages they contain can be used to greatest advantage. Knowing the ways in which the looseleaf is more convenient than the disparate primary and secondary sources from which it is made will make clear why looseleafs in several legal areas have largely supplanted traditional legal research in primary sources. Looseleafs gather the relevant primary and secondary material from different sources, present it in a meaningful arrangement, provide superior indexes and other finding aids, and then *update that material frequently.*

Probably the most valuable thing looseleaf services offer the researcher is that they bring together a targeted collection of relevant full-text primary sources in one place. To illustrate the value of this, imagine for a moment a research question involving an issue of federal taxation. Say that the question involves the tax treatment of a "wash sale." Without a looseleaf service available, the researcher may have to follow a number of steps to find the information. First, he or she might have to consult a legal dictionary to find out the definition of the phrase "wash sale." After determining this, the researcher might consult an annotated federal code in an attempt to find the provision covering this topic. The wash sale rule might be found in the *United States Code*, in which case the researcher would then have to consult the *CFR* to find if there are related regulations, then look in treatises or other material for an explanation of the language in the statutes and regulations. After all that, the researcher might try to find cases interpreting the law, law review articles discussing the application of the law, pending bills or proposed regulations that might affect the law, and so on. Then, at the end, the researcher would have to take steps to update the material reviewed, using the updating method for each different type of source. Clearly, this is an arduous and time-consuming process.

Using a looseleaf service obviates the need to consult all of these different resources because the publishers have done that for you. In the case of the wash sale, the researcher would look up the words in the index, then turn to the appropriate page or paragraph number. There the researcher will find the statute from Title 26 of the *United States Code*, the regulations from Title 26 of the *CFR*, other interpretive rules or guidance from the issuing agency, explanatory or illustrative text written by the looseleaf's editors, citations to secondary sources for further explanation, and so on. All of this appears in one place in the looseleaf, making it truly "one stop shopping" for legal information.

Unlike other secondary sources, looseleafs also have the added advantage of currency. Many interfiled looseleafs (we will discuss the different types of looseleafs below) are updated once per week. Given that most primary and secondary sources are updated much less frequently (some being literally years out of date), it is obvious that researchers can make great use of the currency of looseleaf sources. It is true that the advent of large databases like Lexis Advance, Westlaw, and Bloomberg Law has helped make updating select sources—both primary and secondary—easier for the researcher, but looseleafs offer similar currency along with a host of other advantages to keep them from being readily replaced in the online era.

An often overlooked feature of many looseleafs is that, like other secondary sources, the internal arrangement of the looseleaf is itself instructive. The *Standard Federal Tax Reporter* is arranged according to the Internal Revenue Code sections. Need to know something about a legal issue related to your client's 401(k) account? Simply turn to that section of the looseleaf because its numbering mirrors the Code's numbering. Another example is the *Federal Securities Law Reporter*, which is arranged by the different major securities acts in American history. There are tabbed sections containing material related to the Securities Act of 1933, the Securities Exchange Act of 1934, the Investment Advisors Act of 1940, and so on. Just being mindful of the arrangement of the looseleaf's sections can provide the intellectual outline of the subject matter.

Finally, looseleafs generally succeed in being extremely user-friendly. It is true that many researchers looking glumly at the roughly twenty thick volumes of the *Standard Federal Tax Reporter* might initially be put off by the seeming complexity and sheer bulk of the set. However, a little diligence will pay dividends to the persevering researcher. Because of the rational arrangement of looseleafs, the exceptionally good indexing, the inclusion of a variety of other finding aids, and the nearly universal inclusion of instructions on how to use each looseleaf in the introductory matter of each set, most researchers can use a looseleaf with confidence and great effectiveness after a few minutes of familiarization with the particulars of each. Using a looseleaf is, despite initial appearances, not very difficult.

9.3 TWO DIFFERENT KINDS OF LOOSELEAFS

Legal research guides have for generations divided the looseleaf world into two types; those published like newsletters and those that are the so-called interfiled style. There is no particular reason to depart from this tradition, for in fact there are really only the two different ideas about how to arrange, publish, and keep updated comprehensive information on a legal subject from a wide variety of sources. One can either issue periodic updates, along with updated indexes and finding aids each time, in separate pamphlets that are housed cumulatively in binders, or one can send replacement pages periodically with the idea that pages or sections that have changed in any way since the last packet of pages were issued will be discarded to be replaced by the new pages. A more comprehensive comparison of the two types of looseleaf will help explain how each is used.

The newsletter type is so called because updates are sent at regular intervals in the form of one or more pamphlets. In the *United States Law Week*, for example, each release contains one pamphlet with new Supreme Court opinions, one with Supreme Court docketing and other information, one with general legal news, and so on. Note that along with each release must come an updated, cumulative index, table of contents, and any other finding aids or finding lists that come with that looseleaf set. You should understand that the indexes and other finding aids must be cumulative in nature or the researcher would have to consult a series of index pamphlets, which would be very inconvenient.

Along with a subscription to the *United States Law Week* (used as the example throughout this section because it is the newsletter-style looseleaf most researchers are familiar with), the publisher (Bloomberg BNA, in this case) sends tabbed binders into which the different pamphlets will be filed. The idea here is that all of the pamphlets from each release will be retained (with the exception of the indexes and other finding aids that, being cumulative, could be discarded as each new one is received, leaving only the most current version). With a typical newsletter looseleaf, the publisher will send new, empty binders annually, keeping the bulk manageable. This is not always the case, however. Many different schemes have been tried, and you need to be a little flexible and prepared to conduct a short examination of each new looseleaf you investigate in order to discover the retention pattern for each new title.

By the end of a volume (one year's worth of issues in the case of the *United States Law Week*) the binders will have a full set of pamphlets within each binder. The index and the other finding aids will cover the entire year. The next release will come with new tabbed binders, and the process starts anew. This is worth relating because researchers must determine the dates of coverage of the binder on the shelves. Most libraries keep superseded binders (the *United States Law Week* has been published for many decades), and the researcher may have to consult those older volumes in order to get to information from the relevant time period. It's important also to note that the *United States Law Week* is now available in electronic format (from 1997 to present) only in Bloomberg Law. While this important publication was once available and searchable in full text on both Lexis Advance and Westlaw, it has since been removed (Lexis Advance still has a placeholder for it, but no content). This highlights an oft-overlooked danger of moving to strictly digital access: if you have the print on hand, you can always refer to it again in the future, but if you have only electronic access and something changes (in this case the licensing of the publication), you may lose access even to the things you once were able to read.

The other type of looseleaf is the interfiled type. If you have never turned the pages of one, it might be difficult to fully visualize the description that follows. We strongly recommend that you take a few minutes to familiarize yourself with one or two looseleafs from this category. There is nothing particularly difficult about using these looseleafs, but they are different from anything else in the law library, and may be initially intimidating.

With the interfiled looseleaf, there are no pamphlets issued like a periodical. Instead, each release (as often as each week) comes in a packet with a description of that release's contents, and a set of individual pages replacing the superseded or outdated pages in the set. The act of filing the new release involves discarding the pages to be replaced and inserting the new pages. At any time, the looseleaf is completely current, and none of the text is out of date. The indexes and other findings aids are updated in the same way; they, too, are always current.

Interfiled looseleafs can be large and seemingly complex. An example is the *Standard Federal Tax Reporter*, one of the premier interfiled looseleafs on the market. This looseleaf has now grown to over twenty volumes per year. Each year's *Standard Federal Tax Reporter* is complete unto itself, with an entirely new edition, with new binders and new contents issued each January. Its arrangement is simple; aside from a few volumes of index and finding aids and other material, the vast bulk of the looseleaf is made up of the Internal Revenue Code, section by section, along with the regulations, explanatory text, key decisions, cross references and other material associated with each section. A researcher needing to know about 501(c)(3) organizations need only turn to that section of the looseleaf and find all of the material related to this Code section. It is not hard to imagine why this collocation of related material in Code section order, along with the weekly updating of this material, makes this looseleaf so useful, and so ubiquitous in the offices of tax lawyers. The *Standard Federal Tax Reporter*, as well some other looseleafs of great importance, is also available in electronic format via the IntelliConnect and Cheetah platforms. As compared with the print, however, accessing the same content in electronic format requires a level of familiarly and comfort with the resource that will not come automatically for most people (see **Section 9.8**). In addition, the electronic counterparts come without the helpful index—one of the most valuable aspects of a traditional looseleaf.

With the newsletter looseleafs discussed above, we warned that each looseleaf has its own retention pattern; that is, some start over each new year or volume with new binders, some have other ways to store older issues. The same is true for interfiled looseleafs. The *Standard Federal Tax Reporter*, for example, issues a completely new set of binders each year. Many other interfiled looseleafs, though, do no such thing. (As an aside, why do you think the *Standard Federal Tax Reporter* starts over each new calendar year? It is because, in a very real sense, each year's tax code is a thing unto itself. Someone needing to do research on a tax problem arising in 1999 needs to have a complete set of the laws, regulations and other materials as they were in that year. Very few other legal subjects have such stark temporal divisions year to year.)

For those looseleafs where it isn't critically important to begin anew each year, a variety of other retention schemes are in place. Most commonly, though, the binders are never replaced, new material is merely added for the entire life of the subscription. Since the process of updating involves replacing old pages with new, the age of the binders, the lack of a volume number or date of publication is not an issue. Picture two libraries in the same town. The first subscribes to a particular looseleaf in Year 1 and faithfully files the updated pages each week, year in and year out. The second library subscribes to the looseleaf much later, beginning ten years after the first library. The contents sent to the second library in Year 10 match exactly the text found in the first library, given that the first library has been keeping their copy current by filing replacement pages as they arrive. Many researchers approach a looseleaf title on the shelves of their library, note with despair that the binders seem to be fifteen years old, and conclude that the looseleaf is so out of date that it can be of no use. This is absolutely the wrong assumption to make, of course: as long as the subscription is current and the replacement pages all filed properly, the looseleaf is up to date. But how to tell, then, that the subscription is current, and how to tell that the library has been filing replacement pages as it should?

Recall that the updates are sent periodically in a packet, complete with a description of that release's contents. That description, which resembles a cover letter or transmittal memo, is often referred to a *highlights page*, though specific publishers will use other terms (e.g., *Last Report Letter* in CCH publications). Highlights pages are normally retained in the looseleaf set, usually behind a tab or divider specifically reserved for them. By paging through the highlights pages you can quickly determine if every release has been received and filed. Because the highlights page contains a description of the new developments contained in that release, some lawyers use it as a current awareness tool. If you examined each highlights page in your field's flagship looseleaf as it arrived, it would be like reading a quick weekly update of recent events in the field. You could then decide whether any of the new pages in that release required closer review.

One other feature of the interfiled looseleaf, especially in the large, comprehensive sets, is that the finding aids can often be quite complex. In the *Standard Federal Tax Reporter*, for example, the main index alone is several hundred pages long. There are also a variety of other indexes and finding aids in the set. One typical arrangement in these looseleafs is to have a large general index, along with an index of new developments. This allows the researcher to check quickly for new matter. What constitutes "new" differs from one looseleaf to another. Often, these comprehensive looseleafs reprint cases from a variety of reporters that have to do with the subject matter the looseleaf covers. *Standard Federal Tax Reporter's* associated publication of tax cases, *United States Tax Cases*, is a reprint of tax cases from the primary reporters, along with descriptions of some unpublished cases not appearing anywhere else in print. The indexing in the main looseleaf usually includes a table of cases keyed to the cases volumes. One occasionally finds a table of new cases, too.

The point here is that each looseleaf has a form suited to the needs of the researcher in that particular field. Often, even in the titles produced by a single publisher, there is a bewildering variety of arrangements, finding aids, and other practices. This statement is not made to intimidate; rather, the object is to convince you to take a few minutes to examine the looseleaf's particulars before diving in, and to convince you to take the time to read the instructions for use (often found behind a tab labeled something like "How to Use This Reporter") if you aren't already familiar with its organization. These short instructions can save the researcher valuable time and frustration.

9.4   USING A NEWSLETTER-STYLE LOOSELEAF

Newsletter-style looseleafs are as often used for current awareness as for actual research. Many practitioners read the releases as they are issued, and retain them in their binders for future reference if some development or case or problem calls to mind something read and remembered at some point in the past. Using a looseleaf in this way is simplicity itself, and needs no further explanation.

Using a newsletter-style looseleaf for research is different, but not necessarily difficult. Usually the researcher begins with a topic or subject to be researched. Remember that this type of looseleaf has a cumulative index, updated with each new release, so there is no need to consult any but the most recent version. There are often other, more specific indexes, which could be consulted as well. These looseleafs commonly have tables of contents, tables of cases, tables of statutes, and other aids to research. Depending upon the specific situation of the researcher, one of these tables might be the logical starting point. It is incumbent upon the researcher to investigate the available finding aids to determine which is appropriate for the current research need.

Once the index or finding aid has yielded a citation to the relevant section or sections, the researcher need only turn to the part of the looseleaf indicated. Remember that the looseleaf is constantly being updated, and that even if the search refers to a release from several months ago, it is generally true that there is no need to update beyond what the (updated, remember) index has referred you to.

The thing to bear in mind while researching in a newsletter-style looseleaf is that while these publications attempt to draw together all of the material relevant to specific areas of law, the periodic updating with pamphlet releases makes integrating current information difficult. In rapidly changing areas, the index may point the researcher to the main text and to a series of new matters or new developments sections. The researcher may be forced to trace his or her issue across several different locations within the looseleaf. There is nothing particularly difficult in this; it simply requires a little diligence and some organized thinking and planning.

9.5   USING AN INTERFILED LOOSELEAF

Researching an issue in an interfiled looseleaf presents the researcher with none of the updating issues of the newsletter-style looseleafs, but there are a few different wrinkles worth noting. One of the key features of the interfiled looseleaf is the indexing, which is often incredibly detailed. Researchers used to substandard indexing, such as that found in the *CFR* index, will be greatly relieved to find looseleaf indexing so granular and so thorough that almost any issue can be quickly located within the looseleaf.

Remember, though, that the largest, most complex interfiled looseleafs might have several volumes of indexes and finding aids. It will take the researcher new to that particular title a few minutes to understand how best to begin, and which finding aid to choose.

Another apparent complication of the interfiled looseleaf is the simultaneous use of paragraph numbers and page numbers. Why would this be the case? Imagine an instance where the publisher of an interfiled looseleaf relied exclusively on page numbers. When it came time for the next update, the new release might contain a twenty page discussion of a topic that will replace a one paragraph discussion that came before. The library would discard the single page, replacing it with the twenty new ones. What happens, then, to the page numbers? This is an obviously unworkable situation. The solution is the use of paragraph numbers. In the typical interfiled looseleaf (we say typical because there is always an exception out there somewhere), the paragraph number refers to the smallest, indivisible treatment of a topic. It may be one sentence long or many dozens of pages. In fact, in those looseleafs that reprint judicial or administrative opinions, each opinion is usually assigned one paragraph number. What, then, are the page numbers for? They are only for the library personnel responsible for filing looseleaf updates, and can be ignored by the researcher (except if you suspect a page is missing or some other unusual situation). All of the looseleaf's finding aids refer solely to the paragraph numbers, not the page numbers. Novice researchers are often thrown by the paragraph numbers, but there is absolutely nothing complex or mysterious about them or their use.

The researcher using an interfiled looseleaf should almost always begin with the index or another finding aid. Sometimes the arrangement can be so transparent that the researcher can turn directly to the relevant section (as in our discussion of 501(c)(3), above), but that's risky, for reasons of completeness. After the researcher finds the relevant paragraph citation in the index, then he or she can turn to the appropriate paragraph, and find there the statute, regulation, editorial commentary, cross references to other material, case law, journal articles, and so on. It is this drawing together of text from disparate sources that makes looseleafs so valuable. Coupled with the text being constantly updated, making it unnecessary to spend additional time confirming that statutory, regulatory, and other text is current, the value of looseleafs becomes apparent. In some areas of practice, the comprehensive looseleaf is so pervasive, so thorough, and so indispensable that it is often the only resource the lawyer consults on an average day. Clearly, these looseleafs are seen to be worth their surprisingly high prices because they save the lawyer valuable time by gathering together, arranging, and updating all of the relevant information on a particular area of law. A student graduating from law school with no experience using looseleafs is missing an important part of his or her education.

9.6   WHAT IS NOT IN LOOSELEAFS?

As thorough as looseleaf services can be, it is a mistake to think that everything one might need to find or read on a particular topic will be found in the relevant looseleaf. That is not always the case.

Often, the most recent developments are only described, not reprinted in full text. Very recent opinions are an example of this, as are unpublished opinions. It is very common that the reprinting of opinions can be slower to appear than other types of material. New statutes or regulations are also occasionally represented by only a citation and a brief description. This is not a very big problem, of course, only a mild inconvenience, but it bears noting.

Of more consequence is the fact that few looseleafs publish administrative hearing decisions and other possibly relevant matters. With the Internal Revenue Service, for example, the major looseleafs tend not to reprint Private Letter Rulings, No-action Letters, field manuals, and the like. These materials are printed in other sources. In nearly every field of law covered by a looseleaf service there are some potentially relevant sources the researcher will have to consult other kinds of publications in order to find. Researchers should try to familiarize themselves with the literature in their particular field and consult specialized research guides or the nearest law librarian for help. These omissions are not failings of looseleafs, just a practical limit on the amount of material that can be included in any one publication.

Students are often surprised at the paucity of citations to law review and other journal articles in the typical looseleaf. Since looseleaf services are geared for the practitioner, however, it shouldn't come as too much of a surprise that the publishers focus on primary sources and narrowly tailored commentary on those sources rather than on academic literature. The researcher may wish to supplement looseleaf research with a search for legal journal articles using the indexes or full-text databases described in **Chapter 4**.

9.7   FINDING A LOOSELEAF ON YOUR TOPIC

Once you've determined that your legal research problem is not one easily solved by other means, that it seems likely to require consulting a number of different kinds of primary sources for an answer, that your subject matter is in the kind of heavily regulated area often covered by looseleaf services, and that you don't know the names of any looseleafs that might help, how should you proceed? There are several different ways to look for a looseleaf on a particular topic.

The first thing to do is consult, if it is available, a reference work called *Legal Looseleafs: Electronic and Print* (formerly known as *Legal Looseleafs in Print*). This single-volume work, compiled by Arlene L. Eis and published annually by Infosources Publishing, is an invaluable aid for helping locate a relevant looseleaf. The book has an extensive Title List, which is exactly what it sounds like—an alphabetical listing of looseleafs by title. Following the Title List is a series of indexes, each with references back to the appropriate page of the Title List. The traditional indexes of Publisher and Subject have been part of the publication for years, and the latter is still perhaps the most useful aspect of the book. When appropriate, the Subject Index also includes a geographic element, identifying the looseleaf as specific to a given jurisdiction. Real Property, for example, has its own Subject Index entry, with over 30 looseleafs of general jurisdiction listed. Immediately after it, however, is a separate entry for Real Property—Arkansas, followed by Real Property—California, and so on. In recent years, *Legal Looseleafs: Electronic and Print* has also added a series of Electronic Format indexes, which identify resources that are available in various electronic formats: CD-ROM, .pdf, Online (which means Lexis Advance or Westlaw), Internet (which means other databases like Intelliconnect or BNA or on the open web), and eBook. Using these indexes effectively can allow a researcher to identify a relevant looseleaf publication and also determine whether alternative (non-print) access exists. But what if the law library to which you have access doesn't have a copy of *Legal Looseleafs: Electronic and Print*? Not likely. If a library is large enough and serious enough to own more than a few looseleafs it will also have a copy of this book. If your library does not have this work, check to see if your library has access to the contents of Infosources Publishing's website, which they call LawTRIO, and which contains an electronic version of the contents of *Legal Looseleafs: Electronic and Print*.

If you cannot consult *Legal Looseleafs: Electronic and Print*, you might try to find a relevant product by examining the websites of the largest publishers of looseleafs. All major legal publishers have their catalogues of titles available on their websites. Although many publishers produce annually-updated treatises that are physically in looseleaf format, the list of major publishers of actual *looseleaf services* is surprisingly small. We would recommend searching the websites of Wolters Kluwer Law & Business (CCH, Aspen), Bloomberg BNA, LexisNexis/Matthew Bender, and Thomson Reuters/RIA. These imprints change some over time as publishers are bought up by one another and by other large publishers, but these four imprints together account for the majority of leading looseleaf publications.

Of course, another solution to the problem of locating an appropriate looseleaf is to consult a law librarian. Law firm librarians, law school librarians, court librarians, and many others are familiar with these publications, know how to locate and evaluate them, and are willing to help. Remember that even a publication as useful as *Legal Looseleafs: Electronic and Print* cannot replace the experience and expertise of a librarian whose knowledge and advice you have come to trust. Within any single topic there may be several choices of looseleafs available, and comparing and evaluating the choices is something with which most librarians have considerable experience.

9.8   ONLINE VERSIONS OF LOOSELEAFS

It will come as no surprise to you that many of the leading publishers of looseleaf services have made their contents available electronically. This content is generally provided to subscribers via the web in subscription databases. This has greatly simplified the technical aspects of looseleaf management for practitioners and librarians, but the electronic looseleafs have not yet completely supplanted their print equivalents. The reasons are simple. First, it has proven devilishly difficult to create online interfaces that are as transparent and intuitive as the print versions. Even those who are more comfortable with electronic than print in most instances and are completely comfortable with Lexis Advance, Westlaw, Bloomberg Law, etc. often find the electronic interface of many looseleaf publications confusing. Users must invest a good deal of time to overcome the relatively steep learning curve for each title. Second, while it is generally easy to see precisely how recently a print looseleaf has been updated (remember the highlights page discussed in **Section 9.3**), electronic formats have been slow to make this information readily accessible, instead merely using inexact language like "updated" (without a date) or "current." Third, many electronic versions provide access to the content—particularly for interfiled looseleafs—only in webpage format (no .pdf files), which can pose problems with citation. Despite these drawbacks, which may yet be overcome, the advantages these services offer make them attractive to users committed to learning how to use them. The biggest advantage of the electronic looseleaf over the print equivalent is, of course, the ability to search the full text. As good as the indexing and other finding aids in the typical looseleaf are, the ability to search for specific terms and phrases and retrieve every occurrence is an immensely powerful enhancement. But keep in mind that there can also be times when an expansive result list can become overwhelming and the sense of context and organization so valuable in a looseleaf is lost by not understanding how different sections relate to one another. An electronic looseleaf also benefits from being accessible outside of the library. Although print looseleafs often cannot be checked out from the library because of their constant updates, no such limitation exists with electronic format. Finally, internal hyperlinking from finding aid to section, or from one section to another can, if done correctly, be tremendously appealing when contrasted with the need to go back and forth between different looseleaf binders in print. Because of these benefits, it is very likely that we will see more and more looseleafs available via the online services or on the web by subscription.

Our advice? Don't be daunted by the apparent complexity of the electronic looseleafs. They conform to principles with which you should, by now, be familiar. These services, like their print counterparts, gather together primary and secondary sources from a wide variety of other publications, then arrange them in a meaningful way. They are regularly updated, with dead or moot or superseded language excised. The finding aids are state of the art in most cases, and in the online environment you will also have the option of keyword searching. Remember a few key characteristics shared by all looseleafs regardless of format: they all have instructions for use and they all rely on superior indexes and finding aids. Publishers of the electronic services usually have research support that you can call, email, or chat with for help, and they often have step-by-step tutorials, videos, and other quite elaborate instructional material available for users. Investing a little time before beginning research can save you a great deal of time later.

One final word about electronic looseleafs is in order, and the general principle will hold you in good stead with any electronic source you may use. It is still the case that virtually every source available in electronic format began its life in print form. In almost every case, it is very difficult to use the online version of any publication as effectively, efficiently, and thoroughly if you are not fluent with the print source from which the electronic source is derived. As true as this is for case reporters or annotated codes, it is even more the case with looseleafs, which are such hybrid and complex resources to begin with. It is tempting to log on to the electronic version of a looseleaf on your topic from the comfort of the office or from home, but without a thorough grounding in the print progenitor you will be taking an unnecessary risk. Understanding the organization of a looseleaf by seeing it in print will often do more to help a researcher use that looseleaf in electronic format than any video or tutorial could ever do.

CHAPTER 10

COURT RULES

■ ■ ■

10.1   WHAT ARE COURT RULES AND WHY DO THEY MATTER?

Early in our country's history, it became clear that courts needed the authority to make and enforce rules to ensure the smooth and fair operation of court business. The resulting court rules varied from jurisdiction to jurisdiction. There was also an ongoing question of the power of courts to make rules that were not purely procedural. By the 1930s, the federal court system required a uniform set of court rules that would apply throughout the country. The story of the passage of the first of the federal court rules, the Federal Rules of Civil Procedure (FRCP), is too long a tale to relate here, but the rules represented a great step forward for both the reality and the perception of fairness that the federal courts require.

After the adoption of the FRCP, the federal courts continued to develop rules to govern the operation of the courts and to lay out orderly processes by which parties must conduct litigation. The resulting sets of rules, most notably, the Federal Rules of Criminal Procedure, and the Federal Rules of Evidence, together with the FRCP form the basic rules of federal litigation by which all parties must abide.

In addition to these overarching federal court rules, two other kinds of rules were developed. The first type governs procedures in particular courts: Rules of the United States Supreme Court, the Federal Rules of Appellate Procedure, Federal Rules of Bankruptcy Procedure, and so on. The idea is that each of these courts is so specialized that additional rules are needed to address issues specific to that court. The other type of federal court rule is the body of local court rules. Each federal District Court and appellate court is empowered to enforce rules specific to it. These local rules tend to be more focused on the formalisms of litigation: maximum page lengths for briefs, rules about cameras in the courtroom, or accepted methods of conducting depositions, to name but a few examples.

State courts, too, have their own court rules. Usually printed as part of the state's annotated code, state court rules tend not to vary from court to court within a jurisdiction as much as the federal court rules do. Almost all states have rules that mirror the major federal rules, those related to civil procedure, criminal procedure, and evidence.

Does this matter to the researcher? Definitely. It is critically important for the researcher involved in litigation to understand the procedural requirements of the court where the case will be heard. Without understanding rules related to procedure, for example, a lawyer can miss filing deadlines, have pleadings returned because of improper formatting, delivery method or timing, etc. In general, court rules are intended to be purely procedural, but it is true that unless the procedural rules are understood and followed, a client's substantive rights can be profoundly (and adversely) affected.

Court rules, then, can be thought of as the rules governing any piece of litigation. They are the rules of the game, and one cannot properly plan and execute a case without a clear understanding of their requirements.

10.2   FEDERAL COURT RULES

As mentioned above, the 1930s brought a movement to standardize the procedural rules in the federal courts. The first set of rules promulgated was the Federal Rules of Civil Procedure. These rules were followed a few years later by the Federal Rules of Criminal Procedure. It took another three decades and Congressional action to bring the Federal Rules of Evidence into being. The rules in these three sets have been published in many unannotated and a few annotated versions. The annotations are crucial because these rules are so often the bases of federal appeals, and the annotations track all of these opinions where the rules have been parsed, examined, and applied by federal courts. In addition, there are many helpful secondary sources discussing federal rules that the researcher might consult, and the annotations provide citations to these as well.

10.3   FINDING ANNOTATED FEDERAL COURT RULES, GENERAL AND LOCAL

The three major sets of federal court rules are widely available in a number of formats. Several publishers, for example, produce relatively inexpensive, softbound unannotated sets of the rules for use by law students in first year Civil Procedure courses. The web is also an easy place to find the bare texts of the rules themselves. The most reliable source is a website maintained by the Administrative Office of the U.S. Courts on behalf of the Federal Judiciary, which includes electronic versions of the national federal rules in effect. These rules can be found at the Federal Judiciary website, at http://www.uscourts.gov/rules-policies under the heading "Current Rules of Practice & Procedure." That same website also includes proposed and pending amendments to the nationwide rules of federal courts, and an explanation of the rulemaking process at the federal level. Finally, the "Court Locator" function acts as a portal to individual court websites, which must by law (Section 205 of the E-Government Act of 2002, Pub. L. No. 107–347) include any local rules for specific courts. Whether in print or electronic versions, there are many ways to find unannotated court rules.

That, however, is almost never sufficient to satisfy the researcher's needs. The language of the rule itself is tested, interpreted, and applied in case law. Courts are frequently asked to rule on procedural issues and, not surprisingly, new questions are raised constantly by litigants. In addition, these rules, particularly procedural, evidentiary, and jurisdictional rules, are the subject of a great deal of scholarly investigation. This results in the creation of a wealth of secondary sources to explain, to criticize, to categorize, and sometimes to influence the interpretation and application of court rules. In order to easily locate the entire universe of written material relevant to the understanding and use of federal court rules, the researcher needs annotated rules.

What is in the annotations to court rules, and why are they so important to researchers? In short, the annotated rules act just like an annotated statute. Beyond the mere text of the rule itself, a set of annotated rules also includes relevant references to a variety of sources: the Committee Reports and drafts and other "legislative history" of the rule, judicial opinions construing the meaning and application of the rule, and secondary sources explaining or contextualizing the rule. Together, these disparate materials can tell you what the rule really means in practice.

The easiest places to find annotated federal rules are in *United States Code Annotated* or *United States Code Service*. In these two commercially published versions of the federal code, the major rules sets are reprinted and annotated exactly as are the statutes themselves. In the *U.S.C.A.*, the rules follow Title 18 (Criminal Procedure) and Title 28 (Civil Procedure, Evidence, Appellate Procedure). In the *U.S.C.S.*, the rules are all housed together in dedicated volumes that follow the last Title of the Code. There are also other places where federal court rules are annotated, and in different ways. For a description of where to find important annotated versions of different federal court rules, see **Table 10.A**.

10.4   SECONDARY SOURCES AND FEDERAL RULES

It is certainly true that consulting annotated collections of federal court rules confers a significant advantage over unannotated versions, but the researcher often needs more information or explanation than can be readily gleaned from the annotated source. In that case, especially where explanation or context is what is most needed, it is to secondary sources the researcher should turn. Fortunately for the researcher, there is a wealth of useful, current, and authoritative treatises available to help. In most cases, the treatises have been written by eminent scholars and are compiled in large, comprehensive, multi-volume sets. Some of the most well-respected treatises rank among the handful of top resources in the legal research world.

In a field filled with choices for the legal researcher, several titles stand out due to their authority, clarity, accuracy and explanatory value. The leading offering from Thomson Reuters is *Federal Practice and Procedure*, by Wright and Miller. This monumental work runs to several dozen volumes, is kept current with pocket parts, and covers virtually every aspect of federal civil procedure. Recognized as a leading authority in the field, this work is relied upon by lawyers and courts alike. Part of its appeal for lawyers and researchers is its detailed and strikingly clear discussions of procedural rules. A leading Thomson Reuters product, this source is also included on the Westlaw platform, including an attempt at an index (though as is customary with Westlaw indexes, to browse you would have to go to the index entry and then click the link for the "Table of Contents" of the index).

The competing product from LexisNexis, another comprehensive treatment of federal court rules, is *Moore's Federal Practice* (now in its 3rd edition). This multi-volume treatise, published in looseleaf form, was first published in the 1940s, beginning soon after the promulgation of the Federal Rules of Civil Procedure. *Moore's* provides in-depth explanation and annotation of the federal rules on civil procedure, evidence, and criminal procedure, as well as other related material. On Lexis Advance, this resource is divided into two resources: Moore's Federal Practice—Civil and Moore's Federal Practice—Criminal. Inexplicably, Lexis Advance includes a separate index for the former, but not the latter.

10.5   FEDERAL COURT RULES JUDICIALLY CONSIDERED

Part of the value of the annotated sets of federal court rules and the comprehensive treatises is that they cite and discuss the many opinions which examine, interpret, and apply those rules. As is the case with any other kind of statute (for federal court rules can be so considered for the purposes of the research process), the language of the statute, the history behind its drafting and adoption, and the case law construing it all work together in complex ways, combining to form the "meaning" of the law itself. One cannot answer a question of constitutional law simply by reading the language of the constitutional provision in question, nor can a researcher adequately research a question of jurisdiction, evidence, or procedure generally by referring only to the language of the rule.

In order to do thorough research on a procedural issue, then, it is necessary to find and address the case law. Finding this body of relevant opinions should present few problems because there are tools at hand that make the process essentially a mechanical one. In addition to the normal case-finding methods discussed elsewhere in this book (see **Chapter 5**), there are annotated rules sets and one other major specialized source, *Federal Rules Decisions* (*FRD*). Remember that federal cases are published in the *United States Reports*, *Federal Reporter* and the *Federal Supplement*. The *FRD* covers federal District Court cases discussing federal court rules that are not reported in the *Federal Supplement*. *FRD* is published by Thomson Reuters, and is part of the National Reporter System. In addition to otherwise unreported federal District Court cases, *FRD* contains the texts of articles and speeches related to the federal rules. On Westlaw, the contents of the *Federal Rules Decisions* print publication are divided up into three subsets: Federal Rules Decisions Cases, Federal Rules Decision Articles, and Federal Rules Decisions Rules, the last of which includes speeches and conference proceedings.

10.6　USING CITATORS FOR UPDATING FEDERAL COURT RULES

Both Shepard's and KeyCite make it possible for the researcher to see which cases mention any particular federal rule, in exactly the same way one uses these citators to see which later opinions have mentioned a particular opinion or statute. But why do this? Assuming that federal court rules aren't very likely to be overruled or held unconstitutional, is a researcher really trying to find out if any particular federal rule is still good law? Not really. The reason a researcher concerned with, say, Federal Rule of Evidence 1002 (the best evidence rule) would use a citator is to gather a list of every case that has mentioned this evidentiary rule in order to see how it has been applied and interpreted in a particular jurisdiction or period of time.

Using Lexis Advance, it is easy to Shepardize this evidentiary rule once you have determined the precise citation format required. The Shepard's report indicates that this rule has been cited over 1000 times in judicial opinions, and only once in an opinion by the United States Supreme Court. (This search is also possible in print, of course, by using *Shepard's U.S. Citations*, but you will rarely have the opportunity or need to perform such a search.) What use would a researcher make of this list? It might prove informative to at least look at all the recent cases from the relevant jurisdiction to see how courts have interpreted and applied the rule.

With KeyCite, on Westlaw, the process is much the same. Once you have determined the exact citation form, it is easy to retrieve the full KeyCite report for the relevant rule. Shepard's, by default, returns results in the traditional order (descending order of court, then reverse chronological order), though it does also offer sorting by date and by level of analysis. By comparison, KeyCite (through Notes of Decisions) organizes the citing cases into subject matter divisions, an interesting innovation. One can also limit the KeyCite search to include only cases from relevant jurisdictions and/or time periods (it is possible to limit results in much the same way with Shepard's.) For most rules, KeyCite also provides cross-references to many more secondary sources than Shepard's, which, depending upon your needs, is either very useful or simply a distraction.

10.7   STATE COURT RULES

State court rules operate very much like their federal counterparts. One difference is that there is less consensus on the source of authority for state rules, and practice differs from state to state. Some states consider state court rules to be entirely the province of the state judiciary; that is, that state court rules are nothing more than an example of the judiciary's power to regulate its own business. On the other end of the spectrum, some states hold that only legislative action can create or amend state court rules. In effect, these states consider court rules as just another area of state legislation. In between these two extremes, many states employ a hybrid of the two theories above. In these hybrid states, court rules are considered delegated legislation. The state legislature is the source from which flows the authority to promulgate rules of procedure or evidence, etc., but the legislatures are free to delegate this authority to a rulemaking body, usually the state judiciary. This means that court rules occupy a niche in state law roughly parallel to state regulations.

For the average researcher or practitioner, these distinctions are without much significance. Whatever their ultimate source of power, state court rules have the status of state law, and in most instances are applied and interpreted no differently regardless of the theory under which they were promulgated.

10.8   ANNOTATED STATE COURT RULES

Finding unannotated versions of state court rules is very easy. Virtually every state has made the rules readily available on the state website, but without annotation, of course. In addition, state court rules are available in print and electronic formats in a number of other places. What one almost always needs, however, is an annotated version of those rules. Remember, the text of the rules themselves is only one portion of the information you need to determine what the law is. You also need case law, and occasionally secondary sources as well. You need annotated rules.

Fortunately, in every state that has an annotated code, the court rules are included and annotated. Regardless of the theory of authority under which the rules were promulgated (as discussed in **Section 10.7**), the annotated codes treat court rules as just another state statute. As with the rest of the statutes in the state code, the quality and comprehensiveness of the annotation depends in large part upon which publisher is responsible for the annotated code. It is true in most instances that the publishers do not exert the same effort as that given to annotating the federal code, but one will usually find enough in the annotation to satisfy most research needs.

10.9   TABLE

TABLE 10.A: SELECTED SOURCES OF ANNOTATED FEDERAL COURT RULES

1.   Federal Rules of Civil Procedure

United States Code Annotated. St. Paul, Minn.: West Publishing, 1927– (This set is currently published by Thomson West). Title 28 Rules volumes

Westlaw:

> United States Code Annotated: Statutes & Court Rules > Federal Rules of Civil Procedure (same annotations as in *U.S.C.A.*)

United States Code Service. Charlottesville, Va., 1998– (This set is currently published by LexisNexis). Rules volumes (toward end of set)

Lexis Advance:

> Statutes and Legislation > Court Rules > TOC icon to the right of USCS—Federal Rules Annotated > Expand Federal Rules of Civil Procedure

> Shortcut: type "FRCP" in the home page main search box, click on the TOC icon to the right of USCS—Federal Rules Annotated, and then expand Federal Rules of Civil Procedure (same annotations as in *U.S.C.S.*)

Moore's Federal Practice. 3rd ed. New York, N. Y.: Matthew Bender, 1997– (This set is currently published by LexisNexis).

Federal Practice and Procedure. St. Paul, Minn.: West Publishing (This set is currently published by Thomson West).

2.   Federal Rules of Criminal Procedure

United States Code Annotated. St. Paul, Minn.: West Publishing, 1927– (This set is currently published by Thomson West). Title 18 Rules volumes

Westlaw:

> United States Code Annotated: Statutes & Court Rules > Federal Rules of Criminal Procedure (same annotations as in *U.S.C.A.*)

United States Code Service. Charlottesville, Va., 1998– (This set is currently published by LexisNexis). Rules volumes (toward end of set)

Lexis Advance:

> Statutes and Legislation > Court Rules > TOC icon to the right of USCS—Federal Rules Annotated > Expand Federal Rules of Criminal Procedure

> Shortcut: type "USCS Rules" in the home page main search box, click on the TOC icon to the right of USCS—Federal Rules Annotated, and then expand Federal Rules of Criminal Procedure (same annotations as in *U.S.C.S.*)

Moore's Federal Practice. 3rd ed. New York, N. Y.: Matthew Bender, 1997– (This set is currently published by LexisNexis).

Federal Practice and Procedure. St. Paul, Minn.: West Publishing (This set is currently published by Thomson West).

3.   Federal Rules of Evidence

United States Code Annotated. St. Paul, Minn.: West Publishing, 1927– (This set is currently published by Thomson West). Title 28 Rules volumes

Westlaw:

> United States Code Annotated: Statutes & Court Rules > Federal Rules of Evidence (same annotations as in *U.S.C.A.*)

United States Code Service. Charlottesville, Va., 1998– (This set is currently published by LexisNexis). Rules volumes (toward end of set)

Lexis Advance:

> Statutes and Legislation > Court Rules > TOC icon to the right of USCS—Federal Rules Annotated > Expand Federal Rules of Evidence

> Shortcut: type "USCS Rules" in the home page main search box, click on the TOC icon to the right of USCS—Federal Rules Annotated, and then expand Federal Rules of Evidence (same annotations as in *U.S.C.S.*)

Moore's Federal Practice. 3rd ed. New York, N. Y.: Matthew Bender, 1997– (This set is currently published by LexisNexis).

Federal Practice and Procedure. St. Paul, Minn.: West Publishing (This set is currently published by Thomson West).

CHAPTER 11

LEGAL ETHICS RESEARCH

■ ■ ■

11.1 INTRODUCTION TO LEGAL ETHICS RESEARCH

This chapter is intended to introduce you to researching a legal topic that will have an impact on you throughout your legal career, no matter what field of law you choose. In truth, as important as an understanding of the particulars of legal ethics is, imparting this knowledge is only a secondary goal of the chapter. Our primary goal in this chapter is to expose students to a few new concepts. Most importantly, law students need to know about uniform and model laws, and why conducting research into any state law that began life as a uniform or model law can be different from ordinary state law research. By the end of the chapter you will see that, despite the differences, legal ethics research follows the familiar pattern; there are statutes, several varieties of judicial and other opinions that interpret and apply the statutory language, and secondary sources that are important in helping to explain and contextualize the primary sources.

Another concept with which you should become familiar is the idea of the self-regulating industry. Until the 1970s, the American Bar Association (ABA) considered its ethical rules to be private laws regulating the behavior of members of an industry group with voluntary membership. Many industries have implemented some degree of self-regulation. In the case of the ABA, however, some of the resulting ethical rules might have been held to be private agreements in restraint of trade, which ran the risk of running afoul of the antitrust laws. Once it became clear that the kind of ethical rules the American Bar Association's members felt it was important to abide by might be found to be illegal, the idea of the national bar as a self-regulating industry was largely abandoned. The ABA, from that point until today, has taken the position that its ethics code and rules are models only, and that the ABA merely advocates their adoption by all of the state legislatures. And the state legislatures have acquiesced, to a degree, but not without preserving some important differences from state to state. Because of this history, legal ethics research should be approached first as a matter of state law, but second as a uniform or model law, with all of the research implications we will discuss in this chapter.

11.2   MODEL AND UNIFORM LAWS GENERALLY

The uniform or model law is a concept with which students should be familiar, even from first year courses. Most Contracts courses, as an example, contain at least some examination of the Uniform Commercial Code. Many Criminal Law classes discuss the Model Penal Code. But just what is a model law or a uniform law, how is it different from the laws we have already examined, and what difference does it make to you, the researcher?

In the typical case, a body of scholars, judges, lawyers, and other authorities meets to draft a model or uniform law on a subject, and to urge its adoption by the legislatures of many jurisdictions. This body, no matter how influential, is not making law in any way. In the case of the Uniform Commercial Code (and all the legal ethics strictures we will discuss in this chapter) the proposed uniform law has no legal effect at all until individual states adopt it and make it part of their state law. It is also true that each jurisdiction is free to adopt all or part of the proposed law, or to change any part of it the state wishes. The term "uniform," then, applies only to the source, not to the resulting state legislation, which is often anything but uniform across all jurisdictions.

There are several groups taking the lead in drafting uniform and model laws for adoption by states. Foremost among them is the Uniform Law Commission (ULC), also referred to as the National Conference of Commissioners on Uniform State Laws. Founded well over a century ago, the ULC is now comprised of over 300 scholars, judges and lawyers. These leading figures have been appointed by the various states, and, according to the Conference's website, at http://www.uniformlaws.org, their mission is to provide "states with non-partisan, well-conceived and well-drafted legislation that brings clarity and stability to critical areas of state statutory law." As of this writing, this highly influential group has drafted or contributed to nearly 200 uniform and model laws, from the Uniform Commercial Code (in cooperation with the American Law Institute) to the Model Punitive Damages Act, from the Unclaimed Property Act to the Determination of Death Act. The texts of any acts produced solely by the ULC (so not the Uniform Commercial Code) are available at the ULC website, along with detailed information about the adoption of each act by states. Much of this information is also included as part of the *Uniform Laws Annotated* resource, published in print by Thomson Reuters and available on Westlaw.

11.3   SOURCES OF AUTHORITY—AMERICAN BAR ASSOCIATION ETHICAL CODES AND RULES

The modern system of regulating legal ethics began in 1908 when the ABA, influenced by several state ethics codes and by urging from its membership, published the first national, comprehensive code of ethical lawyer behavior. The ABA Canons of Professional Ethics contained thirty-two canons, adherence to which was required for continued membership in good standing in the ABA. These canons described general rules of conduct, and although they were amended several times over the following decades, the need to replace them with a code better suited to addressing the complexity of modern practice became increasingly clear as the years passed.

The resulting new code, called the ABA Code of Professional Responsibility, was adopted by the ABA in 1969. Several years later, in response to the realization that this private "law" might not withstand antitrust scrutiny, the ABA changed the name of the code to the ABA Model Code of Professional Responsibility, reflecting the idea that the code was a model that state legislatures could use when drafting or revising state legal ethics laws. In fact, many states did just that, and the adoption of the Model Code became widespread in the 1970s.

This radical rethinking of the regulation of lawyer ethical behavior consisted of canons, ethical considerations, and disciplinary rules. The canons and ethical considerations are "aspirational" meaning that they represent goals to which all lawyers should aspire, but there are no penalties for failing to meet one or more of them. One example is that all lawyers should spend a certain number of hours per year on *pro bono* legal work. Failure (or even refusal) to do so exposes the lawyer to no punishment. The disciplinary rules, on the other hand, are "mandatory." The disciplinary rules describe the minimum level of conduct below which no lawyer can fall without being subject to disciplinary action. It is important to be clear about the distinction between the canons and ethical considerations, which are aspirational (describing what a lawyer should do) and the disciplinary rules, which are mandatory (and describe what a lawyer must do).

The Model Code was not without its critics, however. Many lawyers and state legislatures felt that the Code placed too much emphasis on the ethical challenges facing the trial lawyer, and not enough on transactional work and other branches of law. In response to these criticisms, a commission was established by the ABA to draft a new set of ethical guidelines.

In 1983, the ABA approved the adoption of the commission's new guidelines, called the ABA Model Rules of Professional Conduct. Since their adoption, the Model Rules have been amended several times, including a major revision adopted in 2002. The Model Rules are divided into three parts; the subject divisions (called "Titles"), the disciplinary rules themselves, and then the commentary. The Model Rules are very much like the uniform or model laws described in **Section 11.2**, intended to serve as a model that state legislatures or courts can use when passing ethics laws or adjudicating ethics complaints or cases.

Within each of the Titles of the Model Rules there are several disciplinary rules and their associated commentary. The rule itself is stated in simple, black-letter language. The comments seek to clarify or illustrate the meaning of the rule. The comments are usually explanatory in nature, occasionally giving specific examples of how the rule is to be applied in different situations, but are specifically designed not to impose obligations on the lawyer beyond what is found in the rule itself. You might profitably think of the comments as part annotation, part legislative history.

11.4   SOURCES OF AUTHORITY—STATE LAW

Despite the foregoing section on the history of the ABA codes and rules, you must bear in mind that these national models are models only and lack the power of law unless adopted by a state legislative body. Regulation of lawyer ethics and behavior is almost entirely a state matter. The only important exception to the proposition that legal ethics is a matter of state law is that lawyers must follow the rules of court of the federal courts before which they practice, some of which have adopted either the Model Code or Rules themselves. It is also true that certain local bar associations have some responsibility for lawyer oversight and discipline, but the instances in which local rules differ significantly from state law are relatively rare.

The Model Rules have been adopted in whole or in part by several jurisdictions. The legal ethics laws and rules of other states still reflect their Model Code origins. Confusingly, some states have adopted parts of both, or adopted one or the other but with significant departures from the ABA language. California, by way of example, has never adopted language from either the Code or Rules, but since their laws are so similar to those of the ABA models, not even in California's case is the state completely self-contained when it comes to interpreting and applying ethical laws in specific cases. It is not uncommon for California courts to take outside practice and precedents into account. All of this can result in confusion for the researcher, but by following the techniques described in **Section 11.7**, you will be able to conduct accurate and thorough legal ethics research.

11.5   SOURCES OF AUTHORITY— "CASE LAW" PUBLICATIONS

In this section, the phrase "case law" will be interpreted broadly, taking in more than opinions written by judges in actual controversies in the state or federal court systems. Case law, for our purposes in this section, will include ethics opinions from a number of sources in addition to traditional case law. Why? Legal ethics is one of a number of practice areas where the advisory opinion (including the non-judicial advisory opinions by, for example, one or another bar entity) is often used as a test case for a specific set of facts or for interpretation of a particular rule or statute. These opinions are relied upon by lawyers in their practices, and by courts and other disciplinary bodies when adjudicating claims and complaints. In this way advisory opinions are used like case law, and it is a useful fiction to consider them as such.

There is, of course, a body of traditional case law to be researched as well. Legal ethics rules are a matter of state law, and lawyers of a particular state have access to the courts to challenge or appeal a ruling made by the state bar or other entity charged with lawyer discipline. Ordinary state case law research techniques apply in the case of legal ethics as much as for any other area. State and regional digests allow for subject access to cases in specific jurisdictions. The online services allow for full-text searching of cases for specific words or phrases. The difference in the case of legal ethics is that this is only the first step in the process of case law research. There are other sources of "case law" to be investigated.

The researcher should also examine the results of disciplinary proceedings in the state. Though sometimes these proceedings are not published formally, but are instead summarized in the state or local bar association journal, the body rendering decisions will often make them available on its website. In most instances, the "published" decisions are freely available, but in some states access is restricted to members of that state's bar association. Lexis Advance and Westlaw also include some relevant decisions, but with less thorough coverage than of traditional case law. As always, even when full-text searching is available, it can be difficult to isolate only those hearings or other proceedings that concern your specific issue. To mitigate this limitation, some adjudicative bodies also prepare indexes to their own decisions.

Further, there are two publications with which every legal ethics researcher should be familiar. One is the *ABA/BNA Lawyers' Manual on Professional Conduct*, which is jointly published in looseleaf format by the ABA and Bloomberg BNA. Once available on Lexis Advance and Westlaw, this invaluable resource is now available in electronic format only from Bloomberg Law. Among other useful features, this publication contains summaries of, and references to, disciplinary proceedings, court cases, and ethics opinions from every state. Consulting this looseleaf early in your research can save you a great deal of time and trouble. Once you've identified a relevant summary, it is quite easy in most instances to visit the website of the body making the decision to access the full text. The other publication is the *National Reporter on Legal Ethics and Professional Responsibility*, published by University Publications of America. This important resource reprints in full text selected state and local ethics opinions. An archived (not updated after 2011) version of this resource is available on Lexis Advance, but as with the printed version, not all states are included.

These bar association ethics opinions are the final type of case law the researcher needs to consult. The American Bar Association and the bar associations of all 50 states and the District of Columbia, and some local bar associations all publish ethics opinions. These opinions are advisory in nature, that is, they are written prospectively, often in response to inquiries by one or more lawyers. Most states publish their ethics opinions in the state or local bar association journal, while a few states do not publish them at all. Westlaw and Lexis Advance include some state ethics opinions in their databases as well. Most states make ethics opinions available via the state judiciary or state bar association website. Finally, as noted above, the *ABA/BNA Lawyers' Manual on Professional Conduct* contains summaries of state and national ethics opinions. Wherever the ethics opinions from your state happen to be published, they are an important part of your legal ethics research. While it is technically true that these opinions are advisory in nature, state courts often find their interpretations persuasive and choose to follow their advice. In most instances, they have nearly the same precedential weight as actual judicial opinions.

Since 1924, the American Bar Association has issued formal and informal ethics opinions. Again, these are advisory in nature, but courts commonly cite them as authority when interpreting or applying a state statute derived from an ABA model. Formal ethics opinions are issued on matters the ABA deems to be of general interest to the bar. Informal ethics opinions, on the other hand, are more narrowly drawn, addressing a particular situation or set of facts, and are therefore accorded slightly less authority and cited less frequently by courts. Formal and informal ethics opinions are available in specialized print publications of the ABA, on Westlaw, on Lexis Advance, on Bloomberg Law in the *ABA/BNA Lawyers' Manual on Professional Conduct*, and in the *ABA Journal*.

11.6   SOURCES OF AUTHORITY— SECONDARY SOURCES

A wealth of secondary sources exists to help the researcher. As one would expect, there are a great many law review articles written annually on various aspects of legal ethics. Locating and using law review articles should be a routine process to you by now. There are even a few journals specializing in legal ethics issues (such as *Legal Ethics* and the *Georgetown Journal of Legal Ethics*), although one should search broadly since many general law reviews publish articles on legal ethics as well.

There are also many treatises on legal ethics. Too numerous to list here, these works, if carefully chosen by the researcher, can help explicate difficult material, identify lacunae in the rules or case law, track differing interpretations of particular model language across jurisdictions, and so on.

There is also a Restatement that includes a treatment of legal ethics: the *Restatement of the Law; Third, The Law Governing Lawyers*, published by the American Law Institute in 2000 and updated with pocket parts. Like all Restatements, the Restatement of the law governing lawyers was written by an eminent scholar in the field, and reviewed and revised by a committee of expert lawyers, scholars, and judges. The Restatement covers much more than legal ethics, but does include sections that are relevant to legal ethics research. As discussed in **Section 6.2**, Restatements have as their goal to restate, or describe in subject arrangement, an area of the law in declarative or black-letter terms, followed by commentary and illustrations. Although primarily descriptive of current practice, Restatements do urge reform in certain areas or express preferences for one practice or another. Restatements are very influential, often cited in court opinions. If the Restatement contains a section discussing the rule you are researching, it would not be wise to ignore that analysis. Strangely enough, there is no first or second edition of this Restatement. Since the current round of revisions of the Restatements is generally the third, the American Law Institute decided to give this new publication the same edition number as the others.

11.7   HOW LEGAL ETHICS RESEARCH REALLY WORKS

How, then, does one actually conduct research in legal ethics, given its model law origins and state law adoption? Research is only marginally more complicated than any other state law research might be. In general terms, we can lay out the steps you might take when faced with a research problem related to legal ethics.

First, of course, it is necessary to identify the issue at hand. One thing worth mentioning is that lawyers in practice are subject to all of the laws pertaining to all businesses or generally to all professionals in the particular state in which they practice, even if there is no mention of the contested activity in the legal ethics or professional responsibility section of the state code. For example, no matter what provisions, if any, of the Model Code or Model Rules your state may have adopted, all lawyers are prohibited from committing fraud, embezzling money, falsifying tax returns, and so on. The legal ethics rules of a state are in no way an exhaustive list of the legal responsibilities and obligations of the lawyer. Assuming, though, that for purposes of this section you are faced with a question of legal ethics (as opposed to garden variety criminality), how should you proceed once you have identified your issue?

The next step is to consult your state's law. Remember that the legal ethics laws in your state may have been passed by the legislature like any other state law, or they may have been adopted by the state supreme court and thus considered rules of court. Either way, they are the law of your state. The only difference lies in where you need to go to find them. If the legislature has passed the ethics laws like any other state law, your research will begin in your state's annotated code. If your state's supreme court has adopted ethics laws as rules of court, you will need to find where rules of court are published in your state. Most commonly, rules of court are published as a separate pamphlet shelved with the annotated code. Practices vary from state to state, however.

Once you have located your state's ethics laws, the next phase of research involves reading the relevant sections, following any annotations that may pertain to your topic, performing the necessary updating, and all of the usual steps required when conducting state statutory research. You will follow the clues in the annotations, gathering citations to useful primary and secondary sources, which may prove to be sufficient. It may be that your issue is straightforward, making research fairly mechanical.

If, however, you are not so lucky, you will need to dive into the body of material reflecting your law's probable genesis in one or another model code. You may want to examine your law's model source, in an annotated version if available. The ABA publishes annotated versions of the Model Rules and the Model Code, although the Model Code annotations are no longer updated. You may want to consult the *ABA/BNA Lawyers' Manual on Professional Conduct* for tables showing which other jurisdictions have adopted the code or rule you are researching, which makes it possible to find cases, ethics opinions, and additional material from other jurisdictions you might decide to employ in order to bolster your argument. The web is becoming an increasingly convenient and easy place to find state ethics codes and opinions, and even some secondary material as well. A general web search for [state name] legal ethics opinions is likely to prove fruitful, provided that you evaluate the results list carefully. In most instances you'll be looking for a .gov website (if the ethics opinion is produced by the judiciary) or a .org website (if it comes from a bar association).

After exhausting all of the statutory research resources, you should turn to the case law. This includes the state court opinions from your state as well as the related ABA and state ethics opinions to see whether your issue has been considered before. It may be easiest to do some of this research online on Westlaw, Lexis Advance, or Bloomberg Law if your state's ethics opinions are included in those services.

In addition to statutory and case law research, you will also probably want to consult secondary sources. Law review articles can be helpful in certain situations. You must examine the *Restatement of the Law, Third,*

Law Governing Lawyers to determine whether it contains any relevant discussion. Finally, it might prove useful to consult treatises and other scholarly work on legal ethics.

The process here differs only in a few details from the approach you would take to research any matter of state law. The differences have to do with the receptiveness of the state courts to arguments and precedent from other jurisdictions that have adopted the same model rule, or that have considered the ethical issue at hand. In a matter of tort law, for example, an Ohio state court judge would probably not be swayed by a decision on a similar issue from a Utah court. In legal ethics, on the other hand, as in all areas of law heavily influenced by model or uniform laws, you need to take other jurisdictions into account when framing arguments. This is not to say that there is anything like national common law on legal ethics, but there is greater attention to uniformity and consistency here than in some other areas of law.

CHAPTER 12

FOREIGN LAW RESEARCH

...

12.1 INTRODUCTION

As globalization marches on, the importance of foreign law research grows. Even if you only practice law in the United States, you may on occasion be asked to provide legal advice that can involve foreign jurisdictions. For example, companies that sell online or have far flung places of business may need to consider relevant commercial laws from other countries; a U.S. citizen planning to work abroad may have questions about the attendant tax obligations; or estate planning for a wealthy individual could easily involve assets that are present in, and subject to the laws of, a foreign country. In each of those examples and countless others, you may have to research and consider the applicability of laws beyond just those of the United States.

For purposes of this book, written from a U.S. perspective, foreign law is best described as the domestic (sometimes called national) law of some other nation. Take care not to conflate foreign law with international law, which is the law between or among countries (see **Chapter 13**). Even legal researchers who work primarily with domestic (that is, U.S.) law will occasionally be faced with an issue that also involves foreign law. This chapter is designed to give you a framework sufficient to allow you to conduct foreign law research as the need arises, to be supplemented by more specialized texts if required.

Much as when you are faced with doing research in an unfamiliar U.S. state, when conducting foreign research you must first get a sense of what you are hoping to find. In New York State, for example, the highest court is the Court of Appeals and so a researcher would most prefer controlling case law from that court. In the foreign law context, however, determining what you're looking for can be a bit more involved. As a preliminary matter, you must first identify what type of legal system exists in your country of interest.

12.2 TYPES OF LEGAL SYSTEMS

Broadly speaking, there are four families of legal systems in use today—common law, civil law, religious law, and customary law. There are also some jurisdictions that are most accurately characterized as having a mixed law system, consisting of some combination of those four principal systems. In practice, the delineations between the families of legal systems have blurred somewhat in the last century or so, but some general principles still apply.

Both common law and civil law systems, by far the two most widespread types, share general categories of legal materials. Nearly all will include a source of foundational law (almost always written), and some level of legislative, judicial, and executive functions. This means that you'll come across the same types of materials with which you are already familiar—e.g., a constitution, statutes (often arranged into a code), and case law. Legal scholarship or research tools (broadly called secondary sources in the U.S.) can also be found in both systems, though its varied role is perhaps the single largest difference between the two legal systems.

To most readers of this book, a common law system is the most familiar, as it is the basis for the system of law in the United States at the federal level and at the state level in 49 of the 50 states (Louisiana is a mixed common law and civil law system). A legacy of the British Empire, common law systems today are found primarily in countries that once were under British control. Unsurprisingly, this also means that there is a high correlation between common law countries and the use of English. Generally, legal research in a common law system may involve a statute or regulation, but will conclude with a focus on judicial (or quasi-judicial) interpretation. A particular statute may, by its plain language, seem applicable, but if prior judicial interpretation has determined otherwise, the principle of *stare decisis* controls. In a common law system, secondary sources, such as scholarship from legal experts, are often extremely helpful as a research tool but are unlikely to be cited to a court or relied on in its determination.

By contrast, in a civil law system the code is of primary importance. Case law does not create precedent and it is usually afforded little weight when applying the code to a particular set of facts. Legal scholarship, on the other hand, is valued much more highly in a civil law system. If the common law system can be considered an export of the British Empire, the expansive spread of the civil law system was originally a creation of the Roman Empire and is more recently a product of continental Europe and its own colonial history. Jurisdictions influenced by Spain, Portugal, France, etc., now tend to use civil law legal systems.

The third family of legal systems is religious law. In a religious law system, religious doctrines are of the greatest import and are applied or interpreted in a fashion that parallels legal analysis in common law or civil law jurisdictions. Many mixed law jurisdictions are a combination of religious law and either civil law or common law. The law of some jurisdictions is influenced, or to some extent supplied by, the religious systems of Sharia (the most prevalent type of religious law), halakha, and canon law. In many jurisdictions, religious law is limited in its applicability to particular areas of life (e.g., domestic relations).

Finally, the fourth family of legal systems is customary law. Like religious law, customary law is rarely the sole legal system in a particular jurisdiction. More often, it is paired with one of the other three families to form a mixed law system. A workable (if simplistic) definition of customary law in the foreign law context is a system where customs are so well established, widely accepted, and part of the culture that they are given the force of law—despite never being codified or in some cases never even reduced to writing. Today, customary law persists mainly in areas that have a strong indigenous population. In many ways, researching in a customary law system requires a far greater understanding of the culture than does researching in a common law or civil law system. To this end, a researcher may have to make use of more non-legal sources, such as sociological, historical, or anthropological resources.

The differences between families of legal systems go far beyond what is outlined here, including things as fundamental as the difference in the approach of the judicial process (e.g., adversarial vs. investigative). As the world becomes more interconnected, the lines between families have also blurred, including some civil law jurisdictions beginning to place more weight on judicial determinations (though stopping short of the idea of precedent). Nevertheless, identifying the relevant legal system in play allows you, as the researcher, to have a sense of what types of materials you can expect to find, as well as the relative importance of those materials. Some of the most reliable and accessible resources for identifying the relevant legal system (at least in general terms) are listed in **Table 12.A**.

12.3   SPECIFIC JURISDICTIONS

Once you have a basic idea of what family of legal system is used in the relevant country, you'll be better equipped to delve into in-depth research. At this stage, you are less interested in the legal system family and more interested in the quirks of a particular country (or countries). Though this book is not designed to provide detailed information for any non-U.S. jurisdiction, many other resources are available to provide such guidance.

One of the best resources, widely available in academia, is called the Foreign Law Guide (FLG). A subscription database, the FLG is designed to be the most effective starting point for conducting foreign legal research. It includes not only an explanation of the government and legal system for each jurisdiction covered, but also bibliographic information identifying that jurisdiction's primary sources—e.g., any official gazette (a periodical that often includes the first, and sometimes only, publication of the text of a statute); any codifications or compilations of existing laws; any reports or other means of distributing judicial decisions, etc. This information can then be used to locate the relevant resources, sometimes available only in print. Though it does not contain the full text of the resources so identified, the FLG does have a separate section pointing to legal texts, primarily statutes, in electronic format (when available).

From both a practitioner and academic perspective, one of the most useful parts of the FLG—and what separates it from the more simplified non-subscription options—is its subject organization. Statutes from each country covered in the database are arranged according to a common index system. If you are a practitioner who needs to know what Nicaraguan labor laws need to be considered by your client opening a business there, you can get the background on the Nicaraguan legal system and identify the specific law(s) that apply through the FLG. If a reliable translation is available (see **Section 12.5**), the FLG will also include information on where that is located. If you are an academic researcher who wants to write a comparative paper on animal welfare laws across jurisdictions, the FLG can help by identifying which countries have such laws that have been placed into its subject organization.

There are other foreign law research guides, many of which are on the open web. Even the best non-subscription sources, however, must be viewed carefully. They are often created and maintained by experts (e.g., librarians, scholars, practitioners) as a labor of love, or with only minimal compensation. As a result, they are sometimes updated with less frequency than a subscription offering. While the background historical information is settled, and the legal system itself is unlikely to change, references to specific statutes or cases can go stale surprisingly quickly. When selecting a research guide that you will use, pay particularly close attention to the date of the last update (which should be prominently displayed) and do not be afraid to make use of multiple guides to combine the best organization with what appears to be the most current information. **Table 12.B** includes some of the best available sources for research guides.

12.4   FINDING SPECIFIC MATERIAL ONLINE

Once you are armed with a good research guide, you will likely learn that you need a particular statute or judicial decision and, as a practical matter, you are unlikely to have easy access to a wealth of foreign materials in print. Fortunately, there is today considerable material that is produced and distributed in electronic format.

Two sources deserve special mention here. The first is the World Legal Information Institute (WorldLII) (http://www.worldlii.org). WorldLII is a unique hybrid, combining a portal to external information and the hosting of legal databases. As a host, it includes hundreds of databases from over

150 countries. For those countries, plus another sixty or so, WorldLII also provides links to legal materials from elsewhere on the web. Similar to the FLG, a strength of WorldLII is the uniform subject organization it provides. In this regard, it can be a helpful stand-in if access to the FLG is unavailable.

The second is the aptly named "Guide to Law Online: Nations" (http://www.loc.gov/law/help/guide/nations.php), created and maintained by the Law Library of Congress. In addition to links to many jurisdiction-specific research guides, the Guide to Law Online also provides links to legal materials (constitutions, executive materials, judicial materials, and legislative materials). Official sources are provided whenever available, though they are often supplemented by other sources. These other sources are primarily produced by non-governmental organizations (e.g., the World Trade Organization, the World Intellectual Property Organization, the Law Library of Congress itself) and may even include useful (though unofficial) translations into English.

12.5   LEGAL TRANSLATIONS

Translation in the legal context is worthy of a special note. Remember, if you can, when you first were introduced to legal English—perhaps as a 1L in law school. For many students, even native English speakers, learning the language of the law in the U.S. can be a challenge. Some terms are unfamiliar, while other familiar terms convey novel shades of meaning or even completely new meanings.

The language of the law in non-English speaking jurisdictions is similarly complex, and machine translators (e.g., Google Translate) are not nearly up to the task of effectively conveying the legal significance of documents. Even human translations, conducted by laypeople who are fluent in both English and the language of the original document, may not capture the legal nuance of the text. Ideally you will be able to locate, or have made, a translation created by someone possessing both native or fluent command of the languages involved and familiarity with the law. Because of the complexities involved in translating law, even when government agencies provide translations into other languages (often English), these translations are specifically identified as "unofficial" or "for information purposes only." If there is any dispute or conflict between the English translation and the original, the original is what will control.

All of this is not to say that machine translation is valueless in a legal context. Quite the contrary, it can be a nearly indispensable tool to help identify the general subject matter of a particular statute or specific components such as dates. But it should not be the final step that you rely on, because context and nuance are often lost on the machine. Let's take one example, albeit from a non-legal context. In many languages, the concepts of "evening" and "night" are very closely related, using the same or perhaps interchangeable words. Similarly, the concepts of "dress" and "gown" can be roughly equivalent, especially without context clues. Imagine then, you are inviting a non-English speaker over for drinks and you are relying on machine translation to craft the invitation. In recommending proper attire, you suggest an "evening dress," which the machine translation promptly renders as the foreign equivalent of "night gown." Exceedingly similar as individual words, but bringing a dramatically different tone to the invitation. Without any sense of context, this is the sort of error that could be merely embarrassing in daily life, but have significant consequences when applied to legal documents. In general, then, you will be better off (when hiring a legal specialist translator is not an option) relying on a human-prepared translation from a reliable source. Keep in mind, however, that the vast majority of legal materials created in other languages have not been translated into English.

12.6   THE BASIC MECHANICS OF FOREIGN LEGAL RESEARCH

How, then, does research in the law of a foreign jurisdiction proceed? After consulting a good research guide to the country in question, you should have a fair sense of the legal system of that country. You should know how to find the constitution, session laws (called gazettes in many code countries), codes (if any), case law, and important secondary sources. Once you have identified your issue, placed it in its legal context, and identified the primary and secondary sources that might be relevant, research proceeds in a manner that roughly parallels the process for attacking a problem of U.S. law.

Take as an example an issue related to Malaysian income taxation. Your first step would be to consult a good legal research guide for background and a description of the major primary and secondary sources. You might choose to begin with the *Foreign Law Guide* (see **Section 12.2** for more on this resource). From it you will learn that Malaysia is a constitutional monarchy with common law traditions (it was a British colony until the 1950s), but a legal system that is a mix of Islamic law, common law, Chinese customary law, and indigenous Malay law. Also, although nearly all official documents are published in English and Bahasa Malaysia, it is the latter that is controlling. From *Foreign Law Guide* you will also learn about the different primary and secondary sources; statutes, regulations, court reports, and secondary sources.

In the section on Malaysian income taxation, which is the topic that interests us, *Foreign Law Guide* lists all of the revisions of the income tax law and includes links to sources for those laws. It also lists a source for tax regulations, and several treatises on income taxation in Malaysia.

Armed with all of this information, the researcher's process from this point bears a rough resemblance to that of a researcher working on a problem of U.S. tax law. The goal is to gather all of the material relevant to the problem, except that in the case of the Malaysian tax problem there are issues of access to resources, language issues, and the vastly more serious consideration of whether the researcher is sufficiently in command of the details of the Malaysian legal system to allow for placing the results of the research process in their proper context. After consulting a general work such as *Foreign Law Guide*, and keeping the foregoing limitations in mind, the next step might be to consult the statutes and regulations. Finally, you might consult other secondary sources for a discussion of your specific subject matter, such as the *Malaysian Master Tax Guide,* one of the resources recommended by the *Foreign Law Guide*. You might also consult the Malaysian court reports and the *Malayan Law Journal*, which reprints important opinions.

Once you have examined all of the resources available to you, and followed citations and other textual clues where they lead, you have done as much as can be done without hiring specialized counsel. Can you have the same confidence in your results as you could for the same research in U.S. tax law? Almost certainly not. First, very few U.S. libraries will hold all of the Malaysian sources listed in *Foreign Law Guide*. Second, there is a wealth of other potentially relevant information not published at all, not published yet, not in English, or otherwise unavailable to you. Very few jurisdictions publish legal information as thoroughly as the United States does. You will, on the other hand, know a great deal more than you did before, and may have learned enough to solve the legal problem before you. This process is time-consuming and, frankly, fraught with problems and frustrations. But it can be done, and done well, by the informed, diligent, resourceful researcher.

12.7   TABLES

TABLE 12.A: RESOURCES TO IDENTIFY RELEVANT LEGAL SYSTEMS

1.   Foreign Law Guide—Brill Reference

    www.foreignlawguide.com

2.   JuriGlobe—World Legal Systems

    http://www.juriglobe.ca/eng/index.php

3.   The World Factbook, Central Intelligence Agency

    https://www.cia.gov/library/publications/resources/the-world-factbook/

    Specific Legal System field listing (naming available countries and corresponding legal systems) available at https://www.cia.gov/library/publications/the-world-factbook/fields/2100.html

    Also available in print, published annually by the U.S. Government Publishing Office.

4.   *Legal Systems of the World: A Political, Social, and Cultural Encyclopedia.* Santa Barbara, Cal. ABC-CLIO, 2002.

    This 4-volume set is only available in print and includes entries for every country and many sub-national jurisdictions.

TABLE 12.B: SELECTED SOURCES OF ONLINE FOREIGN LAW RESEARCH GUIDES

1.   GlobaLex, Hauser Global Law School Program at NYU School of Law

http://www.nyulawglobal.org/globalex/index.html

GlobaLex is home to over 150 foreign legal research guides, most with regular updates. To access the most recent material, be sure to select the "UPDATE" link rather than the more descriptive title.

2.   Guide to Law Online, Law Library of Congress

https://www.loc.gov/law/help/guide.php

[Go to "Nations," then choose a country and look under the heading of "Legal Guides."]

3.   Columbia Law School, A Selective List of Guides to Foreign Legal Research

http://library.law.columbia.edu/guides/A_Selective_List_of_Gui des_to_Foreign_Legal_Research

4.   Institute of Advanced Legal Studies, University of London, IALS Library Guides

http://libguides.ials.sas.ac.uk/jurisdictions

5.   LLRX—Law and Technology Resources for Legal Professionals

https://www.llrx.com/category/comparative-foreign-law/

Individual articles (research guides) related to foreign law are put into the category "Comparative/Foreign Law," but unfortunately they cannot be easily browsed.

CHAPTER 13

INTERNATIONAL LAW RESEARCH

■ ■ ■

13.1   INTRODUCTION

International law can be defined as the law between or among nations. As the world has grown more complex and interrelated, some system of cooperation among the countries of the world has become increasingly necessary. International law covers matters from the least significant trade, tax, or extradition agreement between neighboring countries to the workings of the largest and most complex intergovernmental organizations, such as the United Nations or the European Union. It is important to understand the distinction between public international law, which is the law among nations as just described, and so-called private international law, which has to do with questions of which nation's domestic law should govern a particular situation. In the United States, we would call these latter issues choice of law or conflicts of law. Private international law falls outside the scope of this chapter.

International law exists in a variety of forms. Two countries may agree on a bilateral treaty, just between them, on any of a number of subjects. Countries in a region may band together for mutual defense, or trade, or to protect the regional environment. Intergovernmental organizations such as the United Nations use their global influence to urge passage of all manner of treaties and other instruments, ranging across the entire spectrum of social, political, military, environmental, and economic issues.

Often, when a nation agrees to become a party or signatory to a treaty or other international agreement, it becomes necessary for that country to change its internal domestic law to fulfill the requirements of the treaty. This new legislation is usually called implementing legislation, and may be a critical part of research on an issue of international law.

There are a number of good introductions to international legal research that go into far more detail than we will attempt here, some of which are listed in **Table 13.A**. There are also, as you might guess, a great many titles published on more specific subjects in international law research. Increasingly, courses in international legal research are being offered at U.S. law schools, and several excellent texts have appeared for use in these classes. One outstanding example, useful to the researcher even outside the confines of any particular law school class, is *International* *and Foreign Legal Research: A Coursebook*, by Marci Hoffman and Mary Rumsey, now in its second edition.

There are also specialized tools to help you locate journal articles about specific topics in international law. The *Index to Foreign Legal Periodicals* is similar to other periodical indexes discussed in this book, except that its coverage is different. *IFLP*, as it is commonly called, is an index of articles about law in systems other than the Anglo-American countries. This tool indexes legal journals regardless of where they are published (in other words, articles about French law published in U.S. journals would be indexed here) or the language in which they are written. It is available in print and on HeinOnline. Another useful journal index is the *Legal Journals Index*, available on Westlaw, which indexes over 700 periodicals having primarily to do with legal issues in the United Kingdom, selected commonwealth countries, and Europe. Both of these indexes are also useful as tools for current awareness. Also remember that U.S. law journals include many articles dealing with aspects of international law, and so the tools referenced in **Chapter 4** are valuable here.

13.2 SOURCES OF INTERNATIONAL LAW

In this context, "sources" does not mean print and electronic resources used for research. Instead, this section contains a very brief answer to the question, "Where does international law come from?" One source is obvious: treaties. In fact, treaties are what most people think of when they think of international law, but there are other sources to consider.

The treaty establishing the International Court of Justice lays out the different sources of international law. Article 38 of this formulation, long the classic and oft-cited statement on the subject, defines the sources of international law as international conventions (e.g., treaties), custom, general principles of law recognized by civilized nations, and (as subsidiary means for the determination of rules of law) judicial decisions and academic writings. These five sources interrelate in such a way as to result in a relatively complex universe of material for the legal researcher to consider. What exactly, for example, is custom? Who decides what the customary practice is? There are answers to these questions, tentative and qualified though they may be, and it is the responsibility of the researcher to consider all of the material that could potentially be relevant when trying to determine just what the law is on any topic.

Despite the fact that there are many potential sources of international law, treaties are by far the most important single source to consider, and their centrality only increases as time passes. It is to treaty research, then, that we turn next.

13.3 TREATY RESEARCH

Much of international law stems from treaties. Treaties come in two basic varieties: bilateral, between two countries and affecting only them, and multilateral, entered into by and affecting three or more countries. Some treaties have well over a hundred signatories. There are treaties covering every conceivable category of human endeavor and interaction. Finding them, determining whether they are in force, locating the implementing legislation, if any, passed by the legislature of a particular signatory nation, and applying the terms of the treaty to your specific situation are the basic activities of treaty research. For a list of websites featuring useful collections of treaties, see **Table 13.B**.

Bear in mind that in the United States there is a distinction between treaties and executive orders, although this distinction does not always exist in other jurisdictions. The difference stems from the U.S. constitutional requirement that treaties can only be entered into with the advice and consent of the Senate. Executive Orders, on the other hand, need not pass any Senatorial review. The majority of international agreements into which the United States enters in the modern era result from executive orders rather than by Senate ratification. In this chapter, however, we will use the term "treaty" in the broader sense, setting aside the mechanism by which the United States joined the agreement.

When the United States is a party to a treaty in which you are interested, finding that treaty becomes easier. There are a number of print and electronic sources to help. Many websites print the texts of treaties to which the U.S. is party. To locate official versions, the date of the treaty takes on additional importance. For older treaties, the best available official source will often be the *Treaty Series* (between 1795 and 1945) or the Statutes at Large (between 1778 and 1949). For the initial slip form of treaties since 1945, turn to *Treaties and Other International Acts Series* (or *"TIAS"*). For many years (between 1950 and 1984), the treaties published in the TIAS were consolidated (years after the fact) into the preferred official source called the *United States Treaties and Other International Agreements* (or *"UST"*). The federal government ultimately pulled the plug on the UST entirely, and no longer produces the TIAS in print. The TIAS is, however, made available in electronic format on the State Department website, with coverage from 1996 to the present. Other treaty sources are listed in **Table 13.B**.

Though finding the text of a treaty is usually not very difficult, special care must be taken to identify the status of the treaty. One needs to know whether the U.S. has ratified the treaty, or needs to. Many treaties do not go into effect until a certain number of countries have signed. Sometimes countries are signatories to a treaty, yet they draft reservations, specifying provisions to which they do not agree and by which they will not abide. This process of finding out whether the treaty is in force and who has agreed to which of its provisions is the real work of treaty research.

For a treaty where the U.S. is a party, several State Department publications will help determine the status of that treaty. *Treaties in Force* is the place to start. It lists and summarizes every treaty currently in force to which the U.S. is a party and consists of two sections. The first section includes bilateral treaties (between the U.S. and one other nation), organized first by country and then by subject. The second section includes multilateral treaties, organized by subject. *Treaties in Force* is produced annually (though a full edition was not published in 2014 or 2015) and is occasionally updated in electronic format on the website of the Department of State at https://www.state.gov/s/l/treaty/tif/.

Along with *Treaties in Force*, you may also consult *Kavass's Current Treaty Index*, a commercial publication available on HeinOnline, for additional information about the status of treaties. Doing a thorough job of updating treaty status information might require you to consult a variety of other sources, too many to discuss or even list here. Any of the good general sources provided in **Table 13.A** and most of the better international research guides will have more detailed instructions. The point here is to know that the information exists, but is not compiled in one convenient location.

If you are faced with the task of doing international research involving treaties, especially when the U.S. is not a party (rendering most of the aforementioned resources inapplicable) the website of the United Nations at https://treaties.un.org may prove invaluable. The incredible wealth of information made available electronically by the UN, including the text of treaties, planning documents, reports, meeting agendas, and more is ever-changing and cannot be completely covered in a brief introduction like this. That being said, there are two resources on the website that must be specifically highlighted. The first is the Status of Treaties page for the Multilateral Treaties Deposited with the Secretary-General. Here the deposited treaties have been arranged into twenty-nine chapters, each related to a particular subject (e.g., human rights, freedom of information, outer space). This subject organization can be used to identify the treaties that may be applicable to a given research problem. Each chapter then has links to the full text of the treaties within, plus a list of participants, effective dates, and declarations and reservations. The second vitally important resource is the United Nations Treaty Series (UNTS) online. The UNTS online includes all treaties and international agreements filed with the UN since 1945, and supports both full-text and advanced search functionality.

13.4   INTERGOVERNMENTAL ORGANIZATIONS

As important as treaty research is, there is much more to international legal research. One interesting development is the rise of the intergovernmental organization, and how the largest of them are beginning to look and act increasingly like governments: legislating, regulating, conducting judicial hearings, and so on. The United Nations, the European Union, the Organization of American States, and a handful of others may, in some sense, be considered to be governments or sovereigns. Conducting legal research in these "jurisdictions" can be thought of as roughly parallel to doing so in any other national jurisdiction, and the patterns of publication hold as true here as in any national system. Let's examine one such system: the European Union. You will see that the familiar types of legal publications exist here as well.

13.5   THE EUROPEAN UNION

The European Union (EU) is an important example of just such an intergovernmental organization. From relatively humble beginnings as a cooperative arrangement among a few European countries, organized to deal with joint steel and coal issues, the EU has grown into a world economic and political powerhouse consisting of twenty-eight nations and regulating business, travel, citizenship, health, and even issuing its own currency. Although the EU itself states that it is not intended to replace the nation-state, for our purposes it is helpful to think of it as its own country, its own jurisdiction.

The EU is an incredibly complex organization, involved in every aspect of European life, from the economy to defense, from environmental law to agriculture. The EU has also developed legal and governmental structures parallel to those of a sovereign nation: a legislature, regulating agencies, various layers of courts with differing jurisdictions, as well as the full complement of documentary support necessary to make public its workings, its laws and rules, and its judgments.

Conducting legal research in EU law is not simple for the novice, but there is a wealth of explanatory material about the EU and specific research guides to help. You should, by now, be able to anticipate the kinds of publications you will encounter and know roughly how they are to be used. You should expect, as an example, that a wide variety of secondary sources will have been produced to help researchers navigate the complexities of EU law. Also, you should expect that the legislature will produce statutes that are first printed chronologically, and that there will be either a commercial or an official arrangement of these laws into subject order to aid in research. You should also expect that there will be something like regulation, and that the same pattern of chronological and subject printing will exist. Finally, you should not be surprised to find case law from courts, perhaps from several levels of courts or courts with different subject matter jurisdiction, and that these cases will be full-text searchable and that there will be a digest or other tool to allow subject access to opinions. Once you have these patterns firmly in your mind you will be able to approach even as complex a legal entity (or a jurisdiction, if you prefer) as the EU with confidence in your ability to find the material you need to conduct thorough and effective research.

13.6   EUROPEAN UNION—SECONDARY SOURCES

As with all legal research, it would be wise to begin in the secondary literature. When approaching legal research in a novel jurisdiction, context is critically important. You need to know the structure of the international body whose law you are researching in order to understand the ways in which the primary sources you will ultimately be using fit together. Secondary sources for international legal research may be thought of as belonging to one of several categories.

Sources describing the organization generally are a good first step. For EU law, there are several informative publications and websites you can consult for help in understanding the EU's different subgroups and how they function together as interlocking branches of government. Only by beginning research with a firm command of the EU's internal structure, the limits of its power, and other basic information, can you conduct useful and accurate research. *Foreign Law Guide: Current Sources of Codes and Legislation,* for example, provides a useful discussion on the legal structure of the EU and its major publications. *Encyclopedia of the European Union* is another good source to consult for basic background. You should also know that Europa, the EU's own website, found at https://europa.eu/, is extremely helpful, with good explanations of the EU's basic structure, functions and documents. The EU also has developed EUR-Lex, a portal for its legal materials. Most of the primary sources we will refer to below can be found at one or both of those websites. After you have gathered enough background knowledge to understand the structure of this organization, and have an idea about what kinds of primary and secondary sources to look for, you will probably find it useful to turn to another kind of secondary source, the research guide.

13.7   EUROPEAN UNION—STATUTES

EU legislation is difficult to research in part because there are at least five different bodies empowered to participate in the process; the European Commission, the European Parliament, the Council, the Economic and Social Committee and the Committee of the Regions. Each of these subgroups has their own publications and websites, their own mandates, powers and procedures, and it can be difficult even for experienced researchers to keep it all straight.

There are several major sources you should be aware of, but bear in mind that you will need to learn more about your subject matter and which body or bodies legislate on this topic before plunging into the primary sources. The *Official Journal (OJ)* is published every business day, and is divided into two series. The L Series contains the texts of new treaties, legislation, directives and regulations. In a sense the L Series is the EU's *Statutes at Large* and the New Rules and Regulations section of the *Federal Register* rolled into one. The other series, the C Series, is the "Information and Notices" section of the *OJ*, and contains resolutions of the various subgroups, proposed regulations, minutes of meetings, notices of Court decisions, and so on. The *OJ* is the single most important source of EU legislative information. It is available in an authenticated and official version online at EUR-Lex. Westlaw and Lexis Advance both contain some coverage of the *OJ* as well, but the coverage and ability to search on those platforms is not as robust as on EUR-Lex, nor as robust as what you are accustomed to for U.S. research. The *OJ*, as you might expect, also has a number of associated indexes and other directories to help researchers gain subject access to the chronologically printed material.

13.8   EUROPEAN UNION—CASE LAW

The European Court of Justice is the highest court in the EU structure. This court decides cases involving the founding treaties and other documents of the EU, their appropriate application, and their interpretation. There are also a series of subordinate courts with different subject matter jurisdiction as well.

The official reporter of the Court of Justice's opinions is called *Reports of Cases Before the Court* (also called *European Court Reports* or *ECR*). Like the *United States Reports*, this official reporter is always a few years out of date. For more current reports, one must turn to one of several unofficial, commercial publications: *European Community Cases* and the *European Union Law Reporter*. These offer more current coverage of EU cases. There are also different ways to get access to EU cases by subject, primarily via EUR-Lex. EUR-Lex includes a "directory" of EU case law, which organizes judgments and orders from the Court of Justice, General Court, and Civil Service tribunal into a consistent classification scheme that has been applied to cases decided since 2010. You can also search the full text of decisions, or browse by court and date within the Court Reports. Using the finding aids associated with the commercial version of opinions can also be helpful and there are a variety of secondary sources available. These are listed and described in research guides and specialized international research texts, such as those listed in **Table 13.A**.

13.9   EUROPEAN UNION—SUMMING UP

The point of the foregoing discussion of the sources of legal information produced by the EU and available for the legal researcher is not to provide a comprehensive description of the EU's legal structure, nor to provide the researcher with a general method or process to employ when faced with a legal problem based on EU law. Rather, the idea here is to show that even as complex an organization as the EU produces basically the same categories of legal publication with which the U.S.-trained law student or lawyer should be fluent. You should know how to look for and work with constitutions, legislation, regulations, case law, and the like. None of these forms of publication should be new to you. What is required before a novice can successfully undertake international law research is a clear understanding of the need to discover the source of the law to be researched, how to find secondary sources to help contextualize and explain the relevant legal structure, and how to find the underlying legal publications necessary to solve the problem. We do not mean to minimize the difficulties these tasks will occasionally present, but we believe solid legal research in foreign or international law can be conducted by the careful and persistent researcher.

13.10 TABLES

TABLE 13.A: TEXTS AND GUIDES TO INTERNATIONAL LEGAL RESEARCH

1. Marci Hoffman & Mary Rumsey, *International and Foreign Legal Research: A Coursebook*, 2nd ed. Boston, Mass.: Martinus Nijhoff, 2012.

2. Anthony Winer, Mary Ann Archer & Lyonette Louis-Jacques, *International Law Legal Research*. Durham, N. C.: Carolina Academic Press, 2013.

3. Marci Hoffman & Robert C. Berring, Jr., *International Legal Research in a Nutshell*, 2nd ed. St. Paul, Minn.: West Academic Publishing, 2017.

4. GlobaLex, Hauser Global Law School Program at NYU School of Law

    http://www.nyulawglobal.org/globalex/index.html

    GlobaLex is home to over 50 international legal research guides, most with regular updates. Some guides are related to specific subjects (e.g., International Criminal Law), while others are designed to aid with research into particular international bodies (e.g., Council of Europe). To access the most recent material, be sure to select the "UPDATE" link rather than the more descriptive title.

5. Columbia Law School, Research Guides

    http://www.law.columbia.edu/library/research-guides

    Includes guides under the following headings within International Law: Commercial Law, Human Rights, Organizations, Treaties, and Miscellaneous.

6. Georgetown Law Library, Research Guides, Treatise Finders, & Tutorials—Foreign & International Law

    http://guides.ll.georgetown.edu/home/foreign-law

7. International Legal Research Tutorial

    https://www.law.duke.edu/ilrt/

    This collaborative project between Duke University School of Law and University of California, Berkeley, School of Law is geared toward students, but includes information helpful to all types of researchers.

TABLE 13.B: ONLINE TREATY SOURCES

1. United Nations Treaty Collection

   https://treaties.un.org/

2. United States, Department of State, Text of International Agreements to which the US is a Party (TIAS)

   https://www.state.gov/s/l/treaty/tias/index.htm

   Includes texts from 1996 to present.

3. Congress.gov

   https://www.congress.gov/

   [Use the link for "Treaty Documents"]

4. European Union Treaties

   http://eur-lex.europa.eu/collection/eu-law/treaties.html

5. Council of Europe, European Treaties

   http://conventions.coe.int/

6. HeinOnline, Treaties and Agreements Library (subscription database)

   www.heinonline.com

7. Organization of American States, Multilateral Treaties & Bilateral Agreements

   http://www.oas.org/DIL/treaties_and_agreements.htm

8. International Committee of the Red Cross, Treaties, States Parties and Commentaries

   http://www.icrc.org/ihl

9. World Treaty Index

   http://www.worldtreatyindex.com

10. World Legal Information Institute, International Treaties Collection

    http://www.worldlii.org/int/special/treaties/

11. Australian Treaties Library

    http://www.austlii.edu.au/au/other/dfat/

12. University of Minnesota Human Rights Library

    http://www.umn.edu/humanrts

13. World Intellectual Property Organization, WIPO-Administered Treaties

http://www.wipo.int/treaties/en/

CHAPTER 14

MUNICIPAL LAW RESEARCH

■ ■ ■

14.1   MUNICIPAL LAW: WHEN, WHY, AND HOW

At the other end of the spectrum from international law lies municipal law. Some legal questions of local provenance require us to turn from focusing on the global village and instead to consider the requirements of our actual village. Preemption by legal requirements imposed by entities higher up the legal food chain need always to be considered (via all the legal research methods outlined in the previous chapters), but sometimes the governing authority will actually turn out to be a local ordinance or a village court legal decision or a city agency regulation.

When will municipal law come into play? Obviously there are local conditions and problems that would stimulate a local government to come up with its own legal strictures and remedies in order to address them. The rules about keeping poultry, for instance, are likely to vary as between a rural community and a big city within the same state. Other issues addressed by local laws are local only because there is a political will to address them locally that does not exist beyond the municipality. Both types of local concern are brought within the limited capacity of the municipality to act by a delegation of power from the state government, i.e., as a matter of state law. These delegations of power are effected via "home rule" statutes that can be found in the usual sources for state law: the codes and the session laws. These home rule statutes furnish (among other things) the outside limits on what the local lawgivers can legitimately undertake, and can thus provide the basis for challenging the validity of local laws.

Many of the subjects with which local laws are concerned cut quite close to the daily life of individual citizens: where they may hang out, where they may swim, what they may put out in their garbage. Accordingly, an individual's own personal rights may be more often impinged upon by these local laws than by the more lofty and institution-oriented state laws. Local ordinances that have furnished the basis for U.S. Supreme Court cases run the gamut from anti-pornography laws to ordinances concerning loitering, noise control, and the permissible size of bread loaves.

The key thing to remember about municipal or local law research is that you should analogize from state or federal law to figure out what to look for. As emphasized throughout the preceding chapters, confidence in the legal researcher comes in part from knowing what kind of material you will need to find (or not find) in order to rest easy about your legal conclusions. This principle is thrown into sharp relief in the municipal law context, where publication can be sporadic, narrowly distributed, or even non-existent. Where the published legal record peters out, you will still have to look for the things that you know must be out there. This may involve going to a tiny back office somewhere and leafing through the contents of a filing cabinet or a cardboard box; it will almost certainly involve calling on the assistance of those on the spot in the locale in question. For more on finding help from those intimately involved with a legal issue, see **Section 15.14**, and for additional details on sources for local laws, see the research guides listed in the **Appendix**.

14.2   MUNICIPAL CHARTERS

What should you assume is out there, regardless of the nature of the municipality? And how can you find it? By analogy from larger legal systems, we would expect there to be some sort of constitutive document. In municipal law that would be two-fold: the state law delegating power to the municipality and the constitutive local document setting up the exercise of that power. In many municipalities the latter document is called the "charter." As with the federal and state systems, researching constitutional issues basically follows the path of statutory research in the same jurisdiction.

14.3   MUNICIPAL "SESSION LAWS"

The next component you would expect to find would be some sort of set of session laws, the raw output of the local legislature. This is where the fun begins: as the 50 states' statutory publication schemes vary from each other, so, too, with the work of thousands of legislating municipalities. The distinguishing characteristic, of course, of municipal legal publishing is the relative smallness of the market. For many years, this meant that most legal information on the local level was not published by the issuing entity (too big an expense for the size of the entity's budget) and could not be published by the commercial sector (too much overhead for the size of the market). Obviously there were exceptions: for example, the New York City market contains many more people than do most of the 50 states; moreover, the place is fairly bursting with lawyers. Additionally, many people outside the city itself have legal interests there to protect. Accordingly, the New York City statutes (called Local Laws) are published in print by two different local commercial publishers. One of them even publishes the Local Laws first in "advance sheet form," in the manner of the *U.S.C.C.A.N.* advance sheets, and then subsequently reprints them in annual bound volumes. But this is far from the norm. For most municipalities, the local laws are only available from the municipality, in unpublished form.

14.4   MUNICIPAL STATUTORY CODES

Session laws are not where the legal researcher starts out anyway, so the absence of a browesable collection of them is not a huge problem. As you well know by now, the starting point for statutory legal research in primary sources is the code: the subject arrangement and compilation of the laws that originally appeared chronologically as session laws. While municipal codes were always at least marginally more accessible than session laws, the big difference today is the internet. Now that the overhead costs of publishing the codes have plummeted, more and more municipalities have taken the plunge of putting their codes out there for public perusal. Many of them have subcontracted out the preparation of their codes on the web to specialists in this function, and the resulting collocation of multiple codes on the websites of the contractors (e.g., Municode, General Code, and Code Publishing Company) has been a boon for comparativists in the municipal area (see **Section 14.6**). Lexis Advance has also accumulated a considerable collection of municipal code material.

14.5   MUNICIPAL DECISIONAL LAW

All this local law making, as might be expected, generates a certain amount of need for clarification when those laws get applied to individuals' circumstances. In addition to identifying any local statute that applies to your case, you will also want to ascertain whether there is any history of relevant decisions. Arrangements for seeking to apply local laws vary from jurisdiction to jurisdiction. Sometimes there is a regular court involved, sometimes a special court specifically charged with enforcing local ordinances. As a preliminary step towards discovering where the relevant decisions would have been generated, you can consult a court organization chart. These charts, locations for which are given in the first paragraph of **Section 5.22**, give rough summaries of the structure of local courts within the schematic layout of the courts for each state. However, the charts are not supported by statutory citations, so you would need to verify their accuracy by doing regular statutory research in the jurisdictional statutes of the state.

As discussed above with respect to the output of federal District Courts, the value of reading through previous decisions from the relevant local courts will mostly reside in their predictive value. The precedential clout of decisions at this level is minimal. Instead, the value lies in trying to figure out what this particular judge or this particular court is likely to do in your case, based on past track record. Note that since these local courts are part of the regular appeals structure, you should research any and all local law issues in the regular state and federal case law universe, to account for the outcome of previous appeals in similar cases.

Finding the actual local decisions, however, can take you outside the sources familiar to you from state and federal research. Only a minute proportion of local court decisions are selected for publication in the regular state reporters or in local legal newspapers. Those that are part of the ordinary world of published decisional law can be located in a number of ways, including the use of state Shepard's citators in print. Many of the print Shepard's volumes for statutory citations include a section listing case and law review citations to local laws within that state. Some of these volumes also include a subject index to the local laws covered, so that comparison between laws in different locales may be easily accomplished. As noted in **Section 5.22**, certain unusually remunerative jurisdictions and subject matters have supported the development of local reporters and/or digests that include cases not reported in the larger structure of state law case reporting.

In many instances, however, local courts may be statutorily or constitutionally designated as courts not of record, meaning that a permanent record of their proceedings is not legally mandated. But even these "inferior" courts usually are required to keep certain records of their activities, and you may find yourself obliged to prevail on someone working with these records to dig them out for you. Some case records can be consultable as a matter of public record, while others may be sealed to the general public for privacy reasons. Seek guidance in these matters from the clerk in charge of records for the jurisdiction. If you already know what jurisdiction is involved, the information about whom to contact is usually only a web search away.

14.6   DOING COMPARATIVE RESEARCH ON MUNICIPAL LAW

In the state law context, the practitioner is likely to undertake comparative statutory research in order to choose a favorable venue for a client's undertaking, or in order to look as far afield as necessary for favorably persuasive interpretation of a statute similar to that in the client's own jurisdiction. Both of these purposes can also, of course, motivate the local law researcher. The latter purpose, the search for analogous and persuasive judicial interpretation can be particularly crucial for the local law researcher because of the relative thinness of an interpretive record for statutes at this level.

However, there is a third reason that many lawyers find themselves interested in finding out about the ordinances of other localities. Each and every community that undertakes code creation is likely to consult with a lawyer as to the fitness and appropriateness of what they want to do. Not to do so would be to invite challenge from state or federal law, or merely to suffer ineffectuality from a poorly drafted and thus unenforceable statute. Thus, drafting and revising of local ordinances is something that many lawyers will encounter in their practice. Accordingly, the legal information market has provided them with several sources of comparative information that enables them readily to compare statutes of many jurisdictions.

One of these sources, mentioned in **Section 14.4**, is the swarm of websites maintained by commercial contractors of municipal code production. In addition to singing the praises of codification of ordinances and promoting their own services to that end, these websites serve as the residence for many of the codes of their respective client municipalities. In most cases each code is separate, and they are generally grouped by state. But the uniform format for each code produced by a given publisher and the simplicity of arrangement, born out of long and repeated experience with what makes these codes work, combine to make dipping into these codes to check out the experiences of other municipalities a relatively straightforward task. The issue of variant nomenclature, however, still exists, since the commercial codifiers are working in each instance with locally-produced ordinance language.

There is, however, a singular tool that draws together references to municipal codes by subject, regardless of the local terminology used: *Ordinance Law Annotations* (formerly titled *Shepard's Ordinance Law Annotations*). This digest-like multivolume compilation collects citations to published decisions (and summaries of the same) that construe or apply municipal ordinances on a particular topic. It also includes references to secondary sources (including treatises, legal encyclopedias, American Law Reports annotations, and law review articles) dealing with those particular municipal law topics. Despite its limitations (only those topics discussed in regularly published cases are mentioned, and no specific code or law citations are provided), this set offers a good jumping off point for comparative analysis of local law topics from Laundries to Libraries, from Ice to Junk, from "Adult Businesses" to Weed Abatement.

14.7   ADMINISTRATIVE REGULATIONS AND DECISIONS ON THE MUNICIPAL LEVEL

As with states and the federal government, the agencies and departments of the executive branch of municipal entities may engage in both delegated legislative activity via agency rules and regulations and in delegated judicial activity via administrative decisions. In New York City this output is captured in a commercially published multi-volume annotated set, *The Official Compilation of the Rules of the City of New York*. Some of that activity is also available on Lexis Advance. This easy accessibility, however, is the exception to the rule: for the most part, research in these materials will involve extensive exploration of byways of the internet, and/or personal contact with the individual agencies.

CHAPTER 15

WHERE THE LAW IS

▪ ▪ ▪

15.1   GENERAL PRINCIPLES

As suggested in the first chapter, research on any legal issue should always consider whether there are statutes, cases, regulations, or administrative decisions (or materials analogous to any of these) that have any bearing on the situation. The subsequent chapters, we hope, have led you to explore the circle of information that surrounds each of these four types of legal authority, and to think about when the search for any of them should become a high research priority for you. Any legal authority might have historical background, commentary, or subsequent applications that either strengthen or undercut its meaning and its usefulness for your purposes. This galaxy of interrelated sources defines, for the legal researcher, where the law is.

We hope, also, that you have come to appreciate how certain principles of legal research come into play over and over again, in many different contexts. Conscientious application of these principles can come to your aid whenever you find yourself thrust into a legal area you have never encountered before. Soon enough, the initially bewildering sources you need to use in such an area will become trusted allies; remembering these general rules will help to make it so.

15.2   LOOK FOR BASIC STRUCTURES

Thinking about what types of material you need to look for can get you oriented even in a totally alien jurisdiction or legal subculture. There will usually be something like a statute (official entities telling people what to do), even if only a constitutional provision, and something like a case (official decisions as to the legality of what people did in certain circumstances). For finding both of these types of material, there's generally going to be something **chronological**, something **subject-based**, and something **name-based**.

Many primary sources appear first in **chronological** order, then are arranged by someone into **subject** order. All branches of government act in real time, performing work in chronological order. Chronicling this work results in a record that is official and accurate, but often largely useless for research. After the chronological record is captured, someone has to arrange all that material in subject order as an aid to practitioners and researchers. Remember the analogies we have observed:

Chronological Order	Subject Order
Session laws	Codes
United States Statutes at Large	*United States Code*
U.S.C.C.A.N.	*U.S.C.A.*
State session laws	State code
Reporter	Digest
Texas Reports	*Texas Digest*
Pacific Reporter	*Pacific Digest*
Administrative Register	Administrative Code
Federal Register	*Code of Federal Regulations*
State administrative register	State administrative code

Remember, too, that even though electronic publication has lessened the time gap between appearance of the chronological record and appearance of the subject-arranged tool, the former is usually still the more official authority. That is, if their content should differ in any way, the chronological record generally controls.

One of the first steps in bringing the chronological record under control is to create an alphabetical index of its contents. A case **name**, boiled down to a condensed form A v. B, will be filed alphabetically in a Table of Cases. Some statutes and cases also receive or develop popular names or even nicknames, and these can be found in a number of ways. We have specifically discussed some methods for doing so in the preceding chapters (the indexing to session laws and codes, *Shepard's Acts and Cases by Popular Names*, and full-text searching, especially in law review articles). Other ways to go fishing for nicknames of cases or statutes include keyword searching in periodical indexes, law library online catalogs, or simply on the web (where, however, you will almost certainly face the problems of too many false drops and lots of erroneous information).

15.3   ESTIMATE WHAT FORM YOUR ANSWER WILL COME IN

As you begin your research, ask yourself what form the answer may take. Is your answer likely to be a statute, a regulation, an article, a definition in a dictionary, a line of cases, or something else? You might have to revise your estimate as you go along (in many instances it is nearly impossible, for example, to predict whether any particular state issue is addressed in that state's statutes or its regulations) but there's no harm in that. By focusing on what form your answer will likely take, it will help you choose your approach and to think clearly about your research strategy. On the other hand, making a guess as to the ultimate, substantive outcome of your research before you begin is almost never helpful, and in fact, can prejudice your search. Don't let hunches about the outcome cloud your thinking about the research process.

15.4   YOUR STRATEGY WILL DEPEND UPON YOUR STARTING POINT. WHAT DO YOU KNOW NOW?

You should know how to start from a known case, statute, article, or issue and move from your starting point to gather all the rest of the relevant material on your topic. As an example, starting with a known case you can use a citator to update it, use its headnotes to find its place (and other similar cases) in a digest, use the tables of cases in secondary sources to find where in a treatise or encyclopedia or law review article your case is discussed. The finding aids and other tools in law books allow you to start anywhere and move forward or backward in time, or laterally to encircle all the sources relevant to your issue in your jurisdiction. There is a real art to framing the issues, imagining the possible arguments, etc., but there are simple mechanical procedures to follow once that is done, in order to gather all the material that is relevant.

15.5   THE LESS YOU KNOW, THE MORE CERTAINLY YOU NEED SECONDARY SOURCES

Context is king in legal research. When faced with a new area of law or a new concept, begin your research in the secondary sources, using them to help you understand the general framework in which your issue can be placed. If you get an assignment related to admiralty law, and you don't know the first thing about admiralty law, you need to start with secondary sources. After you understand a little about your area, then you can proceed to the primary sources you need to solve your problem. Just jumping straight into primary sources with no context can be dangerous and is almost invariably not the most efficient method of researching.

15.6 SECONDARY LEADS TO PRIMARY, BUT THERE ARE OTHER WAYS AROUND THE CIRCLE

The main use for secondary sources is to steer you to primary sources. Sometimes, though, secondary sources lead to other secondary sources. Or you might use a primary source (say, a known case) as a way into the secondary literature (looking up that case in the table of cases in a well-respected treatise or perhaps a Restatement) that will then lead you to further primary sources. You often have to use a variety of sources in different combinations to get from where you are to where you need to be. The more you know about the kinds of finding aids that exist, the better the odds that your work will be thorough, accurate, and timely.

15.7 OFFICIAL PUBLICATIONS ARE OFTEN LESS USEFUL FOR RESEARCH

This isn't very complicated. Official publications often come with two distinct disadvantages: first, they are usually not current; and second, they are not annotated. A good example is the official *United States Statutes at Large*, which is both slow to appear and largely devoid of aids for the researcher, especially when compared with both *U.S.C.C.A.N.* and the government-posted materials on Congress.gov or FDsys.

15.8 HUMAN ORDERING VS. MACHINE RECALL

As you know, keyword searching is very powerful, allowing you to search for specific factual situations, names or phrases. The ability to search through full-text databases using keywords has changed legal research profoundly. The danger in this power stems from the fact that the success of this method of searching depends upon your understanding and control of vocabulary.

The literal nature of machine recall (i.e., the keyword search) means that you sometimes sacrifice recall in favor of precision. High precision means getting a narrowly defined, specific result, and running the risk of missing some relevant material. Using human ordering, such as an index, a table, a table of contents, or especially a digest or other assigned subject headings, the opposite is true: you get improved recall at the expense of precision. High recall means getting a large, inclusive result, including some hits that may not be relevant (for example, you have to wade through all the warrantless search cases to find the ones that involved searches of car interiors).

Every technique, every source, every approach you take involves a trade-off between precision and recall. Ask yourself what compromise you can afford to make at any particular point in your research and what you might do to minimize the risk, and only then pick your source and access method (e.g., full-text searching or using an index). If you have the luxury of a little time, you should use both techniques. For example, as discussed in **Chapter 5**, when searching for cases you might begin with a keyword search on Lexis Advance, Bloomberg Law, or Westlaw, then gather the Key Number(s) from the cases you find, and check the completeness of your result in a digest to see if there is anything you missed. You won't always have the time to do that, of course.

15.9 STATUTORY RESEARCH ONLINE HAS HIDDEN PITFALLS

Typically, statutory research involves using a variety of tabular or columnar material. This material, tables of contents, conversion tables of various kinds, indexes, outlines of titles, etc., are available in the online databases, but they are cumbersome to use in electronic form. Also, codes are arranged in outline form, with titles, chapters, sections, and subsections, with notes and appendices added. This structure can be very hard to visualize online. If you start your statutory research with a search for a particular term or phrase, you'll often click on the likeliest-looking hit and then determine whether it is relevant. If the section does appear to be relevant, you still need to place that section in its larger context to ensure that language in other, related sections doesn't control or alter the interpretation of what you've found in the section your search turned up. For example, it is very common for a definition of terms contained within one section of a code to control the meaning of that term in sections or chapters that follow. Extra caution is called for when you conduct statutory research online because of the more restrictive display that limits what you see at any one time.

15.10 KNOW EXACTLY WHAT LEGISLATIVE HISTORIES ARE, AND WHAT THEY ARE FOR

A legislative history is an attempt to determine the intent of the legislature. The intent of the legislature is one of the arguments you can use when arguing how a facially ambiguous statute should be interpreted. It is not controlling or binding on a court. A legislative history is compiled from all of the published evidence of legislative deliberation. In the federal setting, much of what Congress does is published. Understand, though, that the importance of the major Committee Report (reprinted at least partially in *U.S.C.C.A.N.*) dwarfs the importance of everything else you might find. Remember, too, that many courts and many individual judges are hostile to legislative intent arguments.

15.11   LET SOMEONE ELSE DO THE WORK FOR YOU

There is nothing more satisfying than finding out that some scholar or publisher has already compiled the information you need. Before you dig in to a long research problem, try to think whether it is likely that someone has already done this for you. Many compiled federal legislative histories are readily available if you have access to HeinOnline, ProQuest Congressional, and ProQuest Legislative Insight. Digests gather many of the cases on a particular issue together in one place. Many treatises are filled with information that would be very time consuming to gather from scratch. Always try to find the easiest and most efficient way to do a thorough and accurate job. Librarians can help you find out if someone has done your work for you. Consult them early in your research process.

15.12   BUT DON'T BE AFRAID TO BE THE FIRST, IF NECESSARY!

Stare decisis and binding precedent are, in some sense, fairy tales. You must be able to make an argument, even in the seemingly hopeless case. Remember, every adverse precedent has some basis for distinguishing it from your case; it is your job as the attorney to identify and make that argument. You have to train yourself to step up to the plate: make the distinction, resist the temptation to say there's nothing out there, and work to craft an argument even where the case seems hopeless. And remember, novel arguments are successfully put forward all the time. Just because nobody has made an argument or a distinction before doesn't mean that it is necessarily a losing argument or baseless distinction.

15.13   EVALUATING SOURCES

In legal research, evaluating sources involves balancing what you need and want in terms of **authenticity**, **currency**, and **editorial work** (human-provided connections in and out from the source). Look at the organization of the source, the publisher, the date, the table of contents, and the finding aids and tables. If there is an instructional preface, read it. Even if you've never seen this source before, you'll find that it falls into one of a very few types. You're ready to discern what the source has to offer you in your current situation.

Authenticity can be gauged by considering the publisher, and its relationship with the originator of the material. When dealing with primary sources, is the publisher the originating government entity itself? Is publication of the material specifically delegated to the publisher by that originating government entity? If there is no connection between the publisher and the originating government entity, be alert for motivations that might lead to either biased or sloppy publishing of inaccurately reproduced primary sources, especially in the case of material freely available on the web.

Currency should be appropriate for your needs. One characteristic to look for is specific and accurate indication of how current the information is. If a source claims to be "current" without reference to a particular date, last case reported, last statute included, or something similar, exercise caution. Strangely enough, currency information is often more unambiguously available for print resources than for online material, even though the latter may actually be more up to date.

Evaluating the **editorial** component of a source can involve assessing the authoritativeness of its commentary, the care with which the information has been indexed, or such elements as the clarity of the graphical layout. One factor to consider is the nature and reputation of the publisher. American legal publishing was dominated for many years by two large companies, West and Lawyers' Cooperative. Both publishers produced a full range of legal materials, starting with law reports and branching out into statutes, secondary works, and other practitioners' tools. Other publishers or imprints concentrated on the legal education area, sometimes branching out from there into more general legal works. Specialist publishers developed works designed for practitioners in areas like tax or criminal law, or catered to a local market. Today, American legal publishing, both online and in print, is even more dominated by a few very large companies. Comparatively few independent legal print publishers still function in the United States, but of course independent entrepreneurs aplenty are trying to gain a toehold in the market via the internet.

What are the implications of these industry developments for the researcher? Traditional publishers got involved in evaluation of the material they published because of the capital that would be tied up in producing and distributing that material, and because their reputations were on the line. West, in deciding to publish this book, considered the credentials, education, position, and experience of the authors, as well as the characteristics of the proposed book itself: i.e., some moderate level of vetting went on. A potential reader of this book is entitled to rely to some extent on West's track record of such judgments in the past. The most respected law reviews have a long history of vetting the articles submitted to them: you would expect an article published in one of them to be by an important writer, a famous writer, or at least a good writer.

By contrast, a publishing company without such a track record puts the entire onus of evaluation onto the researcher. Such is the case with many online sources, including some that appear on such mainstays as Westlaw and Lexis Advance. Free portals on the web (e.g., the Legal Information Institute, LLRX, the 'Lectric Law Library, etc.) have varying criteria for choosing links to sources of legal information, but ultimately they do not control the accuracy or the currency of that information. The commercial vendors or consolidators (e.g., Westlaw, Lexis Advance, Bloomberg, and Fastcase) historically have taken some responsibility (not to be confused with legal liability!) for the completeness of their principal database components. If the information was not "out there" electronically from its producer, the consolidator would undertake to get it into electronic form themselves. This expansive undertaking paid off with a legal industry increasingly inclined to focus on those resources available to them on Westlaw and Lexis Advance.

Now that more and more data is becoming available without charge directly from its originators via the internet, researchers need to compare the merits of conducting research on Westlaw and Lexis Advance with doing more piecemeal research via the free sources on the web. Time efficiencies and the greater confidence that comes from familiarity are advantages of Westlaw and Lexis Advance, due to the more or less uniform interfaces within their respective databases. Theoretically, the data available from the major subscription platforms is more complete in many areas. However, since the data does come from a variety of sources and was added to the database in accordance with a great number of different contracts with providers, you cannot rely absolutely on the commercial databases to be complete or accurate. You need, as with all research, to use your professional estimation of what *should* be available, not abdicate responsibility and limit yourself to what *is* available on one or even all such services.

This matter of using your professional judgment when conducting research on Westlaw, Bloomberg Law, and Lexis Advance needs to be underscored. These services, especially Lexis and Westlaw, have instituted elaborate advisory services, available over the phone, by e-mail, or in live chat over the internet. These services can usefully help you zero in on where a particular kind of information is located within that system, or verify the date of currency or non-inclusion of certain data, but that's all. Again, the research is *your* responsibility. Anything you get from the research advisors you must be able to reconstruct or verify using your own logic and your own review of the sources. In practice, you are being paid to exercise your own professional judgment in both research and writing, not merely to parrot the information provided to you by an employee of a commercial database or by someone on the internet.

15.14 AN AFTERWORD: THE WORLD OF UNPUBLISHED INFORMATION

The chapters prior to this one have emphasized the use of information that is published, whether electronically or in print, to the world at large.

But sometimes the information you want is not circulated to the world on a "push" model. The task at hand can turn out to involve the extraction of information that is only made available by its originators on an "as needed" basis. This may involve presenting your "need to know" credentials to someone who is acting as a gatekeeper. Or the information may be freely available to all, but so time sensitive that it is generated fresh for every researcher (e.g., has there been any action on this bill in the last 6 hours?). When you need to rely on working with personal contacts in order to get needed information, the first step is finding someone who can help you.

Websites of entities like legislative committees, government agencies, courts, and law firms usually provide telephone numbers and e-mail addresses for public inquiries. Although directories of these web addresses exist, the best and most convenient way to find them is simply to use a search engine like Google. Put in as much detail as you know about the name of the sub-entity for which you are looking. Unlike print directories of web addresses, print directories of names and phone numbers can still be handy because they pull together a lot of such information into one handy list (see **Table 15.A**). For more specific guidance than can be teased out of the titles people are given in such directories, the individual state guides to legal research (see **Appendix**) usually go into detail about which government office is the appropriate target for different sorts of queries.

When calling a government entity for information, arm yourself in advance with the docket number of the case or the chapter (or bill) number of the law you are calling about. If you don't know the docket number of a case, at least know the official parties' names under which the case would be filed in the court records (e.g., ask for the records from "California v. Powell," not "the Rodney King case"). In general, the more specific names, numbers, or dates you have readily available, the better your likelihood of success because courts and agencies, especially at the state or local level, may have one and only one access point to their records.

If no public entity can or will provide you with the information you need, the private sector may be able to oblige. Figure out from case reports or from newspaper accounts whether a law firm or a particular lawyer is involved in the matter. You can then try and locate that firm or practitioner through a legal directory. Legal directories fall into two basic categories: directories where you pay to be included, and directories that are based on bar licensure records. Specialized directories also exist for particular types of practice. Many directories are subdivided by city, so get as much information as you can from your original source about where the firm or practitioner is located. Many jurisdictions also have services that allow people to look up attorneys and see professional profiles, often including education, licensure, and disciplinary status.

Now go out, do good, and have fun!

15.15 TABLE

TABLE 15.A: SELECTED DIRECTORIES OF HELPFUL PHONE NUMBERS

1. *Federal-State Court Directory*. New York, N. Y.: Leadership Directories.

   Directory of State Court Clerks and County Courthouses. New York, N. Y.: Leadership Directories.

   These annual publications include charts showing the organization of the different court systems, vacancy information, useful phone numbers for each individual court, and much more. Try these books when you have to call around to a bunch of courts or offices.

2. *Law Firms Yellow Book*. New York, N. Y.: Leadership Directories

   Federal Yellow Book. New York, N. Y.: Leadership Directories

   Congressional Yellow Book. New York, N. Y.: Leadership Directories

   Judicial Yellow Book. New York, N. Y.: Leadership Directories

   These "Yellow Books" are from a series published by Leadership Directories. They are also available via the web: see http://www.leadershipdirectories.com for details.

3. *The Martindale-Hubbell Law Directory*. New York, N. Y.: Martindale-Hubbell Law Directory.

   This annual listing of firms requires that you know the city in which the person or firm you seek is located in order to use the print version. The publisher's website at https://www.martindale.com allows users to search by name without a city, which eliminates this problem.

4. Westlaw: Directories > West Legal Directory.

   This directory permits you to search specifically for government or corporate counsel lawyers as well as lawyers in law firms by area of practice. Information from the Directory is also available without charge at Findlaw (http://lawyers.findlaw.com/).

5. Lexis Advance: Directories > Attorney Directories

   This directory is organized by jurisdiction, and covers U.S. states with a separate area for Canadian attorneys and another for international attorneys (meaning anything besides U.S. and Canada).

APPENDIX

SELECTED LEGAL RESEARCH GUIDES FOR EACH OF THE 50 STATES AND THE DISTRICT OF COLUMBIA

• • •

For print resources, always check to see if there is a more recently-published edition. For web-based resources, even if the web addresses change, you will still be able to track most of these down via your search engine of choice.

Alabama:

Blakeley Beals, *State Documents Bibliography: Alabama.* [Chicago, Ill.]: American Association of Law Libraries, 2012. (available on HeinOnline)

Gary Orlando Lewis, *Legal Research in Alabama: How to Find and Understand the Law in Alabama.* Montgomery, Ala.: Gary Orlando Lewis, 2001.

University of Alabama School of Law, Bounds Law Library

http://www.library.law.ua.edu

[click on "Alabama Resources"](links to web sources)

Alaska:

Merrilee S. Harrell, "A Researcher's Guide to Legislative History in Alaska," 30 *Legal Ref. Serv. Q.* 7 (2011)

Alaska Court System page on Legal Research: Alaska Resources

http://www.courts.alaska.gov/library/aklegal.htm

(covers print as well as web sources, including a link to "Information About How to Research Legislative History Online")

Arizona:

Tamara S. Herrera, *Arizona Legal Research.* 2nd ed. Durham, N. C.: Carolina Academic Press, 2013.

Kathy Shimpock-Vieweg and Marianne Sidorski Alcorn, *Arizona Legal Research Guide*. Buffalo, N. Y.: W. S. Hein, 1992. (still useful, and covers some topics not included in Herrera)

Arizona State University, Ross-Blakley Law Library: Research Guides: Arizona

> http://www.law.asu.edu/library/

> (detailed guides on Arizona legal research, including legislative history)

Arizona State Library, Archives, and Public Records—State of Arizona Research Library: Guide to Arizona Legislative History

> http://www.azlibrary.gov/sla/legislative-assistance-and-resources/guide-arizona-legislative-history

Arkansas:

Coleen M. Barger, *Arkansas Legal Research*. 2nd ed. Durham, N. C.: Carolina Academic Press, 2016.

University of Arkansas at Little Rock, William H. Bowen School of Law Library: Research Guides

> http://law.ualr.libguides.com/index.php

> (includes "Arkansas Legislative History" by Kathryn Fitzhugh)

Southwestern Association of Law Libraries Bulletin: Arkansas Legislative History Research Guide, by Kathryn C. Fitzhugh

> http://www.aallnet.org/chapter/swall/bulletin/Fall01/arkleghistory.html

> (includes some additional details that are still useful)

California:

Aimee Dudovitz, Hether C. Macfarlane, and Suzanne E. Rowe, *California Legal Research*. 3rd ed. Durham, N. C.: Carolina Academic Press, 2016.

John K. Hanft, *Legal Research in California*. 7th ed. [St. Paul, Minn.]: Thomson West, 2011.

Daniel W. Martin, *Henke's California Law Guide*. 8th ed. Newark, N. J.: LexisNexis, 2006. (available on HeinOnline)

Amy Atchison and Jennifer Lentz, "California Legislative History," 30 *Legal Ref. Serv. Q.* 127 (2011)

University of California, Berkeley, Boalt Hall School of Law, Law Library: Research Guides: California Guides

> http://www.law.berkeley.edu/library/dynamic/online.php?node=19

> (includes link to "California Legislative History Research")

University of California, Los Angeles, School of Law, Hugh and Hazel Darling Law Library: LibGuides: California Law

> http://libguides.law.ucla.edu/sb.php?subject_id=38886

> (a collection of detailed guides, including one entitled "California Legislative History" by Cheryl Kelly Fischer)

Colorado:

Robert Michael Linz, *Colorado Legal Research*. Durham, N. C.: Carolina Academic Press, 2010.

Robert C. Richards, Jr. and Barbara Bintliff, *Colorado Legal Resources: An Annotated Bibliography*. [Chicago, Ill.]: American Association of Law Libraries, Government Documents Special Interest Section, 2004. (available on HeinOnline)

University of Denver, Sturm College of Law, Westminster Law Library: Research Guides

> http://libguides.law.du.edu/cat.php?cid=10931

> (a collection of guides, with links, including "Colorado Legislative History")

Connecticut:

Jessica G. Hynes, *Connecticut Legal Research*. Durham, N. C.: Carolina Academic Press, 2009.

Lawrence G. Cheeseman and Arlene C. Bielefield, *The Connecticut Legal Research Handbook*. Guilford, Conn.: Connecticut Law Book Co., 1992. (still useful, and covers some topics not in Hynes)

Janet Fusaris, "Connecticut Legislative History," 30 *Legal Ref. Serv. Q.* 17 (2011)

Connecticut State Library: Guide to Connecticut Legislative History

> http://www.cslib.org/leghis.asp

Connecticut State Library: Connecticut Law and Legislation

> http://www.cslib.org/law.htm

Connecticut Judicial Branch Law Libraries: Research Guides

http://www.jud.ct.gov/lawlib/selfguides.htm

Delaware:

Peter J. Egler, *Selective Annotated Bibliography of Delaware State Documents and Other Resources Used in Delaware Legal Research.* [Chicago, Ill.]: American Association of Law Libraries, Government Documents Special Interest Section, 2008. (available on HeinOnline)

Widener University Delaware Law School, Library: Research: Research Guides

http://libguides.law.widener.edu/

(includes "Delaware Legislative History" by Maggie Adams and Janet Lindenmuth)

District of Columbia:

Leah F. Chanin, Pamela J. Gregory, and Sarah K. Wiant, *Legal Research in the District of Columbia, Maryland and Virginia.* 2nd ed. Buffalo, N. Y.: W. S. Hein, 2000.

Georgetown University Law Center, Georgetown Law Library: Research: Research Guides: District of Columbia In-Depth

http://guides.ll.georgetown.edu/dc-in-depth

Florida:

Barbara J. Busharis, Jennifer LaVia, and Suzanne E. Rowe, *Florida Legal Research.* 4th ed. Durham, N. C.: Carolina Academic Press, 2014.

Kathleen Brown, "The Legislative Process in the State of Florida," 30 *Legal Ref. Serv. Q.* 25 (2011)

University of Florida Levin College of Law, Lawton Chiles Legal Information Center: Law LibGuides: Florida Law

http://guides.law.ufl.edu/index.php?gid=5493

(includes "Florida Legal Research" by Shamika Dalton and "Florida Legislative History" by Christopher Vallandingham)

Georgia:

Nancy P. Johnson, Elizabeth G. Adelman, and Nancy J. Adams, *Georgia Legal Research,* Durham, N. C.: Carolina Academic Press, 2007.

Nancy P. Johnson, Nancy J. Adams, and Elizabeth G. Adelman, "Researching Georgia Law (2006 Edition)," 22 *Ga. St. U. L. Rev.* 381 (2005–2006)

Georgia State University College of Law Library, LibGuides: Georgia Legal Research

> http://libguides.law.gsu.edu/georgialegalresearch

Mercer University, Walter F. George School of Law, Furman Smith Law Library: Georgia Research by Denise Gibson

> http://www.law.mercer.edu/library/research/georgia

University of Georgia School of Law, Alexander Campbell King Law Library, Research Guides: "Researching the Legislative History of an Enrolled Georgia Statute"

> http://www.law.uga.edu/researching-legislative-history-
> enacted-georgia-statute

Hawaii:

Richard F. Kahle, *How to Research Constitutional, Legislative, and Statutory History in Hawaii.* 3rd ed. Honolulu, Hawaii: Legislative Reference Bureau, [2001]. Available as a .pdf file at

> http://lrbhawaii.org/how2/how2.pdf

University of Hawaii at Manoa, William S. Richardson School of Law Library: Hawaii Legal Research

> http://law.hawaii.libguides.com/hawaii

Idaho:

Tenielle Fordyce-Ruff and Kristina Running, *Idaho Legal Research.* 2nd ed. Durham, N. C.: Carolina Academic Press, 2015.

Kristen Ford, "Idaho Legislative Histories Revealed," 30 *Legal Ref. Serv. Q.* 33 (2011)

University of Idaho College of Law Library: Legal Research Guides

> http://www.uidaho.edu/law/library/legalresearch/guides

> (links to guides on various aspects of Idaho legal research)

Illinois:

Mark E. Wojcik, *Illinois Legal Research.* 2nd ed. Durham, N. C.: Carolina Academic Press, 2009.

Laurel Wendt, *Illinois Legal Research Guide.* 2nd ed. Buffalo, N. Y.: W. S. Hein, 2006.

Chicago Association of Law Libraries, Government Relations Committee: "Finding Illinois Law: A Librarian's Guide for Non-Lawyers"

> http://chicagolawlib.org/finding-illinois-law/

> (despite the title, has useful information for lawyers unfamiliar with Chicago local law in Chapter 6, "Municipal Law: The City of Chicago and Cook County, Illinois" by Walter Baumann)

University of Illinois College of Law, Albert E. Jenner, Jr. Memorial Law Library: Legislative History—Illinois

> https://wiki.cites.uiuc.edu/wiki/display/legalresearch/ Illinois+Legislative+History

> (detailed guide dealing with print, fiche, and audio sources only)

Illinois General Assembly, Legislative Reference Bureau

> http://www.ilga.gov/commission/lrb_home.html

> (includes link to "Researching Legislative History")

The John Marshall Law School, Louis L. Biro Law Library: Illinois Legislative History Research

> http://libraryguides.jmls.edu/ILlegres

Northwestern Law School, Pritzker Legal Research Center

> http://www.law.northwestern.edu/library/research/illinois chicago/

> (links to bibliographies of materials on Illinois and Chicago law and to a guide to Illinois legislative history)

Indiana:

Indiana University, Maurer School of Law, Jerome Hall Law Library: Compiling State Legislative Histories (with information on Indiana Legislative Documents)

> http://law.indiana.libguides.com/compiling-state-legislative-histories

Valparaiso University Law School Library: Indiana Legal Resources

> http://www.valpo.edu/law/current-students/c-law-library/ indiana-legal-resources

Iowa:

John D. Edwards, Karen L. Wallace, and Melissa H. Weresh, *Iowa Legal Research*. 2nd ed. Durham, N. C.: Carolina Academic Press, 2016.

John Edwards, *Iowa Legal Research Guide*. Buffalo, N. Y.: W. S. Hein, 2003. (available on HeinOnline)

Drake University Law School Library, Resources, Research Guides

> http://libguides.law.drake.edu/

> (includes links to guides on Iowa legal research including legislative history and municipal and county law)

Kansas:

Joseph A. Custer and Christopher L. Steadham, *Kansas Legal Research*. Durham, N. C.: Carolina Academic Press, 2008.

Joseph A. Custer, *Kansas Legal Research and Reference Guide*. 3rd ed. Topeka, Kans.: Kansas Bar Association, 2003.

University of Kansas School of Law, Wheat Law Library: Research and Study Guides

> http://law.ku.edu/research-study-guides

> (includes links to guides to Kansas legislative history materials and to forms specific to particular municipal jurisdictions in Kansas)

Kentucky:

Kurt X. Metzmeier, Tina M. Brooks, Franklin L. Runge, Leah R. Smith, Beau Steenken, and Ryan A. Valentin, *Kentucky Legal Research Manual*. 4th ed. Lexington, Ky.: University of Kentucky, Office of Continuing Legal Education, 2016.

William A. Hilyerd, Kurt X. Metzmeier, and David J. Ensign, *Kentucky Legal Research*. 2nd ed. Durham, N. C.: Carolina Academic Press, 2017.

University of Louisville, Louis D. Brandeis School of Law Library: Legal Research—Research Guides

> http://library.louisville.edu/kentucky-law

> (guides and lists of links pertaining to Kentucky law)

University of Kentucky College of Law Library: Compiling a Kentucky Legislative History

> http://library.law.uky.edu/kentucky_legislative_history

Louisiana:

Mary Garvey Algero, *Louisiana Legal Research*. 3rd ed. Durham, N. C.: Carolina Academic Press, 2017.

Win-Shin S. Chiang, *Louisiana Legal Research*. 2nd ed. Austin, Tex.: Butterworth Legal Publishers, 1990.

Charlene C. Cain, *Louisiana Legal Documents and Related Publications*. 4th ed. [Chicago, Ill.]: American Association of Law Libraries, Government Documents Special Interest Section, 2014. (available on HeinOnline)

Brian Huddleston, "Louisiana Legislative History Resources," 30 *Legal Ref. Serv. Q.* 42 (2011)

Law Library of Louisiana Online Resource Center: Library Research Guides

> http://lasc.libguides.com/library-research-guides

> (includes link to "Louisiana Legislative History Research" by Sara Pic)

Maine:

William W. Wells, *Maine Legal Research Guide*. Portland, Maine: Tower Pub. Co., 1989.

Maine State Law and Legislative Reference Library: Legal Resources

> http://legislature.maine.gov/lawlibrary/research/9196

> (includes links to extensive online primary sources and to "Compiling a Maine Legislative History")

Maryland:

Leah F. Chanin, Pamela J. Gregory, and Sarah K. Wiant, *Legal Research in the District of Columbia, Maryland and Virginia*. 2nd ed. Buffalo, N. Y.: W. S. Hein, 2000.

Katherine Baer, *State Documents Bibliography: Maryland*. [Chicago, Ill.]: American Association of Law Libraries, 2014. (available on HeinOnline)

Maryland State Law Library: Gateway to Maryland Law

> http://www.lawlib.
> state.md.us/researchtools/sourcesmdlaw.html

> (includes link to detailed legislative history guides)

University of Maryland School of Law, Thurgood Marshall Law Library: Research Guides http://www.law.umaryland.edu/marshall/researchguides

(see, in addition to the Maryland Research Guide and the guide to Baltimore City Research, the Maryland sections in the extensive general TMLL Guide to Legal Research)

Georgetown Law Library: Maryland Resources In-Depth

http://guides.ll.georgetown.edu/maryland-in-depth/introduction

Massachusetts:

E. Joan Blum and Shaun B. Spencer, *Massachusetts Legal Research*. 2nd ed. Durham, N. C.: Carolina Academic Press, 2016.

Handbook of Legal Research in Massachusetts, 3rd ed. Mary Ann Neary, editor. Boston, Mass.: Massachusetts Continuing Legal Education, 2009–

The State Library of Massachusetts: Legal and Legislative Resources

http://www.mass.gov/anf/research-and-tech/legal-and-legislative-resources

(includes link to a detailed legislative history page)

Boston University Law Libraries: Massachusetts Legal Research, by Jenna Fegreus

http://lawlibraryguides.bu.edu/masslegalresearch

Western New England University School of Law, Library: Massachusetts Legal Research, by Artie Berns

http://law.wne.libguides.com/researching-massachusetts-law

Michigan:

Cristina D. Lockwood and Pamela Lysaght, *Michigan Legal Research*. 3rd ed. Durham, N. C.: Carolina Academic Press, 2016.

Richard L. Beer and Judith J. Field, *Michigan Legal Literature: An Annotated Guide*. 2nd ed. Buffalo, N. Y.: W. S. Hein, 1991. (still useful, and covers some topics not covered in Lockwood)

Kincaid C. Brown, "Legislative Intent and Legislative History in Michigan," 30 *Legal Ref. Serv. Q.* 51 (2011)

Michigan Legislature, Michigan Manuals

http://legislature.mi.gov/doc.aspx?MichiganManualSearch2

[Select latest manual and open "Chapter III, Legislature" for access to detailed section "Sources of Michigan Legislative Information."]

(note that many online references to this resource link to a much earlier version of the document)

University of Michigan Law Library: Michigan Legislative History

http://libguides.law.umich.edu/milegishist

Wayne State University, Arthur Neef Law Library: Research Guides: Law—Michigan Legal Resources

http://guides.lib.wayne.edu/michlaw

Minnesota:

Suzanne Thorpe, *Minnesota Legal Research*. Durham, N. C.: Carolina Academic Press, 2010.

John Tessner, Brenda Wolfe, George R. Jackson, and Arlette M. Soderberg, *Minnesota Legal Research Guide*. 2nd ed. Buffalo, N. Y.: W. S. Hein, 2002.

George R. Jackson, "Minnesota Legislative History," 30 *Legal Ref. Serv. Q.* 62 (2011)

Minnesota State Legislature, Minnesota Legislative Reference Library: Minnesota Legislative History Guide

http://www.leg.state.mn.us/leg/leghist/histstep.aspx

University of Minnesota Law Library: Minnesota Law Research Guide, by Vicente Garces

http://libguides.law.umn.edu/minnesotalegalresearch

Mississippi:

Kristy L. Gilliland, *Mississippi Legal Research*. Durham, N. C.: Carolina Academic Press, 2014.

Mississippi State Library: Frequently Asked Questions

https://courts.ms.gov/state_library/st_lib_faqs.pdf

(includes a paragraph about Mississippi legislative history)

Missouri:

Wanda M. Temm and Julie M. Cheslik, *Missouri Legal Research*. 3rd ed. Durham, N. C.: Carolina Academic Press, 2015.

Judy Stark, *State Documents Bibliography: Missouri*. [Chicago, Ill.]: American Association of Law Libraries, Government Documents Special Interest Section, 2010. (available on HeinOnline)

University of Missouri School of Law, Library: Legal Research: Research a Topic: Missouri Legislative History, by Cindy Shearrer http://libraryguides.missouri.edu/missourilegislativehistory

Missouri House of Representatives

http://www.house.mo.gov

[click on "Bill Information" and on "General Information"]

Montana:

A Guide to Montana Legal Research. 8th ed. compiled by Robert K. Whelan, Meredith Hoffman, and Stephen R. Jordan. Helena, Mont.: State Law Library of Montana, 2003. Available as a .pdf file from the Montana State Courts at

http://courts.mt.gov/portals/113/library/guides/guide.pdf

Cynthia Condit, *State Documents Bibliography: Montana.* [Chicago, Ill.]: American Association of Law Libraries, Government Documents Special Interest Section, 2015. (available on HeinOnline)

State Law Library of Montana: Guides—Legal Research Guides

http://courts.mt.gov/library/guides

(includes the Whelan, Hoffman, and Jordan work in .pdf with links, and a very detailed Montana Legislative History Research Guide)

Nebraska:

Kay L. Andrus, George E. Butterfield, Troy D. Johnson, and Ann C. Kitchel, *Research Guide to Nebraska Law, 2008.* Newark, N. J.: LexisNexis, 2008.

George Butterfield, Matthew Novak, and Brian Striman, *Nebraska State Bibliography of Legal Resources.* [Chicago, Ill.]: American Association of Law Libraries, Government Documents Special Interest Section, 2012. (available on HeinOnline)

Nebraska Legislature: Legislative Histories

http://nebraskalegislature.gov/divisions/clerk_histories.php

(page outlining the availability of and procedures for obtaining Nebraska legislative history documents)

Creighton University School of Law, Klutznick Law Library: LibGuides—Nebraska Legislative History

http://culibraries.creighton.edu/NebLegisHist

(useful guide to Nebraska legislative history)

Nevada:

Nevada Legal Research Guide. Jennifer Larraguibel Gross and Thomas Blake Gross, editors. Buffalo, N. Y.: W. S. Hein, 2012.

Ann S. Jarrell and G. LeGrande Fletcher, *Nevada State Documents Bibliography: Legal Publications and Related Material.* 2nd ed. [Chicago, Ill.]: American Association of Law Libraries, Government Documents Special Interest Section, 2000. (available on HeinOnline)

University of Nevada at Las Vegas, William S. Boyd School of Law, Wiener-Rogers Law Library: Nevada Legal Research Guides

> https://law.unlv.edu/content/nevada-legal-research-guides

Nevada Legislature: Research Library

> www.leg.state.nv.us/Division/Research/library/

> (legislative history links, including database of compiled legislative histories of Nevada bills)

Supreme Court of Nevada Law Library

> http://lawlibrary.nevadajudiciary.us

> (links to guides and many resources)

New Hampshire:

Linda B. Johnson, Cynthia R. Landau, and Mary S. Searles, *New Hampshire State Documents: A Selective Bibliography.* [Chicago, Ill.]: American Association of Law Libraries, Government Documents Special Interest Section, 2012. (available on HeinOnline)

New Hampshire Judicial Branch, New Hampshire Law Library

> http://www.courts.state.nh.us/lawlibrary/index.htm

> (links to primary sources and to "Compiling a New Hampshire Legislative History" revised in 2012 by Mary S. Searles)

University of New Hampshire School of Law Library: New Hampshire Legislative History, by Cindy Landau

> http://library.law.unh.edu/NHLegHistory

New Jersey:

Paul Axel-Lute, *New Jersey Legal Research Handbook.* 6th ed. New Brunswick, N. J.: New Jersey Institute for Continuing Legal Education, 2012.

Barbara H. Garavaglia, "Using Legislative Histories to Determine Legislative Intent in New Jersey," 30 *Legal Ref. Serv. Q.* 71 (2011)

Karin Johnsrud and Sarah Jaramillo, *New Jersey State Documents: A Bibliography of Legal Resources.* [Chicago, Ill.]: American Association of Law Libraries, Government Documents Special Interest Section, 2011. (available on HeinOnline)

Rutgers Law School Law Library: Research Guides and Pathfinders

> http://libguides.law.rutgers.edu/content.php?pid=702663

> (includes guides to New Jersey legal materials and legislative history)

New Jersey State Library, Law Library

> http://www.njstatelib.org/research_library/legal_resources/

> (links to New Jersey legal materials and to legislative histories compiled by the State Library)

New Mexico:

Theresa Strike, *Guide to New Mexico State Publications.* 3rd ed. [Chicago, Ill.]: American Association of Law Libraries, 2009.

University of New Mexico School of Law Library: New Mexico Legal Research Guide

> http://libguides.law.unm.edu/NM

New Mexico Supreme Court Law Library

> https://lawlibrary.nmcourts.gov/

> (links to various New Mexico law sources)

New York:

William H. Manz, *Gibson's New York Legal Research Guide*, 4th ed. Buffalo, N. Y.: W. S. Hein, 2014.

Elizabeth G. Adelman, Theodora Belniak, Courtney L. Selby, and Brian Detweiler, *New York Legal Research.* 3rd ed. Durham, N. C.: Carolina Academic Press, 2015.

New York State Library—The Legislative History of a New York State Law: A Tutorial and Guide to Library Sources

> http://www.nysl.nysed.gov/leghist/

New York State Library—Legislative Intent

> http://www.nysl.nysed.gov/legint.htm

New York University Law School Library: Research Guides: New York Legal Research, by Gretchen Feltes and Dana Rubin

> http://nyulaw.libguides.com/New_York

North Carolina:

Scott Childs and Sara Sampson, *North Carolina Legal Research.* 2nd ed. Durham, N. C.: Carolina Academic Press, 2014.

Donna Nixon, Nichelle Perry, and Jason R. Sowards, *Guide to North Carolina Legal and Law-Related Materials.* [Chicago, Ill.]: American Association of Law Libraries, Government Documents Special Interest Section, 2010. (available on HeinOnline)

Thomas P. Davis, "Legislative History in North Carolina," 30 *Legal Ref. Serv. Q.* 85 (2011)

University of North Carolina at Chapel Hill, Kathrine R. Everett Law Library: Research Guides

> http://library.law.unc.edu/research/guides

> (links to North Carolina research guides)

North Carolina Supreme Court Library: Legislative History in North Carolina

> http://www.aoc.state.nc.us/www/copyright/library/leghist/llh 2011.html

North Dakota:

Anne E. Mullins and Tammy R. Pettinato, *North Dakota Legal Research.* Durham, N. C.: Carolina Academic Press, 2016.

Rhonda R. Schwartz, "Resorting to Extrinsic Aids: North Dakota Legislative History Research," 30 *Legal Ref. Serv. Q.* 95 (2011)

University of North Dakota, Olaf H. Thormodsgard Law Library: Online Research Links—Legal Research: North Dakota

> http://libguides.law.und.edu/electronic-subscriptions/nd

> (links to sources on web and to North Dakota Legislative History Guide)

Ohio:

Sara Sampson, Katherine L. Hall, and Carolyn Broering-Jacobs, *Ohio Legal Research.* 2nd ed. Durham, N. C.: Carolina Academic Press, 2015.

Melanie K. Putnam and Susan M. Schaefgen, *Ohio Legal Research Guide.* Buffalo, N. Y.: W. S. Hein, 1997. (available on HeinOnline)

Ohio State University, Moritz College of Law, Michael E. Moritz Law Library: Introduction to the State Materials of Ohio

> http://moritzlaw.osu.edu/library/assistance/ohio_intro.php

Ohio Legislative Service Commission: A Guide to Legislative History in Ohio (2010), by David M. Gold and Rich Merkel

> http://www.lsc.state.oh.us/membersonly/128legislative history.pdf

> (Don't worry: "Members Only" is just the title of the publication in which the guide appears!)

Oklahoma:

Darin K. Fox, Darla Jackson, and Courtney Selby, *Oklahoma Legal Research*. Durham, N. C.: Carolina Academic Press, 2013.

Darin K. Fox, *State Documents Bibliography, Oklahoma: A Guide to Legal Research in Oklahoma*. [Chicago, Ill.]: American Association of Law Libraries, Government Documents Special Interest Section, 2009. (available on HeinOnline)

Darla Jackson, "Legislative History: A Guide for the State of Oklahoma," 30 *Legal Ref. Serv. Q.* 119 (2011)

Oklahoma City University School of Law, Chickasaw Nation Law Library: Oklahoma Legal Research, by Tim Gatton

> http://libguides.okcu.edu/lawlibrary

> [click on "Oklahoma Legal Research"]

Oklahoma State Courts Network

> http://www.oscn.net/applications/oscn/start.asp

> [Click on "Legal Research" for links to online sources]

Oregon:

Suzanne E. Rowe, *Oregon Legal Research*. 3rd ed. Revised Printing. Durham, N. C.: Carolina Academic Press, 2016.

Stephanie Midkiff and Wendy Schroeder Hitchcock, *State Documents Bibliography: Oregon, A Survey of Oregon State Legal and Law-Related Documents*. [Chicago, Ill.]: American Association of Law Libraries, Government Documents Special Interest Section, 2009. (available on HeinOnline)

Willamette University College of Law, J.W. Long Law Library: Oregon Law

> http://law.willamette.libguides.com/oregon

> (extensive collection of links and guides)

Lewis & Clark Law School, Paul L. Boley Law Library: Oregon Legal Research Guide

> http://lawlibguides.lclark.edu/oregon

> (extensive collection of links and guides)

University of Oregon Law School, John E. Jacqua Law Library: Research Guides

> http://library.uoregon.edu/law/libraryguides.html

> (includes links to detailed handouts on researching Oregon legislative history and current legislation)

Pennsylvania:

Barbara J. Busharis and Bonny L. Taveres, *Pennsylvania Legal Research*. Durham, N. C.: Carolina Academic Press, 2007.

Joel Fishman, *State Documents Bibliography: Pennsylvania.* [Chicago, Ill.]: American Association of Law Libraries, Government Documents Special Interest Section, 2011. (available on HeinOnline)

Frank Y. Liu, Joel Fishman, Dittakavi N. Rao, and Tsegaye Beru, *Pennsylvania Legal Research Handbook*. 2008 ed. Philadelphia, Pa.: American Lawyer Media, 2008.

Jenkins Law Library: Research Guides

> https://www.jenkinslaw.org/research/guides

> (includes "Pennsylvania Legislative History" by Mike Sweeney, and many other Pennsylvania-specific guides)

University of Pittsburgh School of Law, Barco Law Library: Pennsylvania Legal Research, by Marc Silverman

> http://law.pitt.edu/pennsylvania-legal-research

> (extensive guide, with links)

Rhode Island:

Nanette Kelley Balliot, Tom Evans, and Colleen McConaghy Hanna, *State of Rhode Island and Providence Plantations: Survey of State Documents and Law-Related Materials*. [Chicago, Ill.]: American Association of Law Libraries, Government Documents Special Interest Section, 2013. (available on HeinOnline)

Roger Williams University School of Law, Law Library: Law Guides: Rhode Island Research, by Lucinda Harrison-Cox

> http://lawguides.rwu.edu/RIResearch

South Carolina:

Paula Gail Benson and Deborah Davis Hottel, *A Guide to South Carolina Legal Research and Citation*. 3rd ed. [Columbia, S. C.]: South Carolina Bar, Continuing Legal Education Division, 2014.

University of South Carolina, School of Law, Coleman Karesh Law Library: South Carolina Legal Resources

>   http://guides.law.sc.edu/SCLegalResources/

South Dakota:

Candice Spurlin, *State Documents Bibliography, South Dakota*. 2nd Revised Edition. [Chicago, Ill.]: American Association of Law Libraries, Government Documents Special Interest Section, 2011. (available on Hein Online)

Delores A. Jorgensen, *South Dakota Legal Research Guide*. 2nd ed. Buffalo, N. Y.: W. S. Hein, 1999.

University of South Dakota School of Law, McKusick Law Library: Legislative History Research

>   http://libguides.law.usd.edu/legislativehistory

>   [click on "South Dakota Legislative History"]

Tennessee:

Scott Childs, Sibyl Marshall, and Carol McCrehan Parker, *Tennessee Legal Research*. 2nd ed. Durham, N. C.: Carolina Academic Press, 2016.

Reba A. Best, *Tennessee State Documents: A Bibliography of State Publications and Related Materials*. [Chicago, Ill.]: American Association of Law Libraries, Government Documents Special Interest Section, 2009. (available on HeinOnline)

Lewis L. Laska, *Tennessee Legal Research Handbook*. Buffalo, N. Y.: W. S. Hein, 1977. (available on HeinOnline) (very detailed and still useful)

University of Tennessee, University Libraries: State Law, Legislation and Regulations: The Legislative Process: Guide to Tennessee and other States

>   http://libguides.utk.edu/tnlegs

Texas:

Brandon D. Quarles and Matthew C. Cordon, *Researching Texas Law*. 3rd ed. Buffalo, N. Y.: W. S. Hein, 2012.

Spencer L. Simons, *Texas Legal Research*. 2nd ed. Durham, N. C.: Carolina Academic Press, 2016.

Lynn Murray, *Texas Legal Materials: A Selected Bibliography.* [Chicago, Ill.]: American Association of Law Libraries, Government Documents Special Interest Section, 2014. (available on HeinOnline)

Southern Methodist University, Underwood Law Library: Research Guides A–Z

> http://libguides.law.smu.edu/index.php

> (includes links to detailed guides to Texas topics, including "Texas Legislative Process: An Overview on Finding Texas Legislative History" by Tim Gallina)

Texas Legislative Council: Texas Legislative Information and Resources

> http://www.tlc.state.tx.us/docs/legref/gtli.pdf

> (detailed guide to research on Texas legislation)

Utah:

Jessica C. Van Buren, Mari J.F. Cheney, and Marsha C. Thomas, *Utah Legal Research.* Buffalo, N. Y.: W. S. Hein, 2011.

Mari Cheney, *Utah Legal Resources Bibliography.* [Chicago, Ill.]: American Association of Law Libraries, Government Documents Special Interest Section, 2009. (available on HeinOnline)

Utah Division of Archives and Records Service: Research Legislative Intent and History

> http://archives.utah.gov/research/guides/legislative-history. htm

> (detailed guide)

Vermont:

Cynthia Lewis, Christine Ryan, Jared Wellman, Jane Woldow, and Paul J. Donovan, *State Documents Bibliography: Vermont, An Updated Guide to the Vermont Legal System.* 3rd ed. [Chicago, Ill.]: American Association of Law Libraries, Government Documents Special Interest Section, 2009. (available on HeinOnline)

Vermont Law School, Julien and Virginia Cornell Law Library: Research Guides: Vermont Law Research Guide, by Jane Woldow

> http://libguides.vermontlaw.edu/vermontlawguide/vermontlaw

Paul J. Donovan: Legislative History—Variations on a Theme

> http://www.pauljdonovan.us/law/leghistvt.html

(a variety of old but interesting observations about Vermont legislative history)

Virginia:

Leah F. Chanin, Pamela J. Gregory, and Sarah K. Wiant, *Legal Research in the District of Columbia, Maryland and Virginia*. 2nd ed. Buffalo, N. Y.: W. S. Hein, 2000.

A Guide to Legal Research in Virginia. 8th ed. Joyce Manna Janto, editor. [Va.]: Virginia CLE Publications, 2017.

Margaret Krause and Sara Sampson, *State Documents Bibliography: Virginia*. [Chicago, Ill.]: American Association of Law Libraries, Government Documents Special Interest Section, 2010. (available on HeinOnline)

George Mason University, Antonin Scalia Law School: Law Library Research Guide: Virginia Legal Materials

https://www.law.gmu.edu/library/guides/research/virginia

Washington:

Penny A. Hazelton, et al., *Washington Legal Researcher's Deskbook, 3d*. Seattle, Wash.: Marian Gould Gallagher Law Library, 2002. (available on HeinOnline)

Peggy Roebuck Jarrett and Cheryl Rae Nyberg, *Washington State Documents: A Bibliography of Legal and Law-Related Sources*. [Chicago, Ill.]: American Association of Law Libraries, Government Documents Special Interest Section, 2011. (available on HeinOnline)

Julie Heintz-Cho, Tom Cobb, and Mary A. Hotchkiss, *Washington Legal Research*. 2nd ed. Durham, N. C.: Carolina Academic Press, 2009.

University of Washington, Marian Gould Gallagher Law Library: Washington State Legislative History, by Cheryl Nyberg

http://guides.lib.uw.edu/law/waleghis

Washington State Law Library

http://www.courts.wa.gov/library/?fa=library.research

(links to guides and resources on all topics of Washington law)

West Virginia:

Hollee Schwartz Temple, *West Virginia Legal Research*. Durham, N. C.: Carolina Academic Press, 2013.

West Virginia University College of Law, George R. Farmer, Jr. Law Library: Legal Research Guides http://www.law.wvu.edu/library/research-guides

(includes "Guide to West Virginia Legislative History Research")

Wisconsin:

Patricia Cervenka and Leslie Behroozi, *Wisconsin Legal Research*. Durham, N. C.: Carolina Academic Press, 2011.

Theodore A. Potter, *Legal Research in Wisconsin*. 2nd ed. Buffalo, N. Y.: W. S. Hein, 2008.

Patricia A. Cervenka, "Wisconsin Supreme Court and Legislative History," 30 *Legal Ref. Serv. Q.* 141 (2011)

Wisconsin State Legislature, Legislative Reference Bureau: Reference and Research

http://legis.wisconsin.gov/lrb/library-and-reference/reference/

(links include "Researching Legislative History in Wisconsin")

Wisconsin State Law Library: Legal Research Guides

http://wilawlibrary.gov/learn/legalresearch.html

Wyoming:

Debora A. Person and Tawnya K. Plumb, *Wyoming Legal Research*. 2nd ed. Durham, N. C.: Carolina Academic Press, 2016.

Debora A. Person, *Wyoming State Documents: A Bibliography of State Publications and Related Materials*. [Chicago, Ill.]: American Association of Law Libraries, Government Documents Special Interest Section, 2006. (available on HeinOnline)

University of Wyoming, George William Hopper Law Library: Compiling Wyoming Legislative Histories

http://www.uwyo.edu/lawlib/researchguides/wyohistory.html

Wyoming Legislature: Legislative History of Wyoming Laws

http://legisweb.state.wy.us/leginfo/hiswylaw.htm

INDEX

References are to Pages